Pro RFID in BizTalk Server 2009

Mark Beckner, Mark Simms, and Ram Venkatesh

Apress®

Pro RFID in BizTalk Server 2009

Copyright © 2009 by Mark Beckner, Mark Simms, Ram Venkatesh

ISBN-13 (pbk): 978-1-4302-1837-1

ISBN-13 (electronic): 978-1-4302-1838-8

9 8 7 6 5 4 3 2 1

Trademarked names may appear in this book. Rather than use a trademark symbol with every occurrence of a trademarked name, we use the names only in an editorial fashion and to the benefit of the trademark owner, with no intention of infringement of the trademark.

Lead Editor: Tony Campbell
Technical Reviewer: Mick Badran
Editorial Board: Clay Andres, Steve Anglin, Mark Beckner, Ewan Buckingham, Tony Campbell, Gary Cornell, Jonathan Gennick, Jonathan Hassell, Michelle Lowman, Matthew Moodie, Duncan Parkes, Jeffrey Pepper, Frank Pohlmann, Ben Renow-Clarke, Dominic Shakeshaft, Matt Wade, Tom Welsh
Project Manager: Sofia Marchant
Copy Editor: Damon Larson
Associate Production Director: Kari Brooks-Copony
Production Editor: Laura Esterman
Compositor: Susan Glinert Stevens
Proofreader: Lisa Hamilton
Indexer: Ron Strauss
Artist: April Milne
Cover Designer: Kurt Krames
Manufacturing Director: Tom Debolski

Distributed to the book trade worldwide by Springer-Verlag New York, Inc., 233 Spring Street, 6th Floor, New York, NY 10013. Phone 1-800-SPRINGER, fax 201-348-4505, e-mail orders-ny@springer-sbm.com, or visit http://www.springeronline.com.

For information on translations, please contact Apress directly at 2855 Telegraph Avenue, Suite 600, Berkeley, CA 94705. Phone 510-549-5930, fax 510-549-5939, e-mail info@apress.com, or visit http://www.apress.com.

Apress and friends of ED books may be purchased in bulk for academic, corporate, or promotional use. eBook versions and licenses are also available for most titles. For more information, reference our Special Bulk Sales–eBook Licensing web page at http://www.apress.com/info/bulksales.

The information in this book is distributed on an "as is" basis, without warranty. Although every precaution has been taken in the preparation of this work, neither the author(s) nor Apress shall have any liability to any person or entity with respect to any loss or damage caused or alleged to be caused directly or indirectly by the information contained in this work.

The source code for this book is available to readers at http://www.apress.com. You will need to answer questions pertaining to this book in order to successfully download the code.

I should extend my thanks to the ideas of Alan Weiss,
without whom my books would not exist.
—Mark Beckner

I would like to thank my father, Bruce, for being a shining example of courage
and perseverance in the face of overwhelming odds.
—Mark Simms

I would like to dedicate this book to my parents, Ramachandran and Malathi.
—Ram Venkatesh

Contents at a Glance

Contents

Foreword

In most industries, successful businesses are defined by the products, services, and solutions they create and deliver—in these times of economic uncertainty, a new paradigm of business is emerging. This new-generation business will be different and will be defined and measured by the *effect* it has and the *value* it adds to its shareholders and customers, and its customer's markets—this forces a major rethink on strategies.

Real-time visibility into supply chains and operations is critical for the next-generation business. The promise of RFID is to improve supply chain business processes through global visibility of physical objects—products and other assets. Visibility not just within your own four walls, but also within your trading partners' walls. Visibility is about getting access to new data and then transforming the data into real value.

Visibility enables traceability and authentication of products, enabling critical and life-saving processes such as effective recall, product authentication, brand protection, and chain of custody for pharmaceuticals.

The biggest challenge that companies face today is knowing where to start the journey, and how to get a firm grip on the potential areas of value creation and eventual return on investment. Project teams need to have a balanced focus across the following four pillars of value creation:

Increase revenue: Can this project help me increase company revenue?

Reduce costs: Where will the real cost savings come from?

Optimize assets: Can I find assets and redeploy them?

Reduce risk: Will visibility improve my recall processes, reducing our corporate risk?

The key to unlocking the ROI is a solid understanding of the underlying global supply chain standards such as the GS1 EPCglobal standards, and applying them pragmatically in applications and processes that can capture visibility data and rapidly transform the data into value that has a positive effect on a company's bottom line. In simple terms, if you understand your supply chain processes, it becomes much easier for project teams to drill into the four pillars of value creation within these processes and expose areas of significant business value creation.

RFID has long been thought of as a critical component to such visibility solutions. Over the last decade, there have been major strides in the mainstreaming of RFID technologies for visibility applications in the hardware, software, interoperability, and acceptance dimensions. A lot of ground has been covered, but significant barriers still remain to the ubiquitous deployment of RFID solutions. The challenges now go beyond the physical or technical. As an industry, we need to have scalable ways to create expertise in the community, and transform the art of rolling out RFID solutions into a predictable, manageable process, if we try to make thousands of RFID deployments a reality. The good news is that hope is around the corner! Microsoft's approach to RFID holds the promise to create a hardware/software platform that will be ready for mass deployment—a tall challenge, but one the industry is ready to embark on.

This book is an important step of that journey—it is structured, pragmatic, and fact-based, and has rich content from the learning of three talented authors who are experienced in deployments and in-depth dialog with customers and technology partners. It exposes another one of the key issues in the industry today: the lack of repeatable modular solutions that enhance interoperability vs. the creation of custom islands of functionality. The very different but complementary perspectives of the authors makes it an interesting journey of understanding: Ram Venkatesh was the architect of the Microsoft RFID vision, and he lays out the model behind the approach. Mark Simms and Mark Beckner talk to the technology from a very hands-on user perspective that comes from deep enterprise hardware and software deployments. The result is a cohesive dialog between the creators and the consumers of a platform, which should give you a unique insight into how to leverage the Microsoft platform in your deployment.

We are close to the tipping point with RFID. This book is a must-read for software developers, project teams, and industry consultants; it unlocks secrets to success and provides global thought leadership.

I am reminded of a famous comment by Dr. William Edwards Deming, the great quality guru who stated, "Survival is not compulsory." In my opinion, only next-generation businesses will survive.

John Keogh
Senior Vice President, EPCglobal Canada and Traceability

About the Authors

 **MARK BECKNER** is a technical consultant specializing in business development and enterprise application integration. He runs his own consulting firm, Inotek Consulting Group, LLC, delivering innovative solutions to large corporations and small businesses. His projects have included engagements with numerous clients throughout the United States, and range in nature from mobile application development to complete integration solutions. He is the author of *Pro EDI in BizTalk Server 2006 R2* (Apress, 2007) and a coauthor of *BizTalk 2006 Recipes: A Problem-Solution Approach* (Apress, 2006), and has spoken at a number of venues, including Microsoft Tech Ed.

Mark resides with his wife, Sara, in western Colorado with their dog, Rosco, the Adventure Mutt. He can be contacted at mbeckner@inotekgroup.com for any questions regarding the concepts in this book, or for advice on integration projects, BizTalk implementations, or other consulting endeavors.

 **MARK SIMMS** is a field program manager with Microsoft's CSD Customer Experience group, focused on BizTalk Server and RFID adoption. He has been developing RFID-enabled systems for more than eight years, both with Microsoft and as a cofounder of Cathexis Innovations, and he has been consulting in the software industry since 1994. Currently, Mark focuses on developing field-readiness content and guidance in developing end-to-end solutions on top of BizTalk Server. He also has a blog at blogs.msdn.com/masimms.

 **RAM VENKATESH** is the founder and CEO of S3 Edge Software, which delivers real-time visibility solutions using the BizTalk RFID platform for warehouse visibility, work-in-progress, and high-value asset tracking. Prior to starting S3, he was the software architect for the Microsoft BizTalk RFID platform. While at Microsoft, Venkatesh worked on a number of innovations involving database technologies and the integration of the .NET Framework into SQL Server, and filed more than 30 patent applications along the way.

Venkatesh is well known in the RFID community and has been a featured speaker at several Microsoft and industry events, including the Microsoft Professional Developers Conference, Tech Ed, RFID Journal Live, and the Paris RFID Show. He resides in Hyderabad, India with his wife Ritu and daughter Tara, and can be reached at venkar@s3edge.com for any questions regarding this book, BizTalk, or building RFID solutions.

About the Technical Reviewer

MICK BADRAN operates Breeze Training Pty Ltd, (www.breezetraining.com.au), a niche consulting and training company specializing in Microsoft integration technologies. He is a Microsoft MVP (Windows Server System: BizTalk Server) who consults at several levels based on the connected systems space, dealing with technologies such as MOSS, BizTalk, WCF, and WF. Typically, he provides system architecture guidance and technical mentoring in design and implementation of various solutions.

Mick has been heavily involved in the BizTalk and MOSS spaces since their v1 inception (1999), where he worked closely with Microsoft UK, delivering sessions around Europe. He works closely with Microsoft in both Australia and the United States, around designing BizTalk- and MOSS-based material, and is currently integrating BizTalk R2/MOSS-based solutions— with everything but the kitchen sink!

Mick has also delivered technical instructor-led classroom-based training for more than 12 years.

Acknowledgments

The authors would like to extend their thanks to the following individuals, groups, and inanimate objects.

Ram Venkatesh:

- Damon Larson and Laura Esterman at Apress for their patience and suggestions

- Mick Badran for his insight in technical reviewing and guidance

- Abhishek Agarwal and Anush Kumar from S3 Edge for their feedback and support

- Bala Sriram at Microsoft for encouraging me and my family

- Ritu and Tara for putting up with me while I worked on the book

Mark Simms:

- My amazing wife, Jackie, for letting me disappear for days at a time to work on this book, and for always being supportive

- My parents, Marie and Bruce, for showing me how to become a reasonably useful member of society—it couldn't have been easy

- Steve Taylor, Colin Power, and the rest of the Cathexis crew—for sharing my belief in the Microsoft platform, and helping out with hardware for the book (the one, the only, IDBlue)

- Paul Sanford, for introducing the three amigos

- Krishnan Gopalan, Bindu Thota, and the rest of the BizTalk RFID development team at Microsoft for building such an excellent platform, and for listening to all of our complaints

- Norberto Garcia, John Wyss, and the rest of the Customer Experience team at Microsoft for giving me the opportunity to help improve the product with an excellent group

- Mick Badran, for being a great reviewer, and teaching us things about the product we didn't know

- The humble coffee bean, for fueling this endeavor

- Our editors, for making our words shine

- For all of the excellent hardware developers that bring RFID to life—Valentina Shkolnikov, Lynn Seilo, and the rest of the Alien Technologies crew, Matt Eschbach, Prashant and PV from Motorola, and Dan Bowman from Impinj

Mark Beckner:

- Umm . . . is there anyone left to thank after all of that?!

Introduction

This book is for solution architects, application developers, and IT administrators involved in the development and deployment of a Microsoft BizTalk RFID solution. We address both ends of the spectrum: if you are an RFID solution integrator who wants to learn about deploying solutions based on Microsoft BizTalk RFID, or a Microsoft solution provider who wants to learn about integrating and leveraging RFID technology, this book is for you. To do this effectively, we use a hands-on approach with plenty of exercises and conceptual material, and assume no significant prior exposure to Microsoft BizTalk RFID.

How This Book Is Structured

The intent of this book is to introduce the different aspects of working with BizTalk RFID in the most logical manner possible. The nature of the product lends itself to a linear storyline, rather than a more compartmentalized approach common in programming languages and broader platforms. Because of this, it begins with foundational topics and moves through advanced build and communications, enterprise integration, debugging, and deployment—the same flow as would be seen in a typical BizTalk RFID project.

Chapter 1: We begin with an overview of RFID, the history of the technology, and its role in the marketplace. BizTalk RFID will make much more sense when the full story of RFID is understood.

Chapter 2: We introduce the fundamentals of the BizTalk RFID application, in order to make you aware of the overall scope of the product before trying to develop any single component.

Chapter 3: Digging into actual development, we introduce a "Hello World" application, illustrating the key concepts needed to build more advanced solutions.

Chapter 4: BizTalk RFID Manager is central to the administration and configuration of solutions. This chapter details how to work with and extend the administrative functionality of the application.

Chapter 5: Understanding how to work with the flow of information from RFID devices is the theme of this chapter. The fundamentals of communication and interpretation of this data are critical aspects of component development.

Chapter 6: Continuing on the concepts introduced in Chapter 5, event handling and processing is explored. The discussions and exercises in this chapter introduce how to extend the communication patterns.

Chapter 7: BizTalk RFID Mobile revolutionizes the way RFID solutions can be deployed and maintained, moving core functionality to mobile devices. This chapter explores this aspect of the technology, including how to successfully incorporate it into an organization.

Chapter 8: BizTalk Server is separate from BizTalk RFID, yet there are many mechanisms that exist that allow for the easy integration of the two. Incorporating orchestrations, ports, data mapping, and other integration concepts are the core concepts discussed in this chapter.

Chapter 9: Integrating with other enterprise applications is essential to many BizTalk RFID solutions, and this chapter outlines some of the more common scenarios that developers will encounter, including those involving SharePoint web parts and SQL Server reporting. These applications can be interacted with directly from BizTalk RFID, or using the more robust functionality of the core BizTalk Server engine.

Chapter 10: Debugging and diagnosing solutions is a ubiquitous need, and this chapter explains in detail the options that are available to the BizTalk RFID developer. Performance counters, log files, and exception handling are all discussed in detail.

Chapter 11: This chapter walks through the process of deploying a BizTalk RFID solution to a production environment, and discusses the many considerations needed in a successful deployment.

Chapter 12: There is such a vast array of BizTalk RFID solutions that there is no way to capture all of the concepts that may prove valuable to a reader. This chapter, however, introduces various ideas that may help developers and architects better understand how to deliver and extend the functionality of a solution.

Prerequisities

The exercises in this book assume that you have access to BizTalk RFID and Visual Studio, and can compile and deploy to a development system. The exercises also assume that you're working with BizTalk Server 2009—though most examples will work with BizTalk Server 2006 R2. Some discussion and analysis centers on other systems, such as SharePoint 2007 and SQL Server 2008, though these are not essential to understanding BizTalk RFID.

Downloading the Code

Much of the code used in the exercises in this book is available at www.apress.com in the Books/ Source Code section. (You can also find the source code for any book in the Book Extras area of the book's page.) All examples in this book can be built without the downloadable code.

Contacting the Authors

Feedback and comments are appreciated, and the authors can be reached via the following addresses:

Ram Venkatesh: venkar@s3edge.com

Mark Simms: blogs.msdn.com/masimms

Mark Beckner: mbeckner@inotekgroup.com

CHAPTER 1

■■■

RFID Background Primer

This chapter provides an introduction to radio frequency identification (RFID), the history of the technology, and its uses. It will compare and contrast RFID technology and standards while providing a context for how RFID is used to overcome real-world business challenges.

The intention of this section is not to make you an expert on the "physics" side of RFID technology, but provide enough of a high-level overview to enable informed discussions and choices.

Tracking Stuff: Eyeballs and Lasers

From the dawn of recorded history, through paintings on cave walls, cuneiform tablets from ancient Babylon, tax records from medieval England, all the way up to modern information systems and databases, we have been obsessed with answering the question, "Where is my stuff?"

Advances in information technology (IT) have always been tied to helping us understand the physical world around us, especially those aspects in which we have some special interest or ownership. The foundation of keeping track of things in the physical world around us is identifying assets, pairing a sensor for collecting information with distinguishing features of a specific asset.

For thousands of years, the essential technology used to identify things was eyesight, coupled with a variety of visual cues. These took a variety of forms, such as pictograms[1] and text. Combining these with paper ledgers to form information management systems made it feasible to manage assets at a far larger scale than ever before.

With the advent of computer-based information processing systems, the information about "stuff" started moving out of accounting books and ledgers and into their electronic counterparts. The fundamental link between these electronic records and the physical objects they tracked remained the eyeball, requiring manual data entry to synchronize the digital and physical worlds.

The challenge with the Mark 1 Mod 0 eyeball (a military colloquialism referring to unaided human eyesight) and handwriting is the human factor. The volume of seemingly identical goods began to overwhelm the human component's ability to capture and process information. For example, take the example of a modern supermarket. How would our large markets function if each cashier had to remember the price of each and every type of product in the store, and ring it in manually?

---

1. Such "primitive" methods of identifying objects are more common than one might think. Everything from "no parking" signs to corporate logos use pictograms to visually associate information.

In the late 1960s, the availability of relatively cheap laser technology led to the development of the now ubiquitous bar code technology, allowing assets to be automatically identified, bridging the gap between the digital and physical worlds. In less than 30 years, the technology has pervaded our lives, appearing on nearly every packaged good available for sale.

As the global supply chain came into being, and trends such as just-in-time inventory drove the need for increased efficiencies, several shortcomings in bar code technology became apparent. This is not to say that bar codes aren't an amazing technology that will be with us for a very long time, simply that their basis on optics rules out being able to extend them to handle a number of scenarios.

The key shortcomings of bar codes that became apparent are the following:

Limitation to line of sight: As reading a bar code requires that the reader (either a laser or special camera) can actually see the bar code, there needs to be a line of sight between the scanner and the bar code. This prevents a scanner from reading items that are inside a box (such as a pallet of goods) or otherwise obscured or out of alignment. (Depending on the scanner being used, the bar code may have to be at a very specific alignment to the reader.) In addition to the line-of-sight challenges, bar code scanners can only read one item at a time. As anyone who has ever waited in line at a supermarket knows all too well, this means that every item needs to be scanned individually.

Static content: Once a bar code has been printed, the data encoded cannot be changed without replacing the label.

Data capacity for serialized items: The amount of data that can be contained within a typical one-dimensional bar code (i.e., a standard UPC code) is fairly limited—often a ten-digit number. Although it's well suited to encoding both the manufacturer of a product and the SKU,[2] it doesn't have sufficient capacity to serialize individual assets.

Note *Serializing* refers to the ability to assign a unique identification code to a specific item, rather than an identifying code to that type of item. With a serialized identification number, it is possible to not only identify something as a specific type of item (such as a laptop), but a specific item (such as that laptop).

A number of new bar-coding technologies have been developed that seek to address the data size limitations, such as 2D bar codes. Commonly used in military and logistics applications, 2D bar codes allow encoding of a large amount of information. However, they still suffer from some of the limitations of optics technology (such as requiring a line of sight). In addition, the physical size of these codes often prevents them from being used in applications with space or marketing constraints.

These challenges with both manual asset identification and bar-coding have led to the rise of a new form of automated identification technology: RFID. Rather than optics, RFID utilizes radio waves to communicate identification data.

---

2. *SKU* stands for *stock-keeping unit,* and is used to represent a type of item or packaged collection of like items (such as a box of razors).

Introducing Radio Frequency Identification

RFID is a technology that uses radio waves to pass information between a reader and a tag (analogous to how bar codes use optics to pass information between a scanner and a bar code). In general (although some active flavors of RFID work slightly differently), the sequence of events for reading an RFID tag is as follows (as illustrated in Figure 1-1):

1. An interrogator (i.e., reader) generates a radio signal.

2. A tag receives this signal and transmits back information.

3. This information is passed back to a host computer.

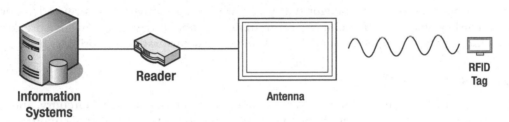

Figure 1-1. *Anatomy of an RFID System*

There are several different types of RFID technology that operate in different frequency bands, draw the power needed for the tags from difference sources, and store different quantities and types of information.

Using radio waves rather than optics opens up several new applications that can be used to drive solutions to business challenges:

RFID technology does not require line of sight. Tags can be read inside of boxes, and through cardboard and wood. Items on a conveyer belt do not require exact alignment with a scanner to be read.

Tags can store dynamic information. RFID tags can hold a large amount of information (from 96 bits to thousands of bytes). This information can be updated in the field. This provides enough information storage for unique, global serialization of assets. Organizations such as GS1 and EPCglobal are leading efforts to provide standard ways of encoding data on RFID tags—the RFID equivalent of UPC codes. These encodings provide standard methods of encoding company IDs, product IDs, and so on.

Tags can provide information security. Certain flavors of RFID technology provide encryption support for accessing data.

Along with its unique advantages, RFID technology also carries some key limitations that need to be taken into account when developing a solution:

The transmission and receipt of radio waves are affected by materials such as water and metal. While it is not impossible to use RFID technology with these substances, special care needs to be taken in choosing appropriate flavors of RFID and deploying the technology.

There are regulatory requirements on which radio frequencies may be used and how much power may be emitted by readers. These regulations vary by country and frequency band.

There are several different types of RFID technology, each with its own unique advantages and disadvantages. Selecting the appropriate technology in developing an asset visibility solution (be it RFID, bar codes, or eyeballs and paper) is a critical factor in the success of the overall solution.

Navigating the Technology Matrix

RFID technology is primarily categorized by its power source (active vs. passive) and frequency band. The key types of RFID technology are outlined in Table 1-1, which provides a breakdown by technology type, frequency band, key advantages/disadvantages, and primary uses.

What's in a Tag?

RFID tags typically consist of the inlay, containing the antenna and digital circuitry, and the *encapsulation* (the physical packaging that surrounds and protects the digital circuitry of an RFID tag, typically a paper label or plastic shell). Many different companies take inlays and provide encapsulations, often in the form of labels, or more ruggedized form factors such as hardened plastic casings for use on reusable pallets. Figure 1-2 shows some examples of typical RFID tags.

Figure 1-2. *Samples of RFID tags*

Active vs. Passive

Passive RFID technology uses the energy provided by the reader to power the RFID tags. In essence, the tag uses the energy provided by the reader as a power source. This gives passive tags a virtually infinite life span, as they have no moving parts and no batteries to deplete. On the other hand, they have a shorter range than active tags, and can only operate when activated by a reader.

Active RFID technology uses an onboard battery to power the RFID tags. This allows active tags to have a longer communication range, and to perform tasks when not within range of a reader. They can also have onboard sensors that allow sampling of temperature, humidity, and physical shock (such as being dropped), in addition to providing identifying information. In contrast, they tend to be a lot bulkier and more expensive than passive tags, and require batteries to be replaced on a regular basis.

In terms of cost, the relatively simple design of passive tags means that they are an order of magnitude cheaper than active tags. While the exact price of tags depends on factors such as technology, vendor, and volume, passive RFID tags often cost on the order of cents, while active tags can cost upward of $100. Table 1-1 lists some of the key RFID technologies.

▪**Note** The *air protocol*, also commonly referred to as the *air interface*, describes the communication protocol used to translate back and forth between electromagnetic waves and information. This is analogous to the Ethernet wire protocol.

Table 1-1. *Summary of Key RFID Technologies*

Technology	Frequency	Typical Range	Common Uses	Advantages	Disadvantages
Low frequency (LF)	125 KHz	1 m	Livestock tracking (cattle)	Mature technology	Little technical innovation
High frequency (HF)	13.56 MHz	1–2 m	Pharmaceuticals, contactless payments cards	Close-range applications, more security options; excellent performance around metal and water	Not suited for highly automated applications
Ultra-high frequency (UHF)	~900 MHz	6 m	Supply chain (pallets, cases, increasing use at item level)	Long range, low tag cost, high technical innovation, common standards	Performance around metal and water potentially challenging
Active tags	433 MHz	50–100 m	Embedded sensors, long-range applications	Greater range, embedded sensor capability	Dependence on battery life, high cost

Passive Readers in Action

All passive RFID systems, regardless of their frequency band and air protocol, share certain common characteristics. Passive RFID systems are composed of readers (interrogators), antennae, and tags. Tags store information, readers manage the logic and communication, and antennae shift electrical waveforms into the appropriate electromagnetic frequency (see Figure 1-3).

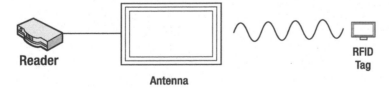

Reader   **Antenna**   **RFID Tag**

Figure 1-3. *Passive RFID*

The basic sequence for communicating with an RFID tag is the following:

1. The reader activates (powers) the antenna. This transmits a carrier wave on the chosen frequency (see Figure 1-4).

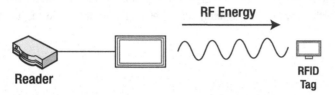

Figure 1-4. *Powering (energizing) the tag*

2. The tag receives the signal (through its built-in antenna), which is used to power up the onboard digital logic (see Figure 1-5). Note that the tag's antenna is tuned to receive a specific range of frequencies, similar to a car radio being dialed into a specific radio station.

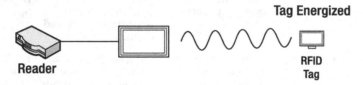

Figure 1-5. *The tag has been energized by the reader.*

3. The reader then modulates data on top of the carrier wave (see Figure 1-6).[3] The specifics depend on the air interface of the particular RFID technology being used (i.e., even within a specific type of RFID, such as HF, different air protocols can be used).

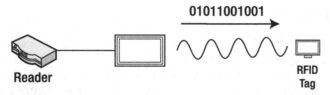

Figure 1-6. *Reader transmitting data to an energized tag*

---

3. *Modulation* is a technical term that refers to layering a data signal on top of a carrier wave.

4. If the tag has been successfully energized, and recognizes the command transmitted from the reader (such as a request for the tag's identifying code), the tag executes that command (see Figure 1-7).

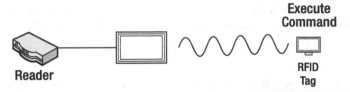

Figure 1-7. *Tag executing command received from the reader*

5. The results of the command (such as the tag's ID) are then sent back to the reader, as shown in Figure 1-8.

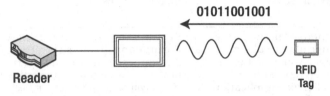

Figure 1-8. *Tag transmitting response back to the reader*

Successful communication between the reader and the tag depends on several factors:

- The reader and tag have to be using a compatible frequency range. If the tag is built for a different frequency than the reader is transmitting, it won't receive any of the power (and hence will not successfully energize).

- The reader's antenna has to deliver enough power to energize the tag. The amount of energy delivered to the tag depends on a number of factors, including the following:

  - Distance from the antenna

  - Orientation between the antenna and the tag

  - Ambient RF noise in the frequency band

  - Environmental factors such as the presence of metal or water

  - Sensitivity of the tag (i.e., the more sensitive the tag is, the more efficiently it will capture energy)

- The reader needs to be speaking the same air protocol as the tag. If the tag doesn't recognize incoming data, it will not respond.

Anticollision

One of the key value propositions of RFID technology is the ability to simultaneously read a large number of tags (e.g., for reading all of the boxes on a pallet while it passes through a loading door). Anticollision algorithms are used to allow multiple tags (and sometimes multiple readers) to share the same bandwidth, in a similar manner to how Ethernet employs a backoff algorithm to allow multiple computers to share the same physical network segment.

Antenna Considerations

RFID antennae come in two primary configurations: *linear* and *circular*.[4] The choice of antenna type has a dramatic effect on read range and fidelity, specifically when using UHF technology, as shown in Table 1-2.

Table 1-2. *Summary of Antenna Types*

Antenna Type	Characteristics	Advantages	Disadvantages
Linear	RF energy radiates from the antenna in a linear pattern. Generally set up in horizontal or vertical orientation.	Generally has twice the range of a circular antenna for a given power level. Best type of antenna for challenging applications (i.e., those involving metal or water).	Requires the tag to be aligned with the antenna. If the tag is offset 90 degrees from the antenna (i.e., horizontal antenna with a vertical tag), reads will be inconsistent at best.
Circular	RF energy radiates from the antenna in a circular pattern.	Does not require a precise tag orientation and alignment to the antenna. Best choice for scenarios that will not present tags in a consistent orientation.	Reduced range (generally half) from a linear antenna for the same power level.

Readers connect to antennae in three primary ways: monostatic, bistatic, and multistatic. Different types of readers support different antenna connections (note that the supported antenna configuration is typically not a configurable option—i.e., you get whatever configuration is used by the reader you buy). The differences, advantages, and disadvantages to each are outlined in the following list:

---

4. There are other types of antennae, such as directional, but these are typically used for niche and certain mobile applications.

Monostatic: The same antenna can both transmit (TX) and receive (RX). Only one antenna is required to read tags in a monostatic configuration (see Figure 1-9).

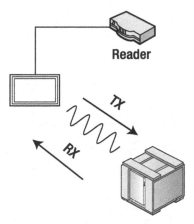

Figure 1-9. *Monostatic: Single antenna for transmitting and receiving*

Bistatic: The reader transmits on one antenna and receives on another. Paired antennae are required (see Figure 1-10).

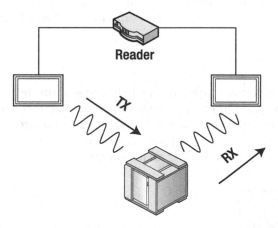

Figure 1-10. *Bistatic: One antenna transmits and the other receives*

Multistatic: Separate antennae are used for transmitting and receiving. The reader alternates between transmitting and receiving on each antenna (see Figure 1-11).

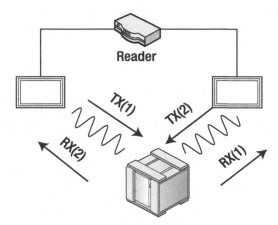

Figure 1-11. *Multistatic: Paired antenna*

Low-Frequency Readers

Operating at 125 KHz, LF readers and tags are the dominant technology in the livestock industry. A stable and mature technology, there is relatively little growth in this space as compared to the HF and UHF spaces. At the time of publication, there are no LF devices supported on the BizTalk RFID platform.

High-Frequency Readers

Operating at 13.56 MHz, HF readers and tags are heavily used in near-field and security-related operations, with a lot of traction in pharmacy applications. There are two primary air interface standards in HF: ISO 15693 and ISO 14443. The ISO 14443 standard has a higher data rate and implements a number of security-related features (such as requiring encryption keys to access data). Figure 1-12 shows an example of a mobile HF reader and an RFID tag.

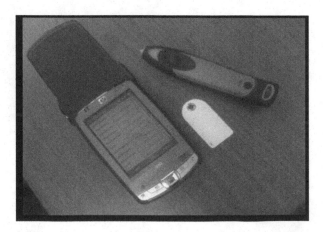

Figure 1-12. *Cathexis IDBlue HF RFID reader, PocketPC, and encapsulated HF RFID tag*

Historically, HF technology has provided far superior performance in the presence of water and metal, though recent advances in UHF have closed the gap somewhat. HF tags also tend to be smaller (in some cases much smaller) than their UHF counterparts, and adapt well to hardened casings for challenging environments.

Even though defined standards exist and the technology is quite mature, there are a number of vendors who have implemented proprietary standards on top of the base ISO 15693 and ISO 14443 standards. When choosing technology in this space, it is very important to be clear about compatibility between the selected readers and tags.

When working with a reader vendor, always ask if a specific tag (model number) can be read by their reader. Compatibility is not guaranteed simply because both reader and tag are based on the ISO 15693 or ISO 14443 protocols.

Ultra–High Frequency Readers

The predominant technology in RFID, especially for supply chain applications, UHF operates around the 900 MHz frequency range (different geographic locations have different regulatory requirements for the allowable range and emitted power levels).

There have been several generations and standards around UHF, but the EPC Class 1 Generation 2 air interface and tag standard (described later in the "Electronic Product Code Class 1 Generation 2" section) has come to dominate the industry.

UHF tags are well suited for use in a supply chain scenario, with a solid combination of good read range and reasonable cost. Although earlier generations of UHF technology were somewhat unreliable in proximity to water or metal, recent advances have greatly improved performance for these scenarios. Figure 1-13 shows an example of a UHF reader.

Figure 1-13. *Alien ALR-9650 UHF reader*

This is not to say that these environments do not present serious deployment challenges, simply that it is no longer impossible to successfully deploy UHF for these types of applications.

Most UHF readers, in addition to the RFID and networking functionality, also include general purpose digital input/output (I/O) ports (often abbreviated GPIO or GPO/GPI). These allow the readers to directly interact with light stacks, air horns, and other I/O devices.

Active RFID Technology

The key differentiator between passive and active RFID is the power source. Whereas passive tags are powered by RF energy from readers, active tags have a built-in power source (usually a replaceable battery). Active tags are usually set to beacon; that is, at a fixed interval, they will broadcast their built-in ID code to be picked up by a series of readers. Due to the built-in power source, active tags can often be read hundreds of feet away.

Some active technology is deployed to implement a *Real-Time Locating System (RTLS)*. In this scenario, information from several different read points is correlated to determine the physical location of a particular tag.

One other key aspect of active technology is the use of sensor tags that have built-in measurement devices. These can measure temperature, humidity, and physical shock (i.e., being dropped). Often deployed in food chain scenarios (i.e., the tag can report if the temperature in a reefer[5] has risen above safe storage levels), they can be used to determine if foodstuffs have been safely transported.

Tag Memory: Reading and Writing

All RFID tags have some amount of onboard memory, varying greatly by vendor and technology type. Some tags (such as most HF tags and some newer UHF tags) ship from the factory with a hard-coded globally unique tag ID (similar to a MAC address). Other tags ship with a default value, which then has to be initialized. The process of initializing these values is commonly referred to as *commissioning*.

Newer tag technologies have improved the ability of vendors to place more memory storage on tags. However, these increased-memory tags carry a burden in production cost and sticker price. While high-memory tags (such as the 64 Kb UHF tag from Fujitsu) enable applications such as storing maintenance histories in aerospace applications, their price point is not suitable for supply chain scenarios.

Thus far, the primary focus of discussion has been on reading data from RFID tags. However, most readers can act as both an interrogator (reading data) and a programmer (writing data). The only key differences between them are the command set used and the amount of power and time required (writing data takes more power and time). Whereas most readers can also program tags, this function is typically performed by an RFID printer or applicator (described in the next section).

Printers and Applicators

So far, this chapter has been focused on readers, tags, and technology. However, the linchpin in any real-world RFID deployment is the commissioning of the RFID tags. This term refers to

---

5. In this context, a reefer refers to a refrigerated truck or rail container.

initializing the RFID tags with the appropriate identifying codes (i.e., in a UHF supply chain scenario, the EPCs), and any accompanying physical packaging (such as a printed label).

RFID printers combine the ability to print physical labels (usually combining textual information, logos, and bar codes) with encoding of data on the tag itself. Once the labels are printed, they are typically manually applied to the target asset.

For use in high-speed, automated scenarios, such as packaged goods rolling off of a conveyor belt in a manufacturing plant, applicators take the print engine and marry it with the ability to automatically apply labels to a given product. While carrying a high price tag, these applicators allow the deployment of RFID technology to scale up to handle high-volume scenarios.

Cutting Through the Hype

RFID technology has been the subject of intense hype, purporting that the technology could track the physical location of assets down to the centimeter in real time, read through bank vault doors, establish an Orwellian state, and allows users to perform wondrous feats of magic. Others have contended that the recent relative lack of buzz around RFID has sounded its death knell.

Neither of these extremes paints an accurate picture of the state of RFID technology. While still early in its adoption phase, RFID technology has reached a level of maturity that is quietly but surely gaining traction in the marketplace by delivering real-world return on investment.

The Science of the Feasible vs. the Art of the Possible

One product of the hype around RFID is the myth that it enables solutions that were not possible without it. This is again losing sight of the true value provided by enabling solutions with RFID. There is no feature provided by adding RFID to a solution that cannot be performed manually.

Dock workers can count boxes, maintenance personnel can fill out work orders, and destination codes can be read from luggage tags, all without the benefit of RFID. If these solutions are possible without RFID, where is the value driving the adoption of RFID?

The key value proposition for adding RFID technology is that it provides a pathway from the possible to the feasible by linking the physical world to the digital. It provides the necessary automation, speed, and accuracy required to bridge the gap between real-world assets and business systems that manage them.

Whereas manual processes provide the first step in bridging the digital divide, RFID technology offers the ability to enable a truly compelling degree of fidelity between the information systems driving your enterprise and your real-world assets. Take the example of receiving a pallet of goods in a warehouse. A dock worker can read all of the box labels and manually enter them into a database. However, the data capture is prone to errors (e.g., was that a box of blue razors or red razors?), and there is a gap between acquiring the data (looking at the boxes and writing the information down on a clipboard) and recording the information (typing it up). Bar code technology provides a first level of data fidelity (reliably identifying the type of product), but does not uniquely identify a specific box of products (which can prove vital in activities such as product recall).

Regardless of the specific technology involved, the fundamental activities remain the same—associating physical assets with digital information. However, the technology (be it eyeballs, bar codes, or RFID) plays a key role in the fidelity and availability of that association.

The Myth of the RFID Solution

Another product of the hype cycle that has surrounded RFID over the past several years has been the phrase "RFID solution," with vendors far and wide touting their technology as a glorious panacea in the provision of such a solution. The phrase obscures the real value provided by RFID technology.

There is no such thing as an RFID problem. There are asset visibility issues, data fidelity problems, and logistical challenges, but there are no RFID problems. Wise use of RFID technology can play a critical role in overcoming these business challenges, but there is no inherent RFID problem that requires an RFID solution.

This insistence on terminology could be seen as mere semantics, but one of the key failings I have observed in the RFID industry over the past five years is the lack of focus on the challenges faced by the end user. Their problem is never "I need to improve read rates in my portal readers," or "This particular tag doesn't read well in proximity to my metal cylinders"—their problem is "I don't know enough about where my assets are," or "The information in my ERP system is out of touch with the real world."

The most important aspect of any system is the value that it provides, not the technology used to enable it. This is why we prefer to refer to the reality of the RFID-enabled solution, rather than the myth of the RFID solution.

For example, picture yourself as a consultant working on implementing a solution at a warehouse for streamlining shipping and receiving activities. If the focus is on delivering an "RFID solution" and diving into readers, tags, and read rates, it's easy to lose sight of the primary goal—driving efficiency in the overall business process. This process stretches all the way from the physical assets being shipped to the key performance indicators (KPIs) viewed at the annual shareholder's meeting. The focus of any solution needs to be firmly centered around the business challenge—not aspects of the technology used to surmount those challenges.

Electronic Product Code Class 1 Generation 2

One of the most important developments in the RFID industry in recent times was the ratification and adoption of the Electronic Product Code (EPC) Class 1 Generation 2 (commonly referred to as EPC Gen 2, or just Gen 2) standard of the EPCglobal standards organization (www.epcglobalinc.org/home/). EPC Gen 2 is an air interface standard that defines how readers and tags communicate.

An industry standards body, EPCglobal has been the lead agency in defining RFID standards for the supply chain industry, based on UHF technology. EPCglobal's mandate is to provide vendor-agnostic standards to provide a common baseline for RFID technology with a focus on industrial (as opposed to academic) requirements.

Designed to overcome some of the limitations of the first-generation EPC standard (known as EPC Gen 1), since its ratification in 2004, EPC Gen 2 has come to dominate the UHF landscape. Offering better performance, 96-bit tag IDs, increased user memory, and important security and privacy features, virtually every UHF reader and tag for sale today is based on EPC Gen 2.

EPCglobal has also led the development of several other standards, definitions, and data formats, such as the following:

Global trade identification number (GTIN): This numbering format provides globally unique identification of products (essentially a global UPC code).

Serialized GTIN (SGTIN): This is a GTIN paired with a serial number, providing unique identification of a specific asset.

Low Level Reader Protocol (LLRP): This is a wire protocol for controlling and receiving data from RFID readers. Several vendors provide native LLRP support in their readers (such as Impinj and Motorola). With BizTalk Server 2009, Microsoft has included support for LLRP readers out of the box.

Electronic Product Coding Information Services (EPCIS): This is a data interchange standard designed to enable enterprises to easily share and exchange EPC-related data both between internal systems and with external trading partners. Still in an early adoption phase, this standard has not seen widespread use.

Information about other EPCglobal standardization efforts and initiatives can be found on the EPCglobal web site (`www.epcglobalinc.org/standards/`).

The 96-bit EPC format contains a manufacturer code, an object type code, and a unique serial number for that object type. The manufacturer code (also known as the EPC manager number) is assigned by EPCglobal. There are several different ways of encoding data into the 96-bit field (defined by a header value), including SGTIN, Global Individual Asset Identifier (GIAI), and Serial Shipping Container Code (SSCC).

Closed-Loop vs. Open-Loop Systems

One of the common discussions in the RFID industry involves closed-loop vs. open-loop systems. A closed-loop system refers to one wherein a single organization owns the assets (i.e., no RFID-related information is shared with external partners). An example of this would be an IT department using RFID to track its laptops and servers.

In an open-loop system, the RFID infrastructure stretches across multiple organizations. An example of this would be a manufacturer of goods exchanging information and tracking goods through delivery to its distributor.

While much of the early hype focused around large-scale open-loop scenarios, closed-loop implementations (if often very large closed-loop implementations) are starting to take center stage as companies deploy RFID within their own walls to drive efficiency.

Applying RFID

So far, this chapter has been very technology-centric. However, as with any technology, the key question is why. What is the purpose of deploying this technology, what problem do we seek to address, and how is the investment justified?

While applicable across a (very) broad range of applications, all RFID technology (and bar codes) relates to correlating digital data with physical assets in an automated, reliable, scalable fashion. The following list describes some of the key industries and scenarios that are adopting RFID as a core technology:

Supply Chain: As perhaps the key industry behind the drive to adopt RFID, supply chain leverages RFID technology to automate tracking the movement of goods (at the pallet, case, and increasingly, item level) between the manufacturer, distribution centers, and retail outlets.

Retail: With increasing adoption and uptake, retail is becoming a key industry for RFID. With the increased automation provided by the technology, industry players are starting to use RFID to do the following:

- Streamline their cycle counts (i.e., counting items on the retail floor and in stock rooms).

- Manage out-of-stock events (if you don't know you no longer have an item on the store floor, you don't know that you need to put more out).

- Improve theft reduction. Systems such as Checkpoint have long been the dominant technology in terms of alerting stores to goods being stolen. However, that technology cannot distinguish between a single pair of jeans being waved in front of the sensor as a decoy, and someone else walking out with 20 pairs.

Manufacturing: This industry is seeing increased use of RFID to automate visibility into processes such as work-in-progress (where an item moves between different stages during manufacture).

The case studies interspersed throughout this book will dive into the innovative ways that many organizations are leveraging RFID technology to enable real-world solutions to business challenges.

Conclusion

RFID technology is the next step along the path of linking information systems with objects in the physical world. Based on radio waves rather than optics, it provides several advantages over bar codes in scenarios requiring high degrees of automation, reading without line of sight, and storage of dynamic data.

Successfully deploying RFID requires careful selection of appropriate technology from the available options (passive vs. active and HF vs. UHF). The intent of this chapter was to provide a high-level overview of some of the key aspects of RFID, and to provide context around integrating information from RFID readers and tags into software systems via Microsoft BizTalk RFID.

If you want to learn more about the physics side of RFID technology, the RFID Solutions Center in Dayton, Ohio (`www.rfidsolutionscenter.com/`) offers in-depth courses on understanding and implementing RFID.

CASE STUDY: WHAT RFID INFRASTRUCTURES LOOKED LIKE PRIOR TO BIZTALK RFID

Industry: Multiple.

Overview: To understand how BizTalk RFID improves processes, a quick introduction to infrastructures prior to its advent is in order. To begin with, if an organization wanted to capture event information from an RFID reader, it generally needed to work directly with the manufacturer of that device to build code to output the information. Then, once this information was made available, they would need to build "middleware" components to catch this information and route it to the appropriate destination. Manufacturers would often request their own proprietary databases to capture this information, and organizations with multiple device types would be left with a scattered and disconnected view of their data. Metrics would be across systems and databases, and would be complex and time-consuming to combine. Updates to readers and components would be difficult and splintered. Exception and error tracking were unique to each reader and each path. Essentially, a united approach to integrating RFID data into the enterprise was elusive, expensive, difficult, and rarely achieved.

Results: Organizations that have incorporated BizTalk RFID have seen a dramatic reduction in the complexity and maintenance of their RFID solutions. By its nature, BizTalk Server combined with BizTalk RFID provide for the integrated infrastructure that enables the capture of events from a multitude of readers and the publication of that information across the enterprise without extensive development of custom objects.

CHAPTER 2

■ ■ ■

BizTalk RFID Architecture and Installation

BizTalk RFID's primary mission is pretty straightforward: to make it easy to build RFID applications on the Microsoft Windows platform. In this chapter, we will explore what an RFID application looks like, and get started on the journey of understanding the mental model of a BizTalk RFID application. Once you have a grasp of this, we will look at the system architecture of BizTalk RFID and the BizTalk RFID device model. Next, different configurations and approaches to installing the application will be outlined.

The key objectives of this chapter are as follows:

- Understanding what a BizTalk RFID application is

- Understanding the process architecture and the BizTalk RFID device model

- Working through installation

- Understanding system architecture and configuration

The BizTalk RFID Process Architecture

As you saw in the previous chapter, the fundamental technology behind RFID is not really new. The technology has been around for a few decades, and has been used with success on several large-scale deployments in military and commercial contexts. Also, there is really no such thing as a single RFID technology. The moniker applies to a collection of protocols, frequencies, power levels, capabilities, form factors, and packaging. The commonality between them is really in the application of the technology—all of them are aimed at automatic object identification. Imagine if you could assign IP addresses to every object in the real world. From a hardware perspective, that is the fundamental promise of RFID. From a solution perspective, that is the just the beginning.

Let's look at the entire analogy and wind back to 1993: imagine that all the computers in the world had network cards with IP addresses. Imagine that you could have a federated collection of servers that could assign names to these IP addresses to make them friendly. This is where we were at the start of the Internet revolution. If we had stopped there, it would have been a really interesting technology that made certain kinds of information sharing possible, but it would not have changed the world. What changed the world was the killer application for IP: the Internet in its full glory of the World Wide Web—ubiquitous, rich, copious, full of searchable content, employing completely new business models like eBay and Amazon, containing rich self-service and collaborative applications, enabling peer-to-peer social networking—the list goes on. And all of them had almost nothing to do with network cards and IP addresses, and everything to do with unlocking the value of the Internet through the power of software.

And that is the role of the RFID application: IP addresses for objects in the real world open the doors to a variety of possibilities, all of which have to be eventually realized in software. The applications for RFID are broad, varied, and rich. We have to confess, one of the amazing things about working on this project was the chance to work fairly closely with partners and customers worldwide, and learn from their descriptions of the scenarios firsthand. The list includes everything from asset tracking (cattle, baggage, people, railway wagons, aircraft components, defense equipment, hospital equipment, office stationery, library books, and fish, to name just a few), to access control, to conventional supply chain visibility, to work-in-progress visibility, to e-pedigree, and everything in between. Phew! RFID scenarios are truly applicable in the vast majority of domains and verticals, and the interest in RFID is truly global: usage of RFID spans manufactures from China; retailers in the United States, Europe, and India; logistics providers in the United States, Europe, Japan, Australia, and South America; and so on. Some analysts and industry experts have started calling this entire class of applications the "extended Internet," or the "physical Internet," which is an apt analogy given the broad promise of RFID applications.

That was the big picture, so to speak. With those scenarios in mind, let us now look at the little picture: as the architects, designers, and developers who have to build out the solutions at the end of the day, the devil (or the fun) is really in the details. What does an RFID application look like? It has the following key requirements:

- It must work well with the hardware layer of readers and tags. Given the diversity of RFID technologies, this is actually a significant task.

- It must be able to interpret the information stored on the tags and reported through the reader. Typically, for a variety of reasons, the information stored on the RFID tag is really an identification code (or a GUID in developer terms, or a license plate number in layman's terms). It rarely has human-readable information directly stored on the tag itself. Understanding this machine-readable binary quantity is the first step to interacting with the physical entity. Note that if you really need the extra storage, certain types of tags (typically HF tags) offer the capability to store 64 Kb or more of data on the tag.

- It must be able to correlate this information with the rest of the contextual information associated with the entity to make real-world sense of the binary ID. Think of this as going from the code to a human-readable description, or from a license plate number to a "vehicle database information record."

- It must be able to use the RFID information to enable better business decision-making for the company. Think of this as the way to leverage the RFID investment to impact the top and/or bottom line for the company. This is a crucial point in the relevance of the solution that you are developing and will typically involve integration with the back-end line-of-business (LOB) system, or the centralized business analytics infrastructure of your enterprise. RFID provides the real-time information stream, but that really needs to be complemented with real-time decision-making to truly utilize the benefits of deploying RFID.

BizTalk RFID addresses the needs of such applications with the following components:

- The Device Service Provider Interface (DSPI), a brand-new device abstraction framework that lets you interact with devices in a uniform, consistent fashion across a rich, diverse set of devices. This is similar to the Windows driver model, but enables a much richer device experience within the familiar .NET programming paradigm.

- A rich object model for retrieving tag information that includes support for the EPCglobal Class 1 Gen 2 protocol.

- A new event-oriented programming application model called the *RFID business process*. RFID business processes provide a declarative experience for authoring an event processing tree that can be deployed and hosted by BizTalk RFID.

- Connectivity components to integrate back into BizTalk Server, SQL Server, and LOB systems.

BizTalk RFID has a layered system architecture (see Figure 2-1). In this section, we will look at the various elements of the architecture, and how they relate to each other.

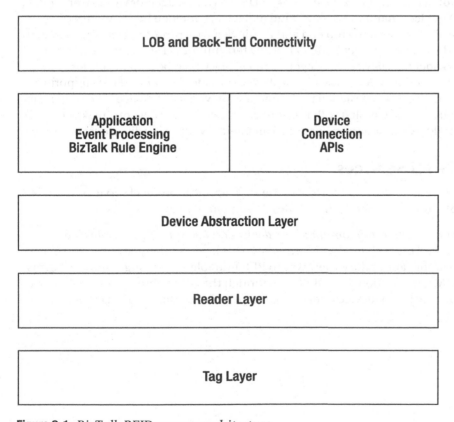

Figure 2-1. *BizTalk RFID process architecture*

The Physical Layer

This is the lowest layer of the system, and it represents the various entities in the physical world that you want to interact with. Typically, it includes RFID tags, bar codes, sensors, and so on. This layer of the system communicates directly with the device above, using RF waves and some over-the-air protocol, most commonly EPCglobal Class 1 Gen 2 these days.

The Device Layer

The next layer up is the device layer: readers, printers, bar code scanners, sensor processors, and everything in between. This layer performs two key tasks: communicating with the physical layer below using the over-the-air protocol, and communicating with the software layer above using some network-based or bus-attached protocol.

The Device Provider Layer

This layer is responsible for communicating with devices and presenting the device using a uniform abstraction to the higher layers of the software. BizTalk RFID introduces a new device abstraction framework called DSPI. You can think of DSPI as a managed device driver model designed with RFID devices in mind. For each kind of device, someone has to write a plug-in that implements this interface on the top end and the device wire protocol at the bottom end. This plug-in is called a *device provider* in BizTalk RFID terminology. Typically, the hardware vendor writes the provider for a device—analogous to how they would be responsible for writing the Windows device driver for a device. While the device provider layer has good support for RFID readers and printers, it was designed to support a wide variety of device types and near-real-time event streams. This, coupled with the application support for events, makes BizTalk RFID a platform to build real-time applications that can interact with a very diverse set of devices.

Application-Level Services

The next layer in the architecture is comprised of the edge application-level services, intended to be directly callable by end user code. It includes three main kinds of services:

> *A set of client APIs for executing commands on devices and getting responses back from them, similar to the ADO.NET model for databases*: This layer is intended to run in-process with your application, and is the easiest way to RFID-enable an existing Windows Forms, ASP.NET, or COM+ application. Note that even though the client library is in-process with your application, the actual device interaction happens in the BizTalk RFID process.

A brand-new hosted application model for event processing, called the RFID business process: This involves designing a process with a set of event handlers, or custom code for handling events, stitched together using an XML definition, similar to how Windows Workflow Foundation (WF) workflows are defined. The process must be deployed into BizTalk RFID and then executed within it. BizTalk RFID as the application host provides a certain level of fault tolerance and reliability, especially on Windows Server.

A way to execute business rules authored using the BizTalk Rule Engine (BRE): BizTalk RFID includes the same rule engine that ships with BizTalk Server 2006 R2. This is great from a BizTalk developer perspective. All the knowledge that you have about authoring rules using the Business Rule Composer and deployment tools will translate directly to BizTalk RFID. The integration between RFID business processes and the BRE is done through the out-of-the-box event handler `RuleEnginePolicyExecutor`.

LOB and Back-End Connectivity

This is the topmost layer in the architecture, and is responsible for collecting, analyzing, and taking actions based on the activity on the edge. Typically, this piece runs in the data center of your enterprise. It includes artifacts such as BizTalk orchestrations that consume RFID data, and Business Activity Monitoring (BAM) reports that depict real-time information derived from the RFID event stream. Other common back-end scenarios for RFID applications include LOB connectivity using the BizTalk WCF LOB Adapter Pack, and analytics using SQL Server Analysis Services.

The BizTalk RFID Device Model

BizTalk RFID has an abstract model for a physical device. Understanding this model is fundamental to how you interact with devices from within BizTalk RFID. In this section, we will cover the basic elements of the model, and how you can interact with them from with RFID Manager and the API. An illustration of this model is shown in Figure 2-2.

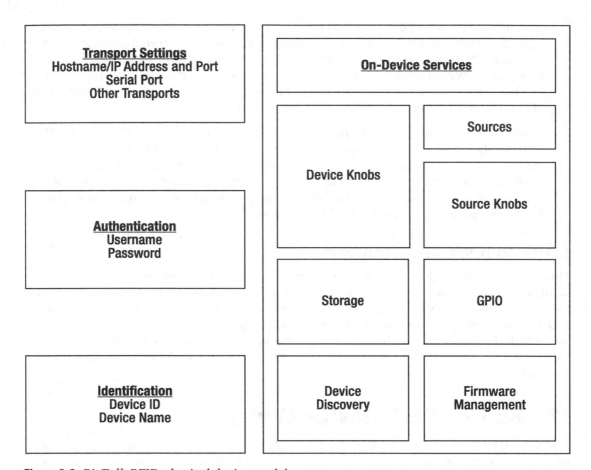

Figure 2-2. *BizTalk RFID physical device model*

Identity

Every device is required to have a unique identity called the *device ID*, which is the basis for identifying devices from BizTalk RFID. Typically, this looks a lot like a MAC ID on a network card, and is not expected to change during the life of the device. Uniquely identifying a device helps BizTalk RFID take actions when the device communicates with it. A device can also have a friendly name, which is used to identify the device both by administrators and applications that want to use the device. If the device does not support a friendly name, the name is managed at the BizTalk RFID layer.

Endpoint

The device is assumed to have a single connection endpoint, through which remote clients such as BizTalk RFID can connect to the device. BizTalk RFID is agnostic to the nature of the endpoint; the device may support TCP/IP, HTTP, Serial Bus, Bluetooth, or some proprietary mechanism. However, the model assumes that the device shall be connectable only through one of these protocols at one time.

■Tip Many RFID readers support more than one protocol (typically serial communications and TCP/IP, or wired and wireless network support). Such readers typically use one interface for initial setup and configuration, and the other for operations. You can work with such devices from BizTalk RFID by using the drop-down box from RFID Manager to select the connection method, and changing it once configuration is done. If you are a provider developer, note that if a device supports more than one transport method, you must return the same device ID for all the transports.

Connection Initiation

The device model assumes that connections are initiated and terminated from BizTalk RFID as and when necessary. For devices that support asynchronous tag notifications, these connections tend to be long-lived. The model assumes that physical connections can be dropped intermittently, and the responsibility for detecting that the connection is down and needs to be reestablished lies with BizTalk RFID. You can use the device statistics tab in RFID Manager to check the number of times the physical connection was opened and the number of failed connections. Note that the true status of the connection really depends on the transport protocol used and that the device provider implements the IsConnectionAlive method correctly.

■Provider authoring tip Some RFID readers support *autonomous operations*, where the reader persists the location of the server of interest and is responsible for setting up the connection to the server on its own. This tends to be useful from a deployment perspective, especially in scenarios where the network connection is dropped or the reader is rebooted. You can work with such devices from within BizTalk RFID as long as the provider supports the functionality to listen for and accept incoming connection requests, and returns the established connection in response to the DSPI SetupConnection call.

Authentication

The model assumes that the device may support some form of authentication when clients attempt to connect to it. This is typically username/password-based, but you can use other forms of authentication and secure communications by using the vendor extensions mechanism.

■Tip The username/password information that is used to connect to the device is managed in a secure fashion by BizTalk RFID. The information is deemed sensitive and is stored in an encrypted fashion in the rfid configuration store. Once set, it cannot be retrieved by RFID Manager; it can only be modified by an administrator (it is write-only information).

■**Provider authoring tip** If you need additional sensitive information to be stored by BizTalk RFID that is per-connection–specific, consider overloading the usage of these fields in the provider.

Discovery

The model assumes that the device has some way of advertising itself when it is booted up. This could be something along the lines of PnP for bus-attached devices, UPnP, mDNS, or any device-discovery mechanism, including the newer Web Services for Devices (WSD) protocols. On device discovery, the provider is responsible for raising a discovery event. BizTalk RFID uses the information in the event to determine if the device is managed by that particular server. If it is not, the administrator is flagged that an unconfigured device was discovered. This explicit model gives administrators control over which devices are owned and operated by a particular server.

■**Tip** Make sure that all the information needed to "identify" the device is part of the discovery information. This must include the device ID, the friendly name of the device, and any other information that will be useful to an administrator when they decide if they should use the device.

■**Tip** For bus-attached devices or devices that are connected to one computer only, there is no ambiguity in whether an administrator can use a discovered device or not. If the device is network-attached, the administrator has to make an explicit choice in whether they want to use the device. This is especially important if there are multiple BizTalk RFID servers on a network, and they are partitioned along some application-defined lines. For example, you may want all the devices in a particular warehouse to be managed by a particular server. In this scenario, you can use the property profile in the discovery packet to indicate which server must manage the particular device.

Knobs

The model assumes that devices have a rich set of settings that control all aspects of the operation of the device, including overall configuration, network configuration, and radio configuration. All of these knobs are exposed as properties by the device. A device can indicate a number of facets about the property, including a logical group that the property belongs to, the type of the property, default values, whether the property is mandatory for operation, and whether it requires restarting the device when the property is changed. The property model also distinguishes between transient properties that will revert to their default values after a device restart, and properties that are persisted across device restarts. The DSPI has a rich model for properties and property metadata, but your mileage may vary based on the extent to which the specific provider that you are using has implemented support for all the configuration settings and options on the device.

■**Provider authoring tip** Transient properties are applied by BizTalk RFID on every connection attempt. This is a good thing. Applying transient properties on each connection attempt takes a lot of the guesswork regarding whether a "transient" knob has the correct value, and makes troubleshooting incorrect property settings a lot easier. The downside is that on every connection attempt, you are going to see change requests for these properties. As an optimization, consider ignoring the property change if the current property value is the same as what is being used by the device.

Management

The model assumes that devices have interfaces through which common management tasks such as firmware updating, rebooting, and resetting can be performed.

Sources

At this point, you should be asking yourself where the RFID functionality on the device is, and how you can use it. All of the previously mentioned parts of the model are agnostic to RFID and apply equally to readers, writers, printers, and lots of devices like bar code scanners and sensors that have nothing to do with RFID. In keeping with the protocol-agnostic theme, a device is modeled as having zero or more sources. The *source* in the name refers to a source of events on the device, typically an antenna or a read point for an RFID reader. However, BizTalk RFID also uses this same source concept to interact with the GPIO ports of a device. If your device has other sources that raise events, such as motion sensors, location detectors, or bar code scanners, consider exposing them as sources. Each source has a set of knobs that can be configured, as well as a switch that lets you enable and disable a source from an application using the BizTalk RFID APIs.

■**Provider authoring tip** Use the System Enabled and User Enabled knobs to differentiate between sources that cannot be used by the system and sources that are available and disabled by a user. For example, if a device has four antenna ports, but only one port has a connection to a physical antenna, you should set the SystemEnabled property on the other three ports to false.

■**Provider authoring tip** Each source has a name, and source names have to be distinct. If you have two sources that have the same name, you need to disambiguate them by prefixing them with something distinctive. For example, you can use the names Antenna1 and GPIO1 to distinguish between an antenna called 1 and a GPIO port with the same name.

The BizTalk RFID Device Model for Applications

The previous section described how BizTalk RFID "thinks" about devices—similar to the Windows driver model that the operating system uses to interact with other physical devices. However, this does not mean applications need to use this model to communicate with the devices. Just like the Win32 .NET APIs provide higher-level abstractions of devices that are more user-friendly than the Windows driver model, BizTalk RFID has a higher-level model that applications should use to talk to devices. This model has two main components:

> *The* DeviceConnection *class*: This is a stand-alone API intended to be loaded into your client application. Use this model if you need to add RFID device interaction into your Windows Forms, ASP.NET, COM+, or other .NET applications, including WF applications that are hosted and called through WCF.

> *The RFID business process*: This is a new hosted application model for designing and deploying business processes that react to RFID events. RFID business processes are described in detail in Chapter 5. For the purposes of this discussion, the main difference between them and the DeviceConnection class is that RFID business processes are fully managed by BizTalk RFID and run within its hosting infrastructure.

The two models are mutually exclusive in the capabilities that they present to the user: using a device connection, you can only execute commands and get responses back; you cannot subscribe to event notifications from the device that are available asynchronously. Using RFID business processes, by default, you can only receive asynchronous events from the device, you cannot execute commands or get responses. If you need to execute commands from within an event handler, you can do so, but you must use the DeviceConnection API and manage the connection in the code for the event handler.

The Device Model Assumed by DeviceConnection

To connect to a device, you just need the friendly name of the device. This friendly name is in a "flat" namespace across all the devices in the system. You don't need any other information to connect to the device from your application, including items like the transport settings or authentication information. All of that is done for you automatically by BizTalk RFID. However, you need to know the name of the machine that the RFID server is running on. This makes the connection model simple to use, while also abstracting out the details of the device transport completely from your application. However, before the connection is permitted, the device security model is used to determine if you have rights to perform the operation—which brings us to the next topic, the device security model.

The Device Security Model

The model is implemented entirely within BizTalk RFID, similar to how the Windows ACL model is implemented completely by Windows, not by the physical storage device. This presents a uniform, consistent view of security for the system across a multitude of devices with different capabilities and requirements. The device security model has two usage patterns that it intends to secure:

Application usage patterns: These typically include executing commands such as an inventory round, or tag manipulation operations such as reading tag data, writing the tag ID, writing tag data, and locking the tag. The user invoking the application must be part of the RFID_USER local Windows group that is created as part of the BizTalk RFID installation. This implies that if you have a user in the RFID_USER group, the user has access to all the devices on the server!

Administrative usage patterns: These include operations such as renaming a device, moving a device from one device group to another, and changing settings on the device, including the RF properties and network settings. Administrative access can be granted in a fine-grained manner. BizTalk RFID has the notion of a *device group*, which is a security container for devices, as well as a container to bind groups of appropriate devices to processes. Devices can belong to exactly one device group, but groups can contain other groups, similar to the Windows folder model. You can add specific local and domain Windows users to a device group and grant them administrative rights on all the devices in the group. The device group security is inheritable down the tree, so you can grant access on the granularity that is appropriate for your scenario.

■**Tip** All users in the local Administrators group on the machine have implicit administrative access to all the devices on the server. If you accidentally lock yourself out, you can log in as a box administrator to fix the security settings.

■**Tip** You can use the folder view in RFID Manager to browse devices. Remember that RFID Manager has two views of devices: the device group view (see Figure 2-3) and the flat view of all devices in the system (see Figure 2-4). Simultaneously, each device would be present in both views, which is potentially confusing, until you understand the purpose of the two views.

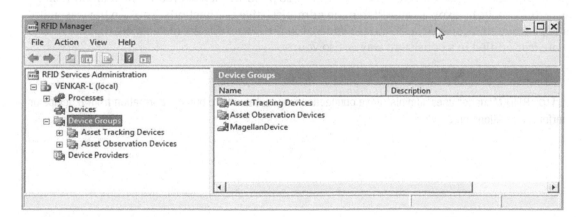

Figure 2-3. *The Device Groups view*

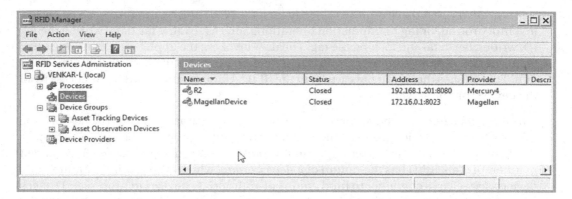

Figure 2-4. *The Devices view*

No device security is applied when BizTalk RFID routes events from devices to RFID business processes. This is because all processes must be deployed and started by an administrator, who implicitly has access to all devices. From a deployment perspective, this feature removes the need to have custom security settings for RFID business processes.

The Concurrency Model for the DeviceConnection Class

Since an application using a device connection is primarily expected to execute commands and receive responses from it using the synchronous command model, BizTalk RFID does not support multiple applications accessing the device at the same instant. This is a good thing. You don't want one application locking a tag and another killing it at the same time. In fact, most devices do not currently even support such an interaction pattern. However, you can have an application and a business process both using the device at the same time. BizTalk RFID takes care of the sharing of the connection for this scenario and the management of the underlying provider objects.

The one exception to this simple model is the usage of device connections by administrators. Administrators may need immediate access to a device, even if another application is using it, perhaps just to browse the settings on the device. To perform such operations in an unobtrusive way, BizTalk RFID exposes an API to open administrative connections. You can have as many such connections open to a device as needed, but the responsibility of ensuring that the device state is modified in a consistent way is also yours.

■**Tip** RFID Manager uses administrative connections when it needs to obtain information from a device or perform operations on the device.

The RFID Business Process Device Model

RFID business processes use the concept of a *logical device* to denote a device. The logical device concept is different from the friendly name of the physical device, and is a concept that is available to that process definition only. Administrators are responsible for binding logical devices to physical devices as part of deployment. The process's model of a device is simple: events emanating from these logical devices are delivered to the process—nothing more, nothing less. The process cannot open device connections to the logical device names, nor can it execute commands or perform other administrative operations on the logical devices. This, of course, does not preclude event handlers from using the physical names of the devices to do all of this, but doing so obviates the benefits from the distinction between logical and physical devices, and the automatic connection management that you get from logical devices. More than one process can receive events from the same physical device. The delivery of the same event to multiple processes is again managed automatically by BizTalk RFID for you.

Table 2-1 describes some of the important differences between the two device application models:

Table 2-1. *Device Application Comparison*

Model Type	Asynchronous Events	Commands	Device Identification	Device Security Applied	Concurrent Usage Allowed
DeviceConnection	No	Yes	Device-friendly name	Yes	No
RFID business process	Yes	No	Logical device name	No	Yes

Installing BizTalk RFID

This section will outline the steps necessary to install BizTalk RFID. It will also provide an overview of the different installation options and the prerequisites involved. Finally, in this section we will walk through an exercise (Exercise 2-1) where we install BizTalk RFID.

BizTalk RFID is intended to be installed at the edge of the enterprise. In this context, *edge* means a site outside a typical data center, such as a manufacturing shop floor, retail point of sale, or even a parking garage, if the items being tagged happen to be cars in a parking lot. To facilitate such deployments, BizTalk RFID comes with its own installer package, and can be installed independently of BizTalk Server 2009. There are three installable components, based on your deployment scenario:

RFID Services: This option installs the server components.

RFID Tools and Client Connector: This option installs the components required to manage the BizTalk RFID server remotely, and for client applications that need to connect to devices that are managed by the BizTalk RFID server.

The RFID SDK: This includes a device simulator, and samples and tools for developing device providers and applications. In a production deployment, you will typically not install this component.

BizTalk RFID is a stand-alone product, but it makes use of a number of other Microsoft technologies in its operation, including SQL Server, MSMQ, MS DTC, WMI, Active Directory, the .NET Framework 3.5 SP1, IIS, and MMC 3.0. For the complete list of requirements, check the latest version of the installation guide, at http://go.microsoft.com/fwlink/?LinkID=58568. Here are some notes for the major dependent components:

- BizTalk RFID stores almost all of its configuration information in a SQL Server database (called RFIDSTORE by default). As part of the installation process (see Exercise 2-1), you need to provide the location and connection information for the SQL Server instance that should be used for the configuration store.

■**Tip** If the SQL Server database is not available, BizTalk RFID cannot run and will shut down. We recommend using a local instance of SQL Server for this configuration database, and using the remote SQL Server option only in advanced scenarios, such as failover.

- BizTalk RFID uses MSMQ as the temporary store for persisting in-flight events from devices that have not yet been consumed by the event processing applications. This usage of MSMQ does not require Active Directory integration, since BizTalk RFID only creates private MSMQ queues.

■**Tip** If BizTalk Server 2006 and BizTalk RFID are installed on the same machine, you must disable the BizTalk Message Queuing (MSMQT) adapter that is part of BizTalk Server to ensure that the usage of MSMQ by BizTalk RFID does not conflict with MSMQT.

- On Windows Server, BizTalk RFID uses IIS as the application host for increased reliability and isolation. If you are running into issues configuring IIS 6.0 for BizTalk RFID, start from the troubleshooting section in the installation document for a few of the common configuration problems.

Exercise 2-1. Installing BizTalk RFID 2009

This exercise will demonstrate how to obtain and install the components needed for BizTalk RFID.

1. First, install MSMQ (this step is for Windows Vista only; it will be different if you're using a different OS). Go to Control Panel ➤ Programs ➤ "Turn Windows features on or off." On the Windows Features dialog, you need to enable Microsoft Message Queue (MSMQ) Server Core only; all the nodes under that can be unchecked (see Figure 2-5).

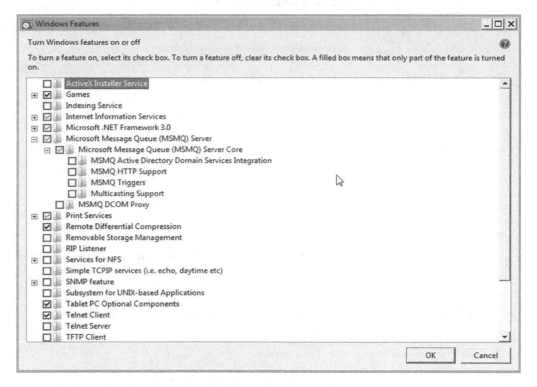

Figure 2-5. *Enabling the required MSMQ components*

2. Install Microsoft Management Console (MMC) 3.0 RTM version (on Windows XP SP3 only). You can download this component from the Microsoft web site.

3. Install IIS (Windows Server only). The instructions for how to install and configure IIS for BizTalk RFID are in the BizTalk RFID documentation.

4. Install SQL Server. The full sequence for installing SQL Server is outside the scope of this book, but any installation of SQL Server 2008 or SQL Server 2005 SP2 (including SQL Server Express) can be used by BizTalk RFID.

5. Install BizTalk RFID. One of the most common questions that we are asked is if BizTalk RFID requires BizTalk Server to be installed on the same machine. The answer is no. If you need just the RFID functionality, you can install just the BizTalk RFID piece on the computer. In fact, if you install BizTalk Server only, the BizTalk RFID components will not even be installed on that machine! When you bring up the BizTalk RFID installer, you will see a screen that looks like Figure 2-6.

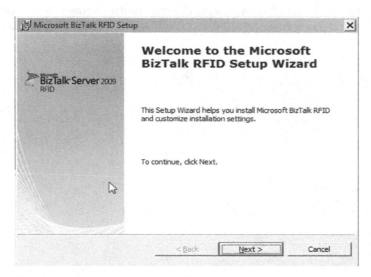

Figure 2-6. *The BizTalk RFID Setup wizard*

6. Click Next until you're past the standard license-related screens. You will be presented with a set of installation options, as shown in Figure 2-7.

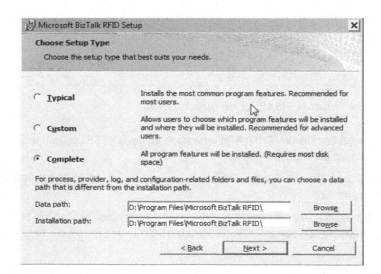

Figure 2-7. *Component installation options for BizTalk RFID*

7. After this, you will configure the SQL Server instance that will be used to hold the RFID configuration store, as shown in Figure 2-8.

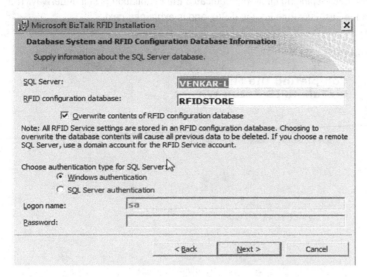

Figure 2-8. *Configuring the SQL Server database instance*

8. Next up, you will specify the RFID service account credentials, as shown in Figure 2-9.

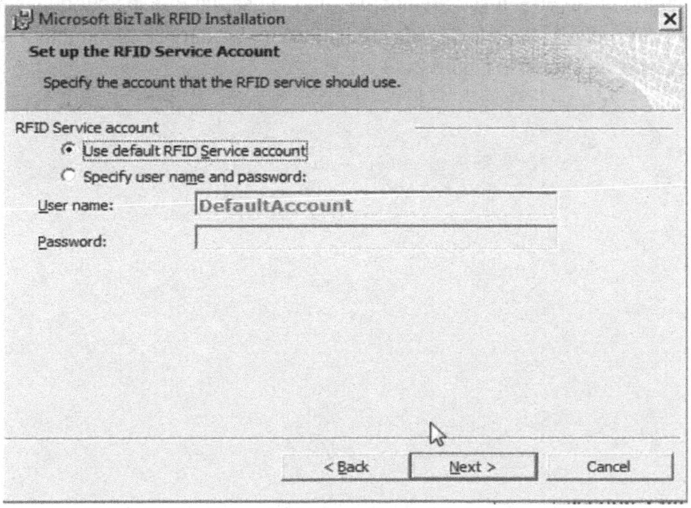

Figure 2-9. *Configuring the RFID service account*

9. At this point, you have provided the installer with all the information that it needs, and it will run to completion. When it is done, you should see a screen confirming that the installation was successful (Figure 2-10). However, you should also see a spinning circle that indicates the installation is still underway. The reason for this involves the Business Rule Engine (BRE), and is explained next.

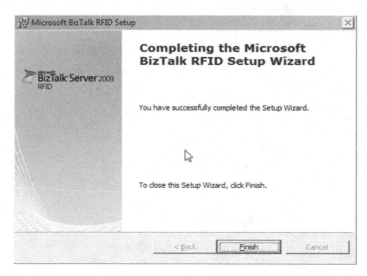

Figure 2-10. *The completion screen for the BizTalk RFID installer*

10. The next step involves configuring the BRE. If you are not planning to use the BRE in your deployment, you can skip this step. If you are, you will need to provide credentials for the service account that will be used by the BRE update service, as shown in Figure 2-11.

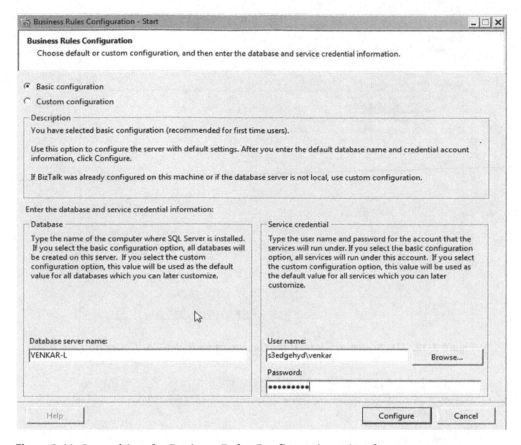

Figure 2-11. *Launching the Business Rules Configuration wizard*

11. Once you have picked the account, you can accept the default options presented (Figure 2-12) and complete the BRE configuration (Figure 2-13).

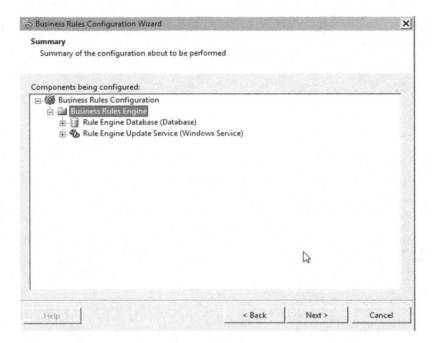

Figure 2-12. *The Summary screen for the Business Rules Configuration wizard*

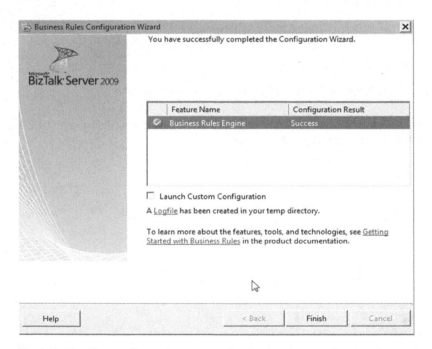

Figure 2-13. *The confirmation screen for the Business Rules Configuration wizard*

All in all, this should have been a pretty painless experience, especially compared to BizTalk Server installs of yore.

Conclusion

In this chapter, we have taken a tour of the abstract model that BizTalk RFID uses to interact with devices. We covered a number of important topics related to device abstraction, including connection management, device security, configuration management, and support for device behaviors. This was followed by a drill-down into the overall architecture of the product, both from a component-layering perspective and a physical process perspective. Moving speedily from the conceptual to the tangible, we finished off the chapter with a quick look at the installation process for BizTalk RFID. Next up, we shall put the installation that we just created to good use by delving into the nuts and bolts of building your first RFID application.

CASE STUDY: IMPROVING MAINTAINABILITY OF RFID INFRASTRUCTURES

Industry: Food.

Overview: A number of food industry–related organizations have implemented RFID infrastructures to track inventory as it moves from one facility to another, and eventually to the shelves. In this industry, the ability to rapidly track and maintain inventory is essential, due to the short shelf life of many products. Ensuring that the latest RFID technology is available for transmission and reading enables these organizations to reduce loss due to slow shipping practices and misplaced inventory. In the past, once an RFID implementation was put into place, it was often difficult to add newer technology without rewriting much of the code that interpreted the information. As these organizations become aware of BizTalk RFID and move to implement it, they are finding that much of the complexity of incorporating various RFID technologies is greatly reduced and their flexibility to respond to market conditions and inventory management is improved.

Results: Adding BizTalk RFID to the enterprise allows adopters to rapidly exchange the underlying RFID components to fit shifting markets and needs without having to rewrite the infrastructure that moves the data to repositories and end user reports.

CHAPTER 3

■ ■ ■

The RFID "Hello World" Application

This chapter will provide a step-by-step walkthrough of creating a basic solution using Microsoft BizTalk RFID and the Contoso device simulator. It will demonstrate the essential end user activities—managing RFID devices and implementing an event processing pipeline.

Overview

This section will provide a walkthrough of building a basic RFID application using BizTalk RFID. It will demonstrate the basic concepts and building blocks, including device providers, devices, processes, and event handlers. It is intended as a quick start to familiarize you with the various components of BizTalk RFID and how they can be applied to implement RFID-enabled solutions.

Our first end-to-end RFID solution, Hello RFID, will implement a basic scenario: capturing data generated by tags passing through a portal reader. It will not address filtering, workflow, I/O, or similar comprehensive features found in real-world applications, as these will be covered in later chapters.

As shown in Figure 3-1, the application will consist of a simulated reader (instead of a real RFID reader—using the simulator that ships out of the box with BizTalk RFID) feeding tag information into a database through BizTalk RFID. The rest of this chapter will walk through how to bring together all of these moving parts into a coherent solution.

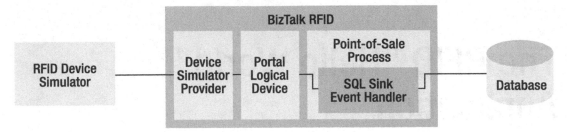

Figure 3-1. *Hello RFID overview*

Using the Device Simulator

The device simulator that ships with Microsoft BizTalk RFID provides basic simulation functionality, including generating tag reads and responding to commands (such as writing data to tags or changing I/O ports). It is a console application with a low level of interactivity (i.e., it dumps information into a console window, but is controlled through a configuration file rather than a runtime interface). Exercise 3-1 shows you how to start the device simulator.

Exercise 3-1. Starting the Device Simulator

This exercise will demonstrate how to start the device simulator and make it available to BizTalk RFID.

1. Start a console by clicking Start ➤ All Programs ➤ Accessories ➤ Command Prompt.

2. Change the working directory to the BizTalk RFID Services device simulator directory by entering the cd command shown here:

   ```
   C:\>cd "\Program Files\Microsoft BizTalk RFID\Samples\
   Device Service Provider\Contoso\ContosoEndToEnd\ContosoDeviceSimulator"
   ```

■**Note** When starting the simulator, if you receive a System.Unauthorized exception error related to the log file not being writable, restart the command prompt with administrative privileges. To do this, click Start ➤ All Programs ➤ Accessories, and then right-click Command Prompt. From the context menu, select Run as Administrator. Continue from step 2.

---

3. Execute the runContosoSimulator.cmd batch file, as shown in Figure 3-2, to start the simulator. Leave the simulator running, as it will be needed in the remainder of the exercises in this chapter.

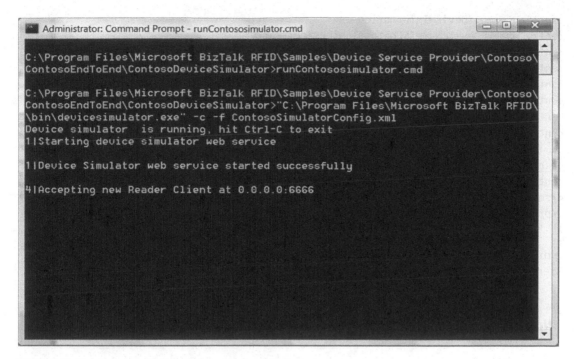

Figure 3-2. *Device simulator running in console*

Starting from the baseline configuration, the device simulator can be tweaked to enable other types of scenarios and tag generation patterns. This is done by manipulating the reader and behavior setting configuration files.

Configuring Settings

A sample configuration file for the device simulator is shown in Listing 3-1. It consists of the header section (defining the number of devices) and a set of device sections (which provide the configuration for the network bindings and behavior module).

Listing 3-1. *Device Simulator Configuration File*

```xml
<?xml version="1.0" encoding="utf-8" ?>
<profile>
<section name="NumberOfDevices">
    <entry name="DeviceCount">1</entry>
</section>
```

```
<section name="DeviceInformation_1">
<entry name="DeviceName">ContosoTestDevice</entry>
<entry name="ConnectionType">TCPIP</entry>
<entry name="IpAddress">0.0.0.0</entry>
<entry name="PortNumber">6666</entry>
<entry name="ProviderId">Contoso</entry>
<entry name="NotificationDataFile">ContosoNotificationConfig.xml</entry>
<entry name="DeviceTranslatorAssemblyPath">
    Microsoft.Rfid.Test.ContosoDeviceTranslator.dll
</entry>
<entry name="DeviceTranslatorConfigFile"></entry>
</section>
</profile>
```

Modification of this file allows configuration of multiple simulated readers with varying setups (depending on the targeted scenario—i.e., number of readers, network paths, etc.). Exercise 3-2 shows you how to modify the simulator for two devices.

■**Note** The 0.0.0.0 IP address in the preceding file means "Use all available IP addresses."

Exercise 3-2. Modifying the Simulator for Two Devices

This exercise will demonstrate how to modify the device simulator to start multiple simulated devices, and make these devices available to BizTalk RFID.

1. Start a console by clicking Start ➤ All Programs ➤ Accessories ➤ Command Prompt.

2. Change the working directory to the BizTalk RFID Services device simulator directory by entering the cd command shown here:

   ```
   C:\>cd "\Program Files\Microsoft BizTalk RFID\Samples\Device Service

   Provider\Contoso\ContosoEndToEnd\ContosoDeviceSimulator"
   ```

3. Create a copy of the ContosoSimulatorConfig.xml file and name it ContosoTwoReader.xml. Modify the contents of this file to match those shown in Listing 3-2. The sections to change are the device name and the network binding (i.e., both readers cannot bind to the same address and port).

Listing 3-2. *ContosoTwoReader.xml Contents*

```xml
<?xml version="1.0" encoding="utf-8" ?>
<profile>
<section name="NumberOfDevices">
    <entry name="DeviceCount">2</entry>
</section>

<section name="DeviceInformation_1">
<entry name="DeviceName">ContosoTestDevice</entry>
<entry name="ConnectionType">TCPIP</entry>
<entry name="IpAddress">0.0.0.0</entry>
<entry name="PortNumber">6666</entry>
<entry name="ProviderId">Contoso</entry>
<entry name="NotificationDataFile">ContosoNotificationConfig.xml</entry>
<entry name="DeviceTranslatorAssemblyPath">
    Microsoft.Rfid.Test.ContosoDeviceTranslator.dll
</entry>
<entry name="DeviceTranslatorConfigFile"></entry>
</section>

<section name="DeviceInformation_2">
<entry name="DeviceName">ContosoTestDeviceToo</entry>
<entry name="ConnectionType">TCPIP</entry>
<entry name="IpAddress">0.0.0.0</entry>
<entry name="PortNumber">6667</entry>
<entry name="ProviderId">Contoso</entry>
<entry name="NotificationDataFile">ContosoNotificationConfig.xml</entry>
<entry name="DeviceTranslatorAssemblyPath">
    Microsoft.Rfid.Test.ContosoDeviceTranslator.dll
</entry>
<entry name="DeviceTranslatorConfigFile"></entry>
</section>
</profile>
```

4. Start the device simulator using the new configuration file (ContosoTwoDevices.xml) by executing this command:

```
"%RFIDINSTALLDIR%\bin\devicesimulator.exe" -c -f ContosotwoDevices.xml
```

5. Check to ensure that the device simulator starts up with two simulated devices by checking the output for devices bound to both ports 6666 and 6667, as shown in Figure 3-3.

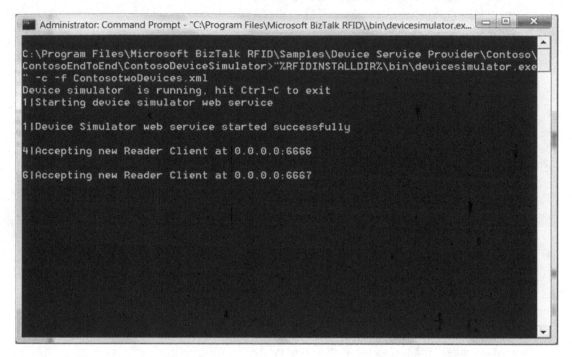

Figure 3-3. *Simulator running two devices*

Configuring Notifications

A separate configuration file configures the behavior of the simulator in the context of which events get raised by the simulator (i.e., which tags it "reads"). A sample configuration file for the ContosoDeviceTranslator behavior module (the default) is displayed in Listing 3-3.

Listing 3-3. *ContosoTwoReader.xml Contents*

```xml
<?xml version="1.0" encoding="utf-8" ?>
<profile>
<section name="Notification">
    <entry name="TimePeriod">10000</entry>
    <entry name="Distribution">EXPONENTIAL</entry>
    <entry name="NotificationErrorRate">0</entry>
    <entry name="WaitAfterNotification">1000</entry>
    <entry name="InitialDelay">100</entry>
    <entry name="Duplicate_Elimination_Time">0</entry>
    <entry name="InfiniteNotification">FALSE</entry>
```

```
    <entry name="ContinuousDataSection">1</entry>
    <entry name="DiscreteDataSection">0</entry>
</section>
<section name="Continuous Data Section 1">
    <entry name="StartingData">1000</entry>
    <entry name="TotalData">10000</entry>
    <entry name="TagType">1</entry>
    <entry name="TagData">SampleTagData</entry>
    <entry name="TagSource">Antenna1</entry>
    <entry name="DelayTime">1</entry>
</section>
</profile>
```

Following are some of the key sections that configure how notifications are sent:

TimePeriod: The minimum time (in milliseconds) between two tag events

InitialDelay: The time delay before posting the first tag

Duplicate_Elimination_Time: The minimum time delay between posting a tag event and posting another tag event with the same tag ID

InfiniteNotification: If set to true, allows tags to be sent continuously

Distribution, NotificationErrorRate, and WaitAfterNotification are not meant to be end user configurable. Do not modify these variables.

Notifications can be configured in either a discrete or a continuous set. The primary continuous configuration variables are as follows:

StartingData: The initial tag ID. Subsequent tag IDs will increment from this value.

TotalData: The total number of tags to send. If InfiniteNotification is set to true, after this number of tag events has been raised, the cycle will start again.

TagType: The numeric tag type used in the raised events.

TagData: The starting tag data field. Subsequent tag data values will increment from this value.

TagSource: The "source" (or antenna) from which these events will be raised.

Exercise 3-3 presents an example of modifying the simulator behavior.

Exercise 3-3. Modifying the Simulator Behavior

This exercise will demonstrate how to modify the device simulator to send a specific sequence of tag events.

1. Create a copy of the ContosoNotificationConfig.xml file and name it ContosoNotificationConfig.bak.

2. Edit the ContosoNotificationConfig.xml file and modify the contents as shown in Listing 3-4. This adds a second source (Antenna2), which will raise tag events with a different tag type and starting ID.

Listing 3-4. *ContosoTwoReader.xml Contents*

```xml
<?xml version="1.0" encoding="utf-8" ?>
<profile>
<section name="Notification">
    <entry name="TimePeriod">10000</entry>
    <entry name="Distribution">EXPONENTIAL</entry>
    <entry name="NotificationErrorRate">0</entry>
    <entry name="WaitAfterNotification">1000</entry>
    <entry name="InitialDelay">100</entry>
    <entry name="Duplicate_Elimination_Time">0</entry>
    <entry name="InfiniteNotification">TRUE</entry>
    <entry name="ContinuousDataSection">2</entry>
    <entry name="DiscreteDataSection">0</entry>
</section>
<section name="Continuous Data Section 1">
    <entry name="StartingData">1000</entry>
    <entry name="TotalData">10000</entry>
    <entry name="TagType">1</entry>
    <entry name="TagData">SampleTagData</entry>
    <entry name="TagSource">Antenna1</entry>
    <entry name="DelayTime">1</entry>
</section>
<section name="Continuous Data Section 2">
    <entry name="StartingData">5000</entry>
    <entry name="TotalData">10000</entry>
    <entry name="TagType">2</entry>
    <entry name="TagData">SampleTagData</entry>
    <entry name="TagSource">Antenna2</entry>
    <entry name="DelayTime">1</entry>
</section>
</profile>
```

You'll use the file from Listing 3-4 in subsequent exercises (since events aren't raised until a connection is made from BizTalk RFID, the results of this exercise won't be apparent until Exercise 3-5).

Creating a Device in BizTalk RFID

Now that we've established a simulated device to which to connect, the next step is to configure BizTalk RFID to recognize and connect to that device. This will take part in two stages: adding the (Contoso) simulator provider (Exercise 3-4) and adding that device to BizTalk RFID (Exercise 3-5).

Exercise 3-4. Adding the Simulator Provider

This exercise will demonstrate how to register the Contoso simulator provider with BizTalk RFID (this is not done by default during installation).

1. Start RFID Manager by clicking Start ➤ All Programs ➤ Microsoft BizTalk RFID ➤ RFID Manager.

2. Expand the computer name and click Device Providers. Right-click Device Providers to bring up the context menu, and click New Provider, as shown in Figure 3-4.

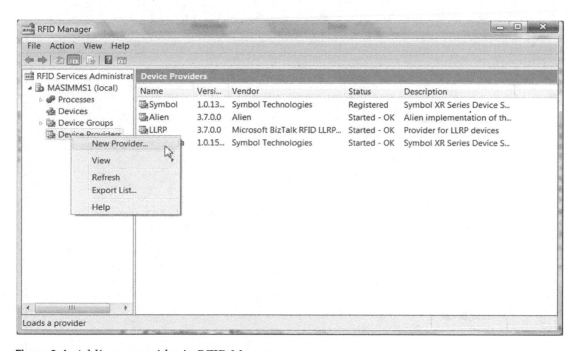

Figure 3-4. *Adding a provider in RFID Manager*

3. From the New Provider dialog, fill in the name field with the value **Contoso**.

4. Click the Browse button and navigate to the C:\Program Files\Microsoft BizTalk RFID\bin directory. Select the Microsoft.Rfid.ContosoDeviceProvider.dll file.

5. Click the Register button to load the provider into BizTalk RFID. The New Provider dialog should now resemble Figure 3-5. Note the ability to configure settings at a provider level (however, the Contoso provider contains many "fake" configuration properties simply for the sake of demonstrating how to implement such properties).

6. Ensure that the "Start the provider" check box is checked.

7. Click OK to finish adding the provider. It should now be visible in the list of registered providers. Note that the other providers loaded in Figure 3-4 are not available out of the box. This screenshot was taken on a machine with several real device providers already loaded.

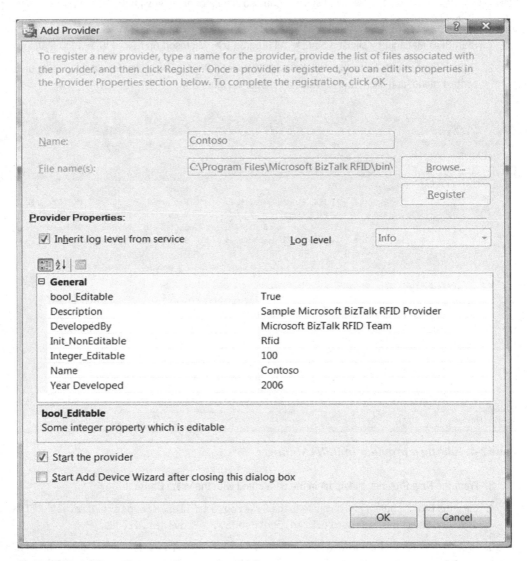

Figure 3-5. *Adding the new Contoso provider*

Exercise 3-5. Creating a Device in BizTalk RFID

This exercise will demonstrate how to add a device in BizTalk RFID.

1. Ensure that the simulator is running and bound to port 6666 (as per Exercise 3-1).

2. Start RFID Manager by clicking Start ➤ All Programs ➤ Microsoft BizTalk RFID ➤ RFID Manager.

3. Expand the computer name and click Devices. Right-click Devices, and then click New Device from the context menu, as shown in Figure 3-6.

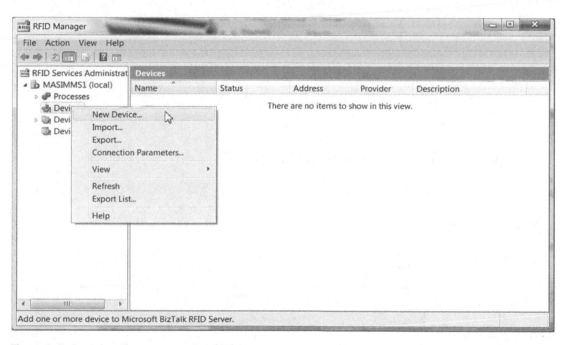

Figure 3-6. *Starting the New Device dialog*

4. From the Add Device wizard, ensure that the Add Single Device radio button is selected, and then click Next.

5. From the list of available providers, click Contoso to highlight it. Click Next to proceed to the next step.

6. As shown in Figure 3-7, type in the loopback address **127.0.0.1** and a port number of **6666** in the appropriate fields. Click Next.

7. From the Add Device to a Group dialog, click Next. At this stage, you will leave the simulated device in the default device group (also known as the *root device group*).

8. On the Authentication dialog, leave the username and password empty, and click Next.

9. Provided that the simulator is running and the network information is correct, the Properties dialog should resemble the one depicted in Figure 3-8. Click Next to proceed to the final step.

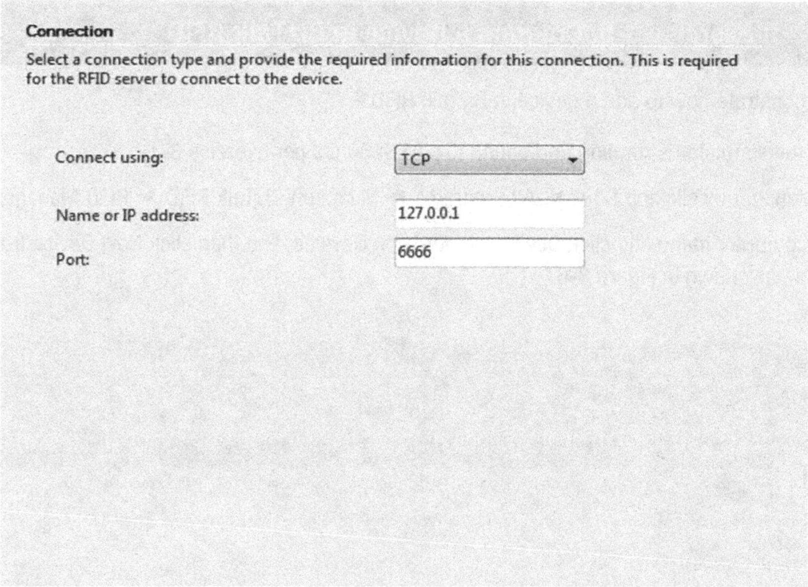

Connection

Select a connection type and provide the required information for this connection. This is required for the RFID server to connect to the device.

Connect using: TCP

Name or IP address: 127.0.0.1

Port: 6666

Figure 3-7. *Configuring connection information*

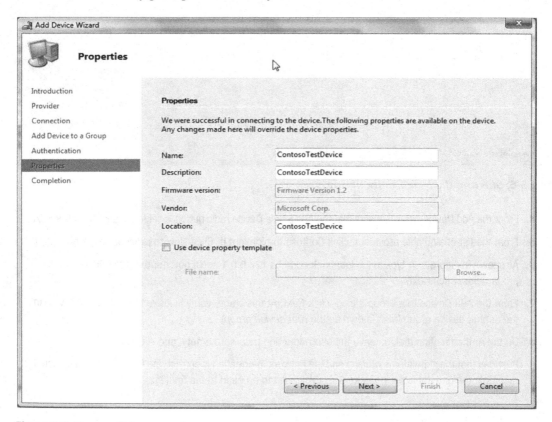

Figure 3-8. *Successful connection*

10. From the Completion dialog, click Finish to complete the process of adding the device. The device should now be visible in the Devices list in RFID Manager, as shown in Figure 3-9.

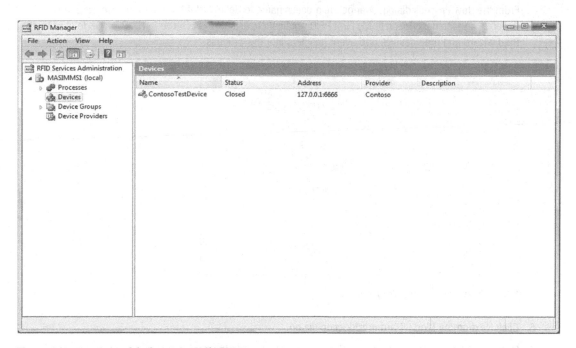

Figure 3-9. *Device added to BizTalk RFID*

Creating a Process

In the previous two sections, you set up the device simulator and created a device binding for it in BizTalk RFID. The final piece of setting up our first BizTalk RFID application involves binding the device into a process, and is explored in Exercise 3-6.

This will tell BizTalk RFID to automatically establish a connection to the device and store received tag events in a SQL Server database (using the SqlServerSink event handler).

Exercise 3-6. Creating a Process in BizTalk RFID

This exercise will demonstrate how to create a process in BizTalk RFID, and bind devices and event handlers to create an RFID application.

1. Ensure that the simulator is running and bound to port 6666 (as per Exercise 3-1).

2. Ensure that the simulated device is defined (as per Exercise 3-5).

3. Start RFID Manager by clicking Start ➤ All Programs ➤ Microsoft BizTalk RFID ➤ RFID Manager.

4. Expand the computer name and click Processes. Right-click Processes, and click New Process from the context menu.

5. From the New Process dialog, change the process name to HelloWorldRfid, the tag-processing mode to Reliable, and the description to My First RFID Application, as shown in Figure 3-10. Click OK to start the Bind wizard and map devices and event handlers into this process.

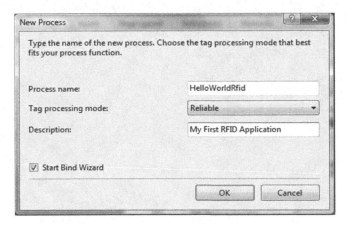

Figure 3-10. *Defining the process*

6. Click Next on the Bind wizard introduction dialog.

7. From the Bind Process to Logical Device dialog, click New. In the Logical Device Name dialog, type **MyLogicalDevice**. Click OK to close the dialog.

8. MyLogicalDevice should now be registered. Click its check box to enable that logical device, as shown in Figure 3-11. Click Next.

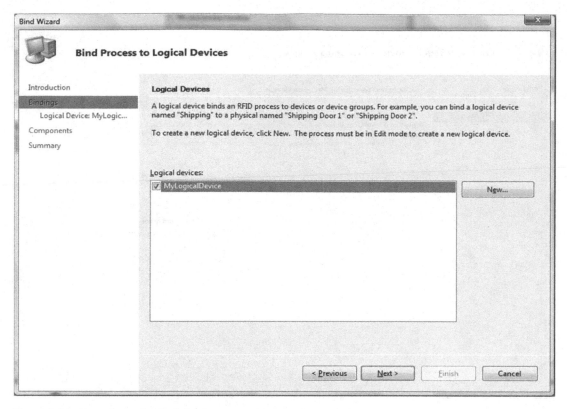

Figure 3-11. *Creating a logical device*

9. From the "Configure logical device – MyLogicalDevice" dialog, expand the ContosoTestDevice node to display the available sources. Click the ContosoTestDevice check box to bind it (and its child sources) to this process, as shown in Figure 3-12. Click Next.

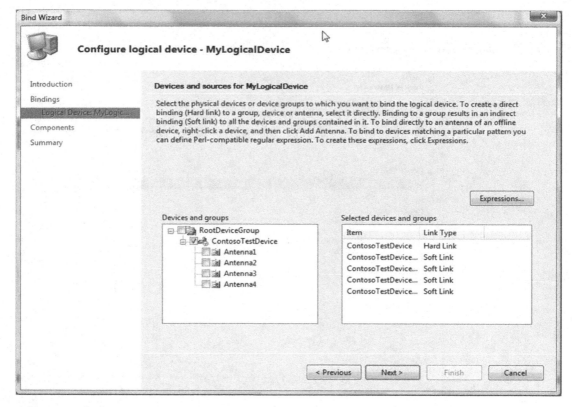

Figure 3-12. *Selecting devices and sources*

10. From the Configure Components dialog, click New Component. From the Add Component dialog, select the SQL Server Sink component and click Add, as shown in Figure 3-13.

11. From the Add Component Instance dialog, as shown in Figure 3-14, type in an instance name of **SqlSink**, and click OK.

12. Click Close on the Add Component dialog to finish configuring the SqlServerSink event handler. Click Next to proceed to the final step in the Bind wizard.

13. From the Summary of Changes dialog, as shown in Figure 3-15, click the "Start the process when I click Finish" check box. Click Finish to close the Bind wizard and start the process.

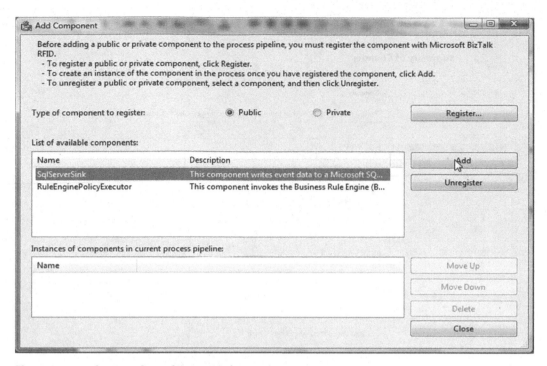

Figure 3-13. *Selecting the SqlServerSink component*

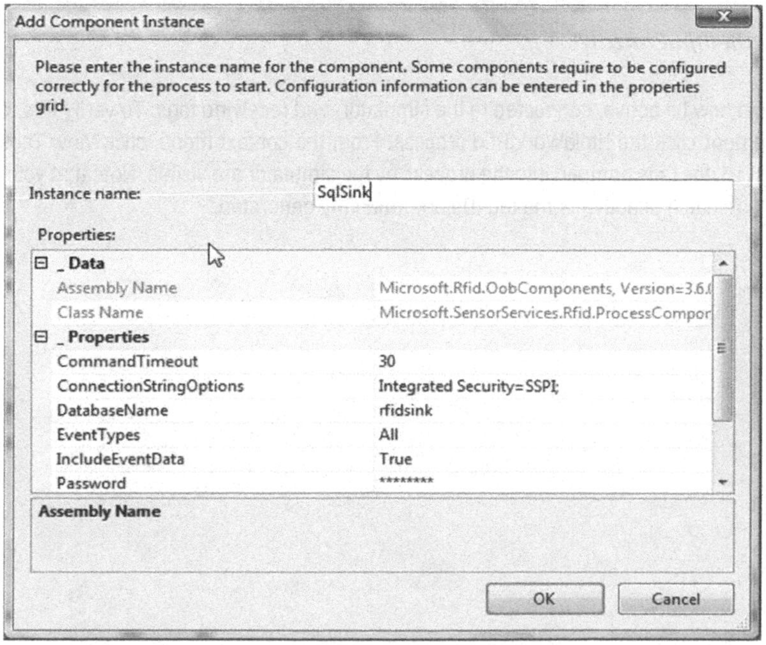

Figure 3-14. *Configuring the event handler*

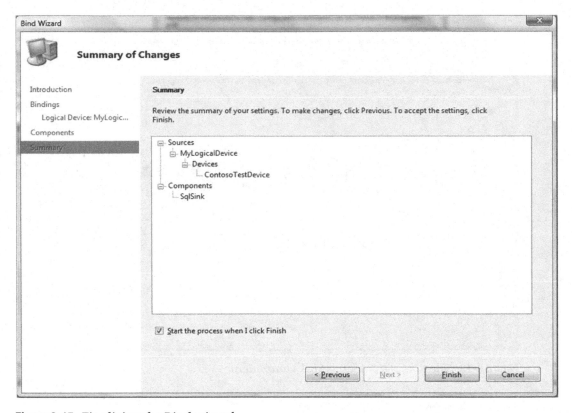

Figure 3-15. *Finalizing the Bind wizard*

14. The process should now be active, connected to the simulator, and receiving tags. To verify this, wait a few seconds, and right-click the HelloWorldRfid process. From the context menu, click View Tags. As shown in Figure 3-16, the tags pumped into the process by the simulator are visible. Note that your View Tags screen will not match exactly, as the tag IDs are randomly generated.

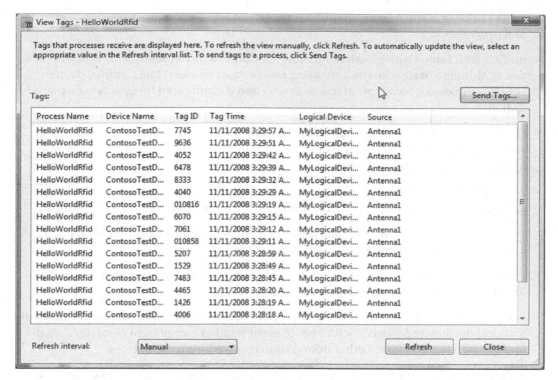

Figure 3-16. *Viewing tags received in the process*

Conclusion

After reviewing the basics of RFID technology and BizTalk RFID, in this chapter you developed your first end-to-end application. Using RFID Manager to configure providers, devices, and processes, you captured a stream of information flowing from the RFID device simulator and captured it in a SQL Server database. The following list describes the key components of the end-to-end application developed in this chapter:

- RFID Manager is the primary graphical interface, used to configure providers, devices, and processes.

- BizTalk RFID ships with a basic simulator, the Contoso device simulator, which allows you to simulate basic scenarios involving one or more readers. The Contoso device simulator does not have a graphical interface, and is configured by modifying a pair of XML files.

- Device providers are the "drivers" of the BizTalk RFID world. In order to connect to a vendor's RFID hardware, you will first need a compatible provider for that hardware. Multiple providers (and multiple versions of a vendor's provider) can be run concurrently.

- BizTalk RFID devices consist of a device provider, transport information (such as the IP address and connection port), and credentials (typically a username and password).

- Device groups are used to associate physical readers matching a particular characteristic, such as management location or device type.

- Logical devices are used to associate physical readers with logical constructs, such as a location zone or entry portal (e.g., Dock Door A).

- BizTalk RFID processes combine a set of logical devices, which are composed of a set of physical devices and sources, with a set of event handler components that filter, shape, and forward tag events and other information received from the devices.

Building on the hands-on foundation of creating your first end-to-end application, the next chapter will dive into the features and functions of RFID Manager.

CASE STUDY: SIMPLE BUSINESS INTELLIGENCE THROUGH TAG TRACKING

Industry: Retail.

Overview: A high-cost-technology company tracks its inventory by collecting tag reads as merchandise leaves the store. Items over a certain price point have an RFID tag placed on them. As these items leave the store, either after purchase, after return to the manufacturer, or after theft, their tags are read and kept in a centralized database. Numerous reports are generated from this data, including a simple dashboard report that is kept on the screen at all times. This report enables the management and sales associates to make immediate decisions around real-time discounts available for customers. For example, if the report indicates that a certain number of items have left the store on any given day, sales associates can begin to offer larger discount incentives to sell additional items on that same day.

Results: With basic business intelligence available to the organization as a whole, employees can interact more intelligently with customers. Due to the high value of the items being sold, this RFID infrastructure pays for itself through increased sales performance based on visibility into inventory.

CHAPTER 4

■ ■ ■

Using RFID Manager

This chapter introduces BizTalk RFID's graphical management interface: RFID Manager. It provides detailed walkthroughs of the fundamental tasks involved in using RFID Manager, including provider registration, device management, and process configuration. It also includes a brief introduction to using the command-line management tool, the RFID Client Console (rfidclientconsole.exe), to perform common administrative tasks.

Overview of RFID Manager

RFID Manager is the fundamental graphical management tool for administering and configuring BizTalk RFID–based applications. Introduced in Chapter 3, it provides a visual interface for managing the basic building blocks of any RFID application: providers, devices, device groups, and processes.

Built on top of Microsoft Management Console, RFID Manager can independently connect to a set of BizTalk RFID servers; meaning that while multiple BizTalk RFID servers can be managed from a single, potentially remote management console, management operations are tied to a specific BizTalk RFID server.

Note None of the screens in RFID Manager automatically refresh their content. If you do not see the expected information displayed, always refresh the display by clicking Action in the menu bar, and then clicking Refresh.

Permissions

The security permissions required to perform administrative tasks through RFID Manager are the same as are required for any interface to BizTalk RFID (be it RFID Manager, a custom application, or the rfidclientconsole.exe application covered at the end of this chapter). The user account executing the application needs to be a member of the RFID_USER group on the local machine. Adding a user to the appropriate security group is covered in Exercise 4-1.

Note that when accessing a remote BizTalk RFID server, one of the following must be true:

- Both of the machines belong to the same Active Directory organization, and the user account on the calling machine is in the RFID_USER group on the target machine.

- Both machines have matching accounts (username and password identical) that are members of their local RFID_USER groups.

■**Note** On workstations running Microsoft Windows Vista with User Access Control (UAC) enabled, processes accessing BizTalk RFID need to run with *elevation* (i.e., explicitly run as Administrator).

If you encounter security-related issues on Vista machines with UAC enabled (i.e., permission denied), it may be necessary or advisable to disable UAC.

Exercise 4-1. Granting BizTalk RFID Access to a User Account

This exercise will demonstrate how to enable the current Windows user account for BizTalk RFID access.

1. Open a command prompt. If you're running Vista with UAC enabled, make sure to run the command prompt as Administrator by right-clicking the command prompt menu item and selecting Run As Administrator.

2. Execute the whoami command, as shown in Listing 4-1. This prints out the current username, to be used in the next step.

3. Execute the net localgroup command, as shown in Listing 4-1. This adds the specified username to the local RFID_USER group.

4. Log out! The security group list for the current user is only refreshed during login. If you try to access BizTalk RFID before logging out and logging back in again, the current user's group permissions will not have refreshed.

Listing 4-1. *Using whoami and net localgroup to Add the Current User Account to the RFID_USER Group*

```
C:\Windows\system32>whoami
Administrator
C:\Windows\system32>net localgroup RFID_USER "Administrator" /add
The command completed successfully.
```

Connecting to Servers

By default, RFID Manager connects to the local instance. To manage remote BizTalk RFID servers with RFID Manager, do the following:

1. Ensure that you have the requisite permissions (as covered in the previous section).

2. Right-click the RFID Services Administration node in RFID Manager (as shown in Figure 4-1), and then click Connect.

3. From the Select RFID Server dialog (shown in Figure 4-2), type in the hostname of the target instance, or use the Find feature to look up BizTalk RFID servers registered in Active Directory (Windows Server 2003 and Windows Server 2008 only).

The remote RFID server will now be available from the list of registered servers in BizTalk RFID.

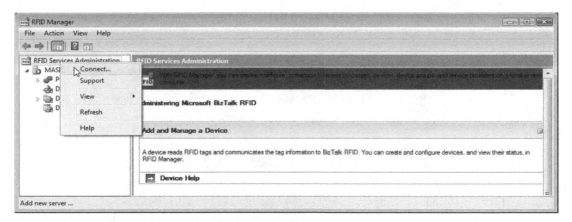

Figure 4-1. *Connecting to another BizTalk RFID server*

Figure 4-2. *Selecting the remote RFID server*

Managing Server Properties

A small number of server-wide properties can be configured through RFID Manager. To view these, right-click a server name in RFID Manager, as shown in Figure 4-3, and click Properties. The server properties are broken out into three groups: general, logging, and advanced. The general properties are read-only, and relate to the server name, build number, OS version, and SQL Server version (these are useful for diagnostics).

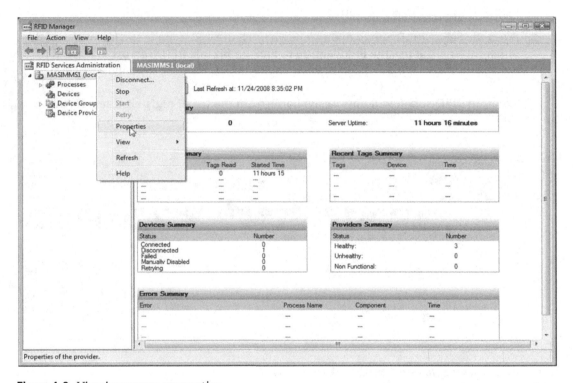

Figure 4-3. *Viewing server properties*

The logging properties, as shown in Figure 4-4, allow tweaking of the log file location name and content of the log files. In general, it should not be necessary to modify the core server log file settings, unless seeking to increase the amount of server log detail during diagnostics. Due to the sheer amount of data produced and the associated overhead, it is not recommended to set the log level above Info on a production server.

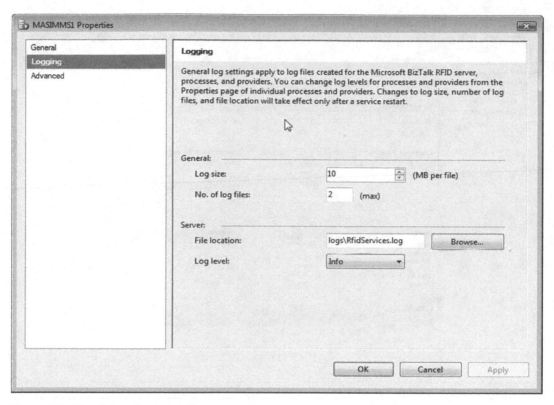

Figure 4-4. *Changing the server log properties*

RFID Manager Server Dashboard

The RFID Manager server dashboard is the display shown when a server name is selected, as shown in Figure 4-5. This server snapshot displays high-level information and statistics about the instance. This includes recent tag reads, active processes, and configured devices. Note that the display does not automatically refresh (use the Refresh button at the top left of the display window).

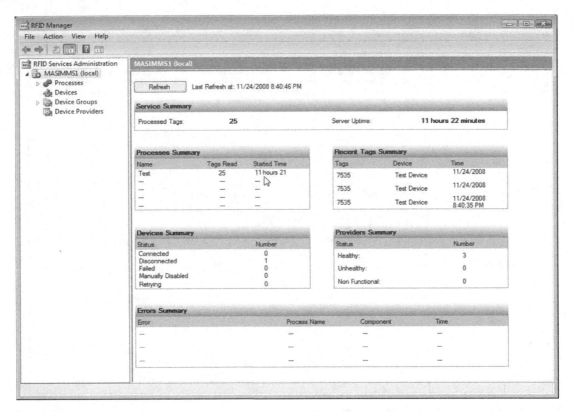

Figure 4-5. *BizTalk RFID server dashboard*

Managing Providers

As shown in previous chapters, providers are the "drivers" of the BizTalk RFID world. They abstract away the specifics of connecting to devices from vendor A as opposed to those from vendor B, while allowing each vendor to surface properties and features specific to their devices. Providers, and their development model—the Device Service Provider Interface (DSPI)—are at the heart of one of the key value propositions for BizTalk RFID: allowing RFID applications to be largely[1] device agnostic. In order to connect to a device, a provider for that device (or collection of devices from that vendor) is necessary.

---

1. There will always be device-specific aspects to any RFID implementation, due to both the physics involved (i.e., the antenna power attenuation level property will usually have dramatically different effects on two different models of readers) and the desire to utilize vendor-specific features (such as tag directionality; i.e., determining the relative direction of motion of a given tag).

■**Note** Included in BizTalk Server 2009 is the LLRP provider (part of the standards pack). Low Level Reader Protocol, or LLRP, is a wire protocol definition that describes a communication standard between middleware platforms such as BizTalk RFID and RFID readers.

When properly implemented, any LLRP-compliant middleware package can communicate with any LLRP-enabled RFID reader. At the time of publication, a variety of RFID readers, including models from Motorola and Impinj, support LLRP. In addition, BizTalk RFID Mobile (discussed in Chapter 7) uses LLRP to communicate between mobile devices and the BizTalk RFID server.

The practical aspect of this is that the Microsoft LLRP provider can connect to any LLRP-enabled RFID device, although not all of the vendor's "secret sauce," or specific features such as directionality, may be available.

A registered provider in BizTalk RFID consists of the base provider assembly (or DLL file) and a name under which to register that provider. This means that multiple versions of a provider from a single vendor may be registered concurrently (or even multiple copies of the same provider, though there is limited practical use for this).

When a provider is registered, a directory is created under `Microsoft BizTalk RFID\Providers`. This directory will contain the provider assembly, any dependent libraries or files (note that these have to be manually copied or placed into the provider directory by an installation application), and the provider log files.

Each provider has initialization and runtime properties, as defined by the developer of the provider. Initialization properties can only be set before the provider is started, while runtime properties may be changed dynamically while the provider is running.

The process for adding a provider was introduced in Chapter 3; the exercises in this section illustrate several other common tasks related to managing providers. Exercise 4-2 covers removing an extant provider, and Exercise 4-3 covers changing the properties of an installed provider.

Exercise 4-2. Removing a Provider

This exercise will demonstrate how to remove a running provider, using the Contoso (simulator) provider.

1. Open RFID Manager and click the Device Providers node. The Contoso provider should be in the list of registered providers (from the exercises in Chapter 3). If the Contoso provider is not registered, follow these steps (see Exercise 3-4 for more details):

    a. From the New Provider dialog, fill in the name field with the value **Contoso**.

    b. Click the Browse button and navigate to the `C:\Program Files\Microsoft BizTalk RFID\bin` directory. Select the `Microsoft.Rfid.ContosoDeviceProvider.dll` file.

    c. Click the Register button to load the provider into BizTalk RFID. Ensure that the "Start the provider" check box is checked.

    d. Click OK to finish adding the provider. It should now be visible in the list of registered providers.

2. Right-click the Contoso provider in the list of registered providers, as shown in Figure 4-6. Note that there is no option to remove the provider. Running providers cannot be deleted (note that the status for the provider is Started – OK); they must first be stopped.

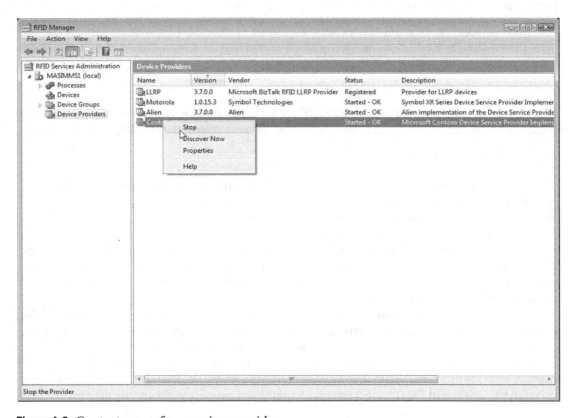

Figure 4-6. *Context menu for running provider*

3. Click Stop to stop the provider. If there are devices registered against this provider (as should be the case if you have completed the exercises in Chapter 3), the warning shown in Figure 4-7 will appear. Click Yes to force the provider to stop.

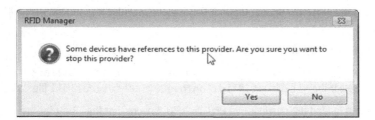

Figure 4-7. *Warning displayed if devices are registered*

Note On a production system, stopping a provider with active device references (i.e., active devices using that provider) will cause all connections to those devices to be dropped. If there are several devices active with references to this provider, it may take some time to close all of the open connections before stopping the provider.

4. Once the provider has been stopped and is in the Registered state, as shown in Figure 4-8, it can be deleted. Right-click the provider name and click Delete.

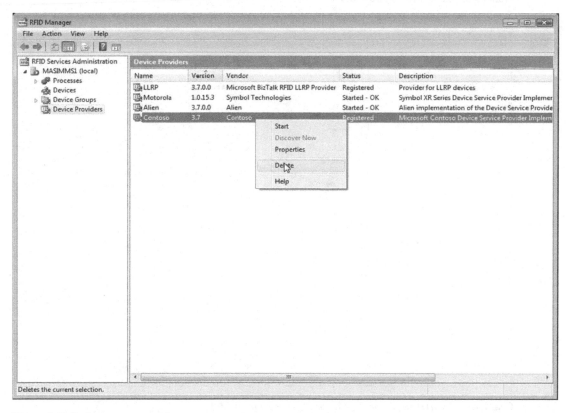

Figure 4-8. *Deleting a provider*

Exercise 4-3. Changing Initialization and Runtime Properties

This exercise will demonstrate how to change the initialization and runtime properties of a provider, using the Contoso provider as the sample case.

1. Open RFID Manager and click the Device Providers node. The Contoso provider should be in the list of registered providers (from the exercises in Chapter 3). If the Contoso provider is not registered, follow steps 1a through 1d from Exercise 4-2.

2. Right-click the Contoso provider and click Properties. In the property dialog that appears, click Runtime Properties, as shown in Figure 4-9.

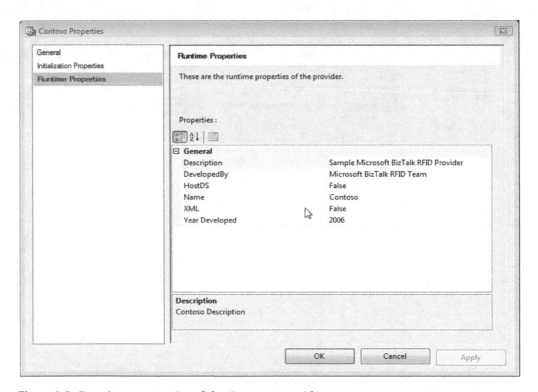

Figure 4-9. *Runtime properties of the Contoso provider*

3. Click the Description text field. Change the text in the Description field to **Changing my Description**, as shown in Figure 4-10. Click Apply to change the property.

4. Click Initialization Properties. The property page that appears will be grayed out—initialization properties cannot be changed while the provider is running. Before you can edit these properties, you will need to stop the provider. Click Cancel to close the properties dialog.

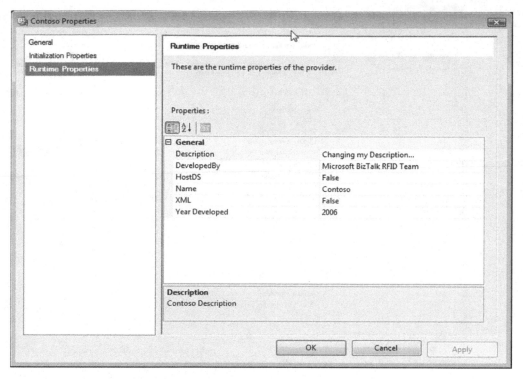

Figure 4-10. *Changed description property*

5. Right-click the Contoso provider, and then click Stop.

6. Right-click the Contoso provider, and then click Properties. Click Initialization Properties.

7. In the properties dialog, as shown in Figure 4-11, uncheck the Inherit Log Level check box, and then select the Verbose logging option from the Log Level drop-down.

8. Click Apply to change the logging level, and then click OK to close the dialog.

9. Right-click the Contoso provider, and then click Start.

■**Note** The provider is now set to produce verbose logging output, which is often useful in debugging hardware-related issues. Note that this tends to produce large amounts of logging output and reduces the overall provider response time. Verbose output should be used only during debugging and diagnostics.

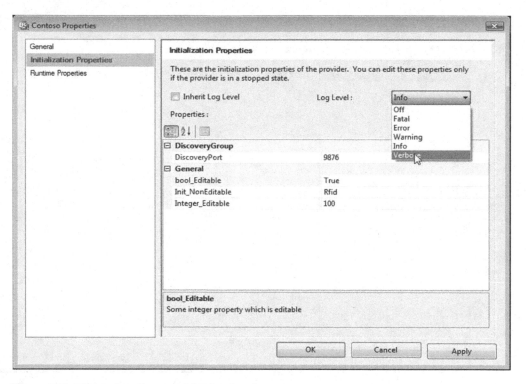

Figure 4-11. *Changing the provider log level*

Managing Device Groups

Device groups are used to group sets of similar devices. The most common use for this would be to group devices by administrative function or type. Device groups can be nested to create hierarchies.

For example, to simplify firmware updates, all Motorola devices could be placed into a MotorolaReaders device group. Within that device group, two subgroups could be created—one for XR450 readers and one for XR440 readers (two different models of Motorola readers). Then, when performing a property template update, all of the Motorola readers are accessible by iterating through a device group, rather than looking up reader information.

Another potential use for device groups is organizing readers by location (Warehouse A, Warehouse B, etc.) or organizational structure (product readers/test readers, though this is a bad example—production devices and test devices should ideally be managed from different BizTalk RFID instances). Exercise 4-4 demonstrates working with device groups.

■**Note** Device groups are not well suited for mapping logical constructs, such as locations or zones. This type of association should be performed using logical devices in processes (as explained later in this chapter).

Exercise 4-4. Working with Device Groups

This exercise will demonstrate how to create device groups and move devices between different device groups.

1. Open RFID Manager and click the Device Groups node. If there are any readers not assigned to a device group, they will be visible in the Device Groups list.

2. Right-click the Device Groups node and click New Group.

3. In the New Group dialog, as shown in Figure 4-12, type in the name **Vendor X Readers**, and a description of **All readers from vendor X**.

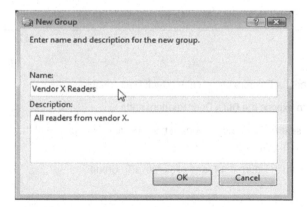

Figure 4-12. *Creating a device group*

4. Expand the Device Groups node to expose the Vendor X Readers node. Right-click the Vendor X Readers node and click New Group, as shown in Figure 4-13.

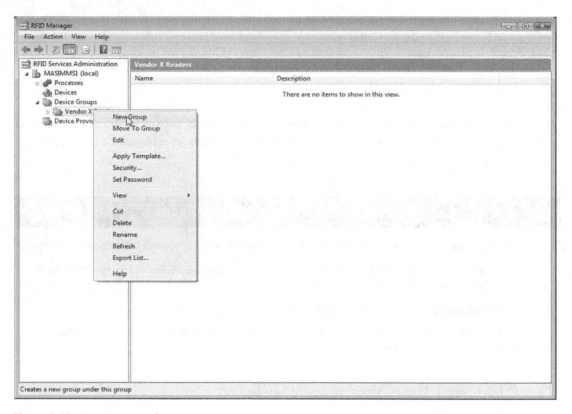

Figure 4-13. *Creating a subgroup*

5. Create a device group within the Vendor X Readers group called Dock Door Readers.

6. Expand the Vendor X Readers node to expose the Dock Door Readers node.

7. There should be registered devices visible in the Device Groups list, as shown in Figure 4-14. If there are no devices visible, repeat Exercise 3-5 to add a new reader.

8. Right-click one of the readers, as shown in Figure 4-14, and click Move To Group.

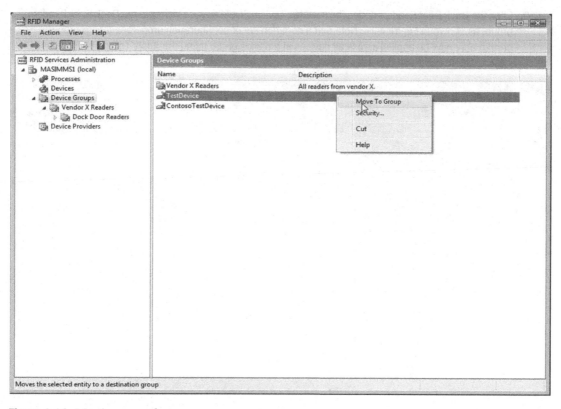

Figure 4-14. *Moving a reader*

9. From the group selection dialog, as shown in Figure 4-15, select the Dock Door Readers node.

Figure 4-15. *Selecting a device group*

10. Click the Dock Door Readers node. The selected device should now be visible in the Dock Door Readers group, as shown in Figure 4-16. Note that a common set of configuration properties (i.e., a property profile) may now be applied across all devices in a device group using the Apply Template command.

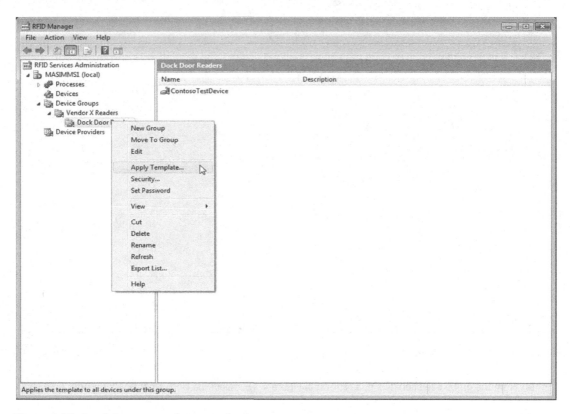

Figure 4-16. *Applying a template to a device group*

Managing Devices

RFID devices are the foundation of any RFID-enabled solution. Having reviewed how to manage providers (for supporting devices) and device groups (for organizing collections of devices), the next core feature of RFID Manager to examine is the actual management of devices. As introduced in Chapter 3, RFID Manager allows you to register (create) new devices within BizTalk RFID, configure their properties, and view their reported tags.

Importing and Exporting Devices

Devices in BizTalk RFID are defined by a record containing the device's provider and transport properties. These records may be exported and imported, allowing devices to be provisioned (i.e., created and initialized) from XML files, and the registered devices on a BizTalk RFID instance easily backed up and restored. Exercise 4-5 demonstrates how to export and import device definitions using RFID Manager.

Exercise 4-5. Exporting and Importing Devices

This exercise will demonstrate how to export and import devices using RFID Manager. Note that this technique also works between different machines; devices may be exported from one machine and imported on another (provided that the appropriate providers are registered on the remote machine).

1. Open RFID Manager and click the Devices node. If there are any readers not assigned to a device group, they will be visible in the Device Groups list.

2. Right-click the Devices node, and then click Export, as shown in Figure 4-17.

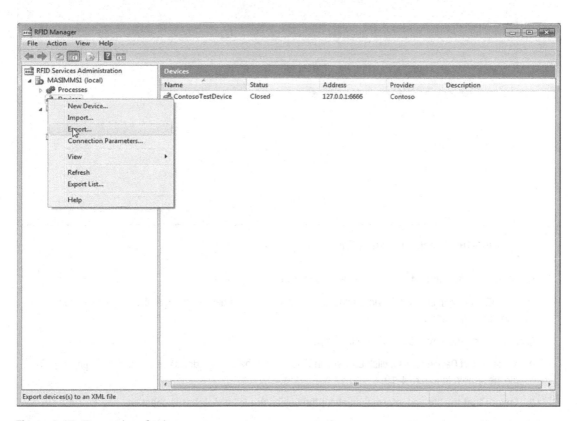

Figure 4-17. *Exporting devices*

3. From the Export Devices dialog, shown in Figure 4-18, click the Add All button to move all available devices to the "Selected devices" list.

4. Click the "Name and connection only" radio button to include only the device name and provider/transport information in the export file. You can also include the device properties by selecting the "All device properties" radio button; however, this option requires that all of the devices be online in order to retrieve their property profiles.

5. Click the Browse button, and select a location such as `C:\Windows\temp\DeviceExport.xml`.

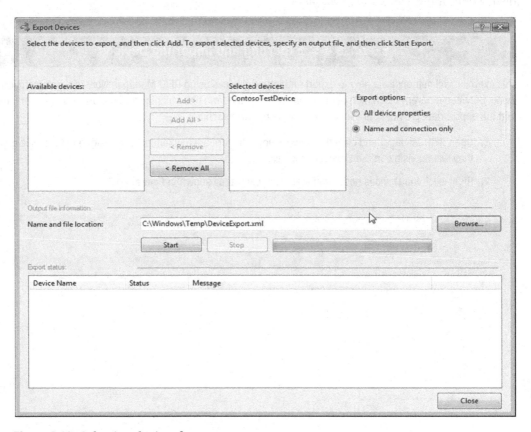

Figure 4-18. *Selecting devices for export*

6. Click the Start button to export the data, as shown in Figure 4-19.

7. In RFID Manager, click the Devices node. Delete any registered devices by right-clicking the device name and clicking Delete.

8. Right-click the Devices node and click Import.

9. In the Import Devices dialog, click Browse, and then select the `C:\windows\temp\DeviceExport.xml` file, as shown in Figure 4-19.

10. Ensure that the "Import information about the device group" check box is checked.

11. Ensure that the "Add the device to the RFID server, even if the device is offline" check box is checked.

12. Click the Start Import button to import the device file.

13. Right-click the Devices node in RFID Manager and click Refresh. The imported devices should now be visible in the Devices list. Note that if devices being imported are offline, the import process may take some time.

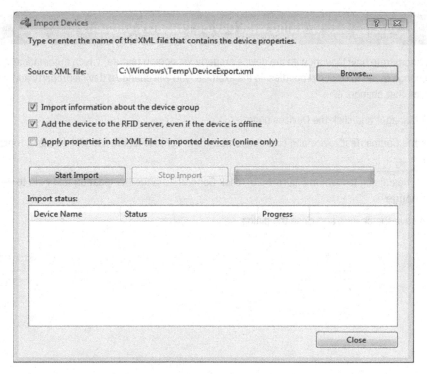

Figure 4-19. *The Import Devices dialog*

Device Configuration

Device configuration is a vital component of any RFID system. If RFID devices are not properly configured, both in general and for specific scenarios, then they will not behave as intended. Being familiar with the standard and vendor-specific configuration properties and how they affect your chosen vendor hardware is an important component in successfully delivering RFID systems.

BizTalk RFID provides a comprehensive and flexible configuration system, exposing a wide variety of configuration properties. Collections of configuration properties are referred to as *configuration profiles*, and can be exported and imported as XML files (as alluded to in previous sections). Whenever a device property is modified,[2] a record of that change is automatically created, allowing administrators to see if any device properties have been inadvertently changed, and revert them if necessary. Exercise 4-6 demonstrates how to use the device version table to review and roll back configuration changes.

---

2. Other than the Source:Port Output Value property, which controls the digital output port on readers supporting digital I/O.

Exercise 4-6. Working with Device Property Versions

This exercise will demonstrate how to work with the device property versioning feature, which automatically saves and versions each change made to device properties. In the exercise, you will change a device property and use the version list to roll back that change.

1. Open RFID Manager and click the Devices node.

2. Right-click the ContosoTestDevice and click Properties. If the ContosoTestDevice is not visible, repeat Exercise 3-4.

3. In the properties dialog (shown in Figure 4-20), click General. Change the location text field to **Random Change**.

4. Click OK to save the change and close the dialog.

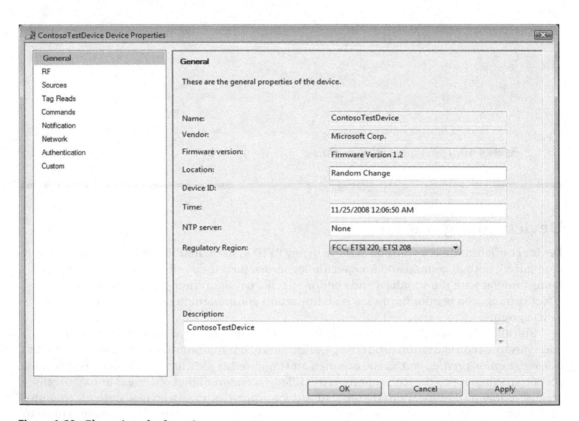

Figure 4-20. *Changing the location property*

5. In the Devices node of RFID Manager, right-click the ContosoTestDevice and click Versions. From the "Device versions" table, select the top two records, as shown in Figure 4-21 (note that the "Device versions" table on your computer may look slightly different).

6. Click Diff to view the differences between the two versions.

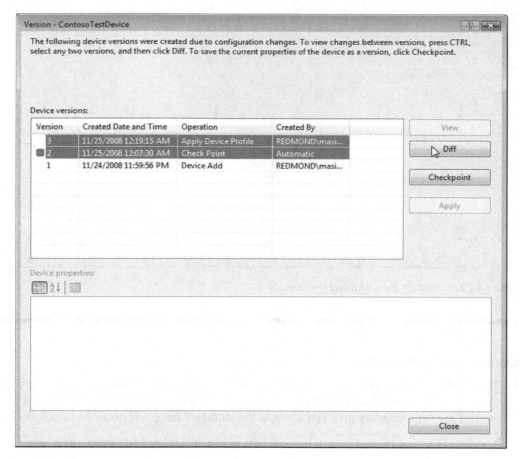

Figure 4-21. *Viewing device changes*

7. As shown in Figure 4-22, the Location property has been changed from ContosoTestDevice to Random Change.

8. Click Close to close the dialog.

9. From the version dialog (shown previously in Figure 4-21), select the second version record from the top. Click Apply.

10. Right-click the ContosoTestDevice and click Properties. Click General and check the value of the Location field. It should now be reverted to the ContosoTestDevice value.

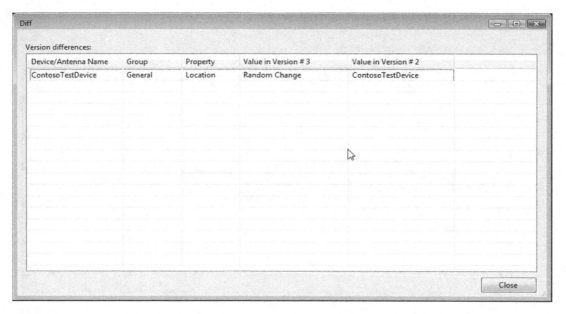

Figure 4-22. *Isolating the changed properties*

Standard Device Properties

BizTalk RFID defines a set of standard device properties that are commonly supported by RFID readers, as well as a set of custom properties that are defined by the individual hardware vendor. Properties are organized by property groups; the standard property groups are as follows:

General: Device-related properties, such as name, location, and device time.

RF: Radio-related properties, such as the RFID air protocol and RFID scanning mode.

Sources: Configuration of the antennae and digital I/O sources. Each source can be individually configured. Used to enable or disable individual antennae, as well as set properties such as the gain/attenuation (power level).

Tag Reads: Configuration of reader-side filtering and reading properties, such as duplicate elimination time.

Commands: Configuration of properties related to sending and receiving data to the reader, such as the request timeout.

Notification: Configuration of how the device reports asynchronous events to BizTalk RFID.[3]

Network: Network configuration settings, such as the IP address.

Authentication: Security-related information, such as the username and password.

Managing Device States

RFID Manager allows the management of device states; the primary uses of this feature are to manually disable a device or manually reenable a device after it has gone into a fail state. If a device is bound to a process and is not available (offline, not connected, etc.), after a certain number of tries BizTalk RFID will automatically set the device into the fail state. Once a device is in a fail state, the only way to reactivate the device is to manually enable it.

To manually disable a device, do the following:

1. In the Devices node of RFID Manager, right-click the device name.

2. Click Disable.

To manually enable a device, do the following:

1. In the Devices node of RFID Manager, right-click the device name.

2. Click Enable.

Managing Processes

Processes are the primary method of gathering data from RFID readers, filtering and enriching the data, and integrating the information into other systems and applications. Introduced in Chapter 3, RFID Manager allows configuration of all facets of RFID processes. Creating a new process was demonstrated in Exercise 3-6 utilizing the Bind wizard, which streamlines defining the readers and event handler components that make up a process definition.

The RFID Manager process view (see Figure 4-23) shows a sample process overview. This view displays some key process metrics (uptime and tags read), as well as information about errors and recent tags read.

---

3. RFID readers typically have a synchronous command channel (which is how BizTalk RFID connects to the device, issues configuration changes, etc.) and an asynchronous notification channel (how the reader posts events to BizTalk RFID).

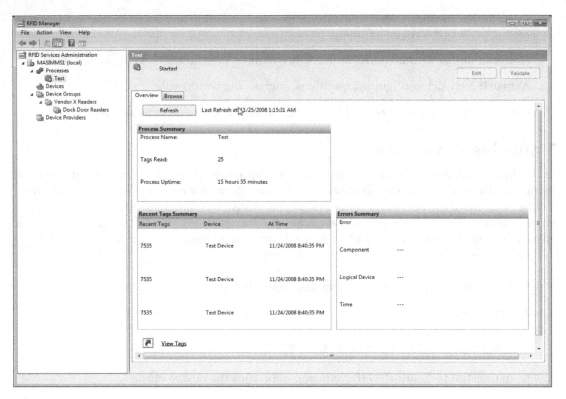

Figure 4-23. *RFID Manager process view*

Switching to the details browse view (see Figure 4-24) shows the device and event handler mappings that make up the process definition. Note that as this process is running, the bindings cannot be edited.

Note In order to edit the process bindings, the process first has to be stopped. To stop a process, right-click the process name and click Stop.

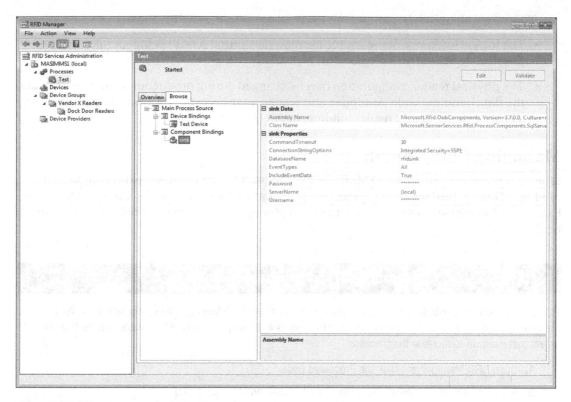

Figure 4-24. *Viewing process bindings*

Understanding Logical and Physical Devices

Logical devices are used in RFID processes to provide an abstraction or indirection layer between physical readers and logical constructs such as doors or portals. Rather than inferring these types of information from physical properties, such as antenna names, the best practice is to use logical readers to provide associations. For example, given a single reader with four antennae—two antennae covering portal A and the other two covering portal B—the best practice would be as follows:

1. Create two logical devices, Portal A and Portal B.

2. Assign two antennae to Portal A and two to Portal B.

This usage of logical devices provides several important benefits:

- The logical inference of the source location (i.e., portal A or B) is independent of the physical device.

- The physical reader configuration may be changed during production without modifying the data handling code. Antennae and readers may be switched around, requiring only a change to the logical reader binding, not to the code.

Managing Components

When a process is stopped, RFID Manager may be used to edit the device and component bindings. This can be done either by executing the Bind wizard or by directly editing the bindings. Exercise 4-7 demonstrates how to use the RFID Manager to edit device bindings and component properties.

Exercise 4-7. Editing Process Bindings

This exercise will demonstrate how to edit process bindings using RFID Manager. The sample process for this example is the HelloWorldRfid process created in Exercise 3-6. If this process is not available in RFID Manager, repeat that exercise to recreate the process.

1. Open RFID Manager and click the Processes node.

2. If the HelloWorldRfid process is running, right-click it, and then click Stop.

3. As shown in Figure 4-25, once a process has been stopped, it can be edited. Click the Edit button to be able to modify the process configuration and bindings.

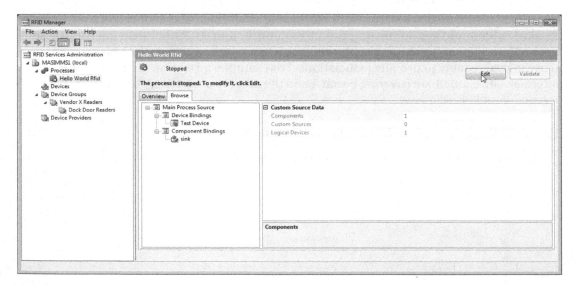

Figure 4-25. *Editing a process*

4. Once the process has been set into edit mode, either the device bindings or the component bindings may be edited. As shown in Figure 4-26, select the Test Device node, and click Bind to edit the logical device bindings.

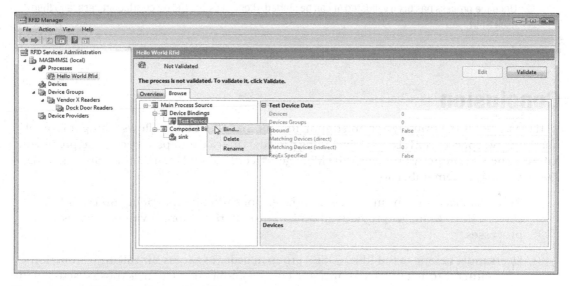

Figure 4-26. *Editing the device bindings*

5. Click Cancel to close the dialog without making any changes.

6. Right-click the `sink` event handler, and click Edit to modify the parameters of the `SqlSink` event handler, as shown in Figure 4-27.

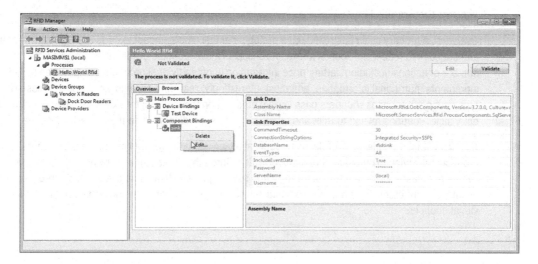

Figure 4-27. *Editing the event handler properties*

7. Click Cancel in the sink properties dialog to close it without making any changes.

8. Before the process can be started, you need to check it to ensure that it is a valid process (i.e., that the configuration makes sense). To do this, click the Validate button.

9. Once the process has been validated, it can be started. Right-click the HelloWorldRfid process, and then click Start.

Conclusion

RFID Manager is the primary administration tool for BizTalk RFID. It allows configuration of nearly every aspect of BizTalk RFID, including providers, device groups, devices, and processes. Knowing how to properly leverage RFID Manager is a critical skill in mastering BizTalk RFID. The key things to remember are

- RFID Manager is the primary user interface application for managing BizTalk RFID servers. RFID Manager provides administrative interfaces for providers, devices, and processes.

- Users must belong to the RFID_USER group in order to access BizTalk RFID functionality, either through RFID Manager or a custom application (such as those discussed in Chapter 6).

Building on this introduction, we'll now begin exploring development of custom applications.

CASE STUDY: GREATER PRODUCT DETAIL AND REAL-TIME COST SAVINGS

Industry: Grocery/retail.

Overview: A grocery chain has rolled out a prototype model where shopping carts are equipped with an embedded RFID reader and coupon tracker. As shoppers move around the store, they are able to perform a number of actions, including getting price information about individual products, recipe ideas based on ingredients, nutritional information, and most interestingly, real-time savings via coupons. These real-time coupons appear as shoppers pass certain products on the shelves; for example, when passing the dairy aisle, coupons related to milk and other dairy items are displayed on the embedded device.

Results: With the greater level of detail available at a glance, shoppers are better able to determine what products they wish to purchase. Products advertised through the real-time coupons have seen a rise in overall purchases within the test program. If the system proves viable, it is likely that the program will tie into a membership program, where additional savings and information can be tailored to the individual shopper.

■ ■ ■

CHAPTER 5

Asynchronous Event Processing in BizTalk RFID

One of the key tasks that every RFID application has to perform is managing the flow of information from the RFID devices. BizTalk RFID includes a brand-new application model for robust, low-latency event processing. This application model streamlines the handling of common tasks related to event processing applications, in the same manner that ASP.NET has streamlined the process of authoring web pages. Just like ASP.NET, the event processing model includes a description of the application, the ability to incorporate custom components from third-party software vendors, a hosting model, and deployment and configuration support.

This chapter will examine different aspects of the application model, including the design-time experience, the binding and deployment experience, and how to monitor and troubleshoot RFID applications.

This chapter begins with a brief overview of the application model using a very simple scenario. This is followed by a set of exercises designed to get your hands dirty with the specifics of the model. Finally, it concludes with detailed topic-by-topic descriptions of the aspects of the model.

If you want to see the detailed explanations before you dive into the exercises, you can skip the exercises and come back to them at the end.

What Is a BizTalk RFID Process?

A BizTalk RFID process (or an RFID process, for short) is a declarative model for specifying the flow and format of event processing. It is declarative in the sense that the definition of an RFID process is expressed through an XML-based description, rather than through C# or VB .NET code. As a declarative model, it is similar to both the BizTalk Server definition of orchestrations and pipelines and the Windows Workflow Foundation (WF) XOML definition of a workflow. Just like a WF workflow is the model that stitches a set of activities together, the RFID process defines the order in which a pipeline of EventHandler components should be executed for a given event.

The original intent and design of RFID processes have always been focused on enabling low-latency, large-volume event processing. This focus is what differentiates the RFID process from other model-based workflow descriptions. Once an RFID process is created and deployed into BizTalk RFID, it should be thought of as a distinct background service that is hosted by

BizTalk RFID. These RFID processes run within the RFID background service, and have no direct interaction with the desktop. While an RFID process can be designed to accept user input, these types of scenarios are generally better served through the use of a synchronous application (as described in Chapter 6), or through external messaging/queuing approaches.

To illustrate how an RFID process works, let's walk through a small scenario, pictorially depicted in Figure 5-1. Assume a warehouse with a single exit gate equipped with an RFID reader, and that goods leaving the warehouse through this gate have an attached RFID tag at both the pallet and case level. The goal is to automatically generate outbound shipment confirmations as pallets leave the warehouse. You can do this with an RFID business process, where you will collect real-time business-relevant information automatically, and send it to a back-end server for processing. Once you have installed and configured the RFID process that implements this "automatic" workflow, it needs to run without interruption or requiring manual user input.

**Pallet is sent out through
portal at the exit dock door**

**Shipment confirmation needs
to be generated and sent
electronically to recipient**

Figure 5-1. *Pictorial description of a shipment confirmation scenario*

The physical deployment for this scenario is outlined in the physical deployment architecture in Figure 5-2. Typically, the RFID reader will be connected to the BizTalk RFID server using a network connection.

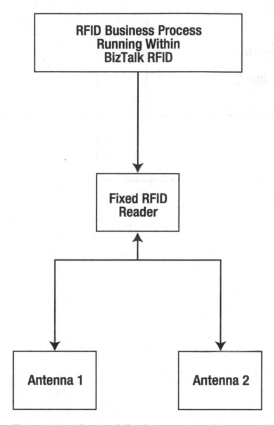

Figure 5-2. *Physical deployment architecture for the shipment confirmation scenario*

The logical flow of events for this scenario is depicted in Figure 5-3.

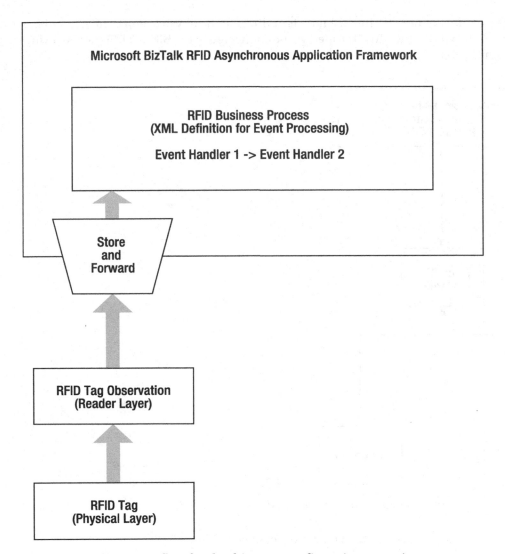

Figure 5-3. *Logical event flow for the shipment confirmation scenario*

To implement this scenario, there are five key elements to the BizTalk RFID process application model:

The XML description of the process: Typically called the *RFID process definition*, this describes the paths that will be taken by the different event types at runtime, and the EventHandler components, which are individual units of code that will be invoked to actually handle the event. Each segment of processing, including the sources of events and the event handlers that will process the events sequentially, is called a *logical source*. The logical source may be thought of as a pipeline segment for event processing. Every RFID process has at least one logical source. The logical source can itself be composed of *child logical sources*— other pipeline segments that feed into the parent logical source. This allows a sophisticated event processing tree to be built up out of individual pipeline segments.

The EventHandler: This is a fragment of .NET code capable of receiving events in the context of an RFID process. Within an RFID process, events are passed through a chain of EventHandler components. Each EventHandler class adheres to a specific contract that defines how various types of events are sent and received, as described in the "Event Processing Application Model" section. For your simple shipment confirmation scenario, assume that you have an EventHandler component called CreateShipmentConfirmation that transforms RFID events into a shipment confirmation notice. The declarative nature of the RFID process model and the formal contract implemented by EventHandler components allow you to plug this functionality into any other business process that requires this functionality in a reusable fashion.

The store-and-forward abstraction: This completely decouples the events from the physical RFID devices that raised the events. BizTalk RFID introduces the concept of a logical device to deliver such events to the business process.

The logical device: Logical devices are "virtual" readers that are used to provide a link between physical devices and processes, as well the ability to group readers and sources by their logical function. Logical devices have a name and are bound to a set of real devices at deployment time (of the RFID process). Using logical devices, rather than directly connecting physical event sources, allows the complete separation of design-time and deployment-time concerns. Additionally, it allows the same process definition to be reused across different physical topologies.

Binding: This is the process of associating the business process with real readers and antennas, which ensures that events are actually delivered to the process. In the preceding scenario, the gate reader is a logical device that is bound to the physical readers on the warehouse exit door. When designing the RFID process, the exact physical RFID configuration to be used may not yet be known (e.g., one reader with four antennae, two readers with two antennae each, etc.). Without having all of this information in advance, you still need a method of assigning a collection of event sources into a logical group (i.e., a logical device).

To summarize, the design-time support, reusable components, and flexible deployment possibilities are the key value propositions behind the RFID process model. It allows developers and third-party vendors (independent software vendors, or ISVs) to create event handler libraries that can be reused across a variety of business scenarios and RFID processes. The EventHandler is the fundamental extensibility mechanism exposed by BizTalk RFID for event processing. All of the samples and scenarios presented in this book, including integration scenarios with external systems such as the Business Rule Engine (BRE) and Business Activity Monitoring (BAM), will be performed using EventHandler components.

Hands-On Exercises

Now that we've looked at the theory, Exercises 5-1 through 5-5 will look at how you can author RFID processes in practice. The RFID process is typically defined using RFID Manager and the process-creation Bind wizard. RFID process definitions may also be created in .NET or via direct XML definitions, but these are generally more difficult and error-prone methods. Finally, once you have created an RFID process, you can export the definition as XML and import an existing definition using RFID Manager or the command-line console client.

Exercise 5-1. Creating an RFID Process That Uses Out-of-the-Box Event Handlers

In this exercise, you will create an RFID process that uses out-of-the-box event handlers (i.e., event handlers that are a standard part of BizTalk RFID) to create RFID processes through RFID Manager.

1. Create a new process with RFID Manager, using the New Process option on the Processes node (see Figure 5-4).

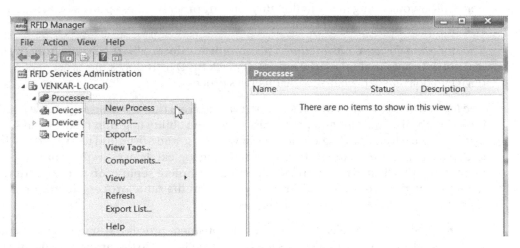

Figure 5-4. *Creating a new RFID process from RFID Manager*

2. In the New Process dialog (shown in Figure 5-5), pick the default value of Transactional for the tag-processing model. The descriptions of the various tag-processing models are covered in the "Executing RFID Processes" section of this chapter. Ensure that the Start Bind Wizard check box is checked; this launches the wizard that will complete the rest of the authoring process.

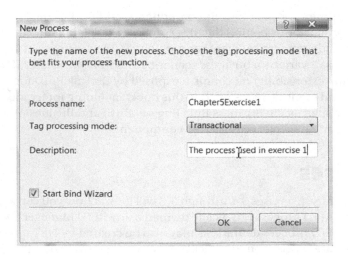

Figure 5-5. *The New Process dialog in RFID Manager*

3. This brings up the first screen of the Bind wizard. Click Next, and then click the option to create a new logical device (see Figure 5-6).

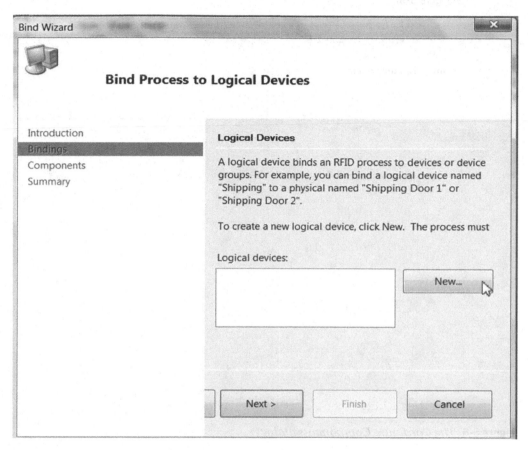

Figure 5-6. *Creating a new logical device in the Bind wizard*

4. When prompted, enter the descriptive text for your logical device (see Figure 5-7).

Figure 5-7. *The Logical Device Name dialog*

5. Click Next to bring up the Configure Components dialog (see Figure 5-8). Click the New Component button, and pick the `SqlServerSink` component when presented with the list of available components (see Figure 5-9).

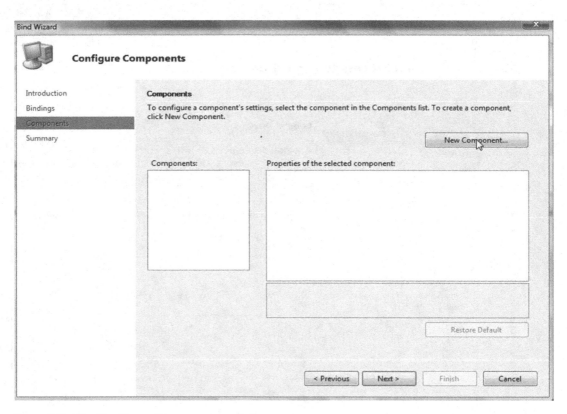

Figure 5-8. *The Configure Components dialog*

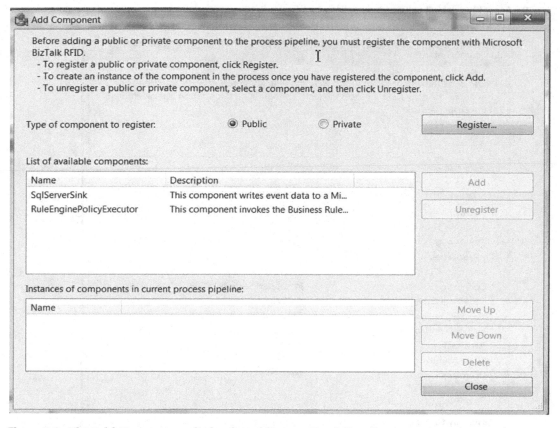

Figure 5-9. *The Add Component dialog for adding an EventHandler component*

6. Accept the default values for all options (see Figure 5-10).

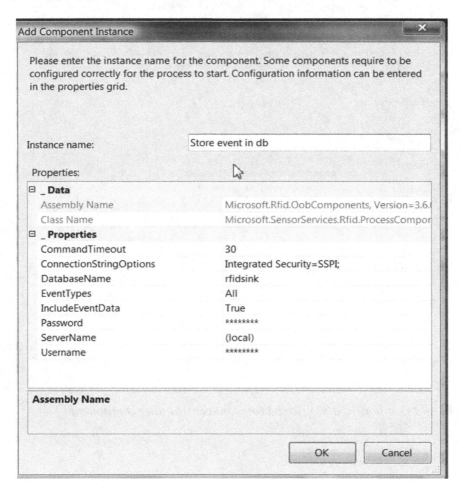

Figure 5-10. *SqlServerSink event handler properties*

7. There are no more components in this process, so you can click Next to complete the Configure Components step in the wizard (see Figure 5-11).

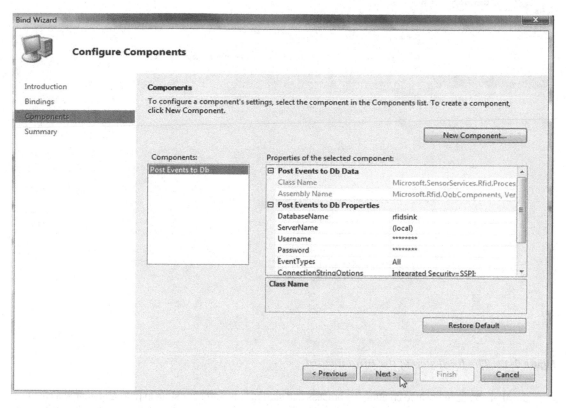

Figure 5-11. *Completing the Configure Components step in the Bind wizard*

8. You are done! Ensure the "Start the process when I click Finish" check box is checked (see Figure 5-12), and click Finish on the Bind wizard.

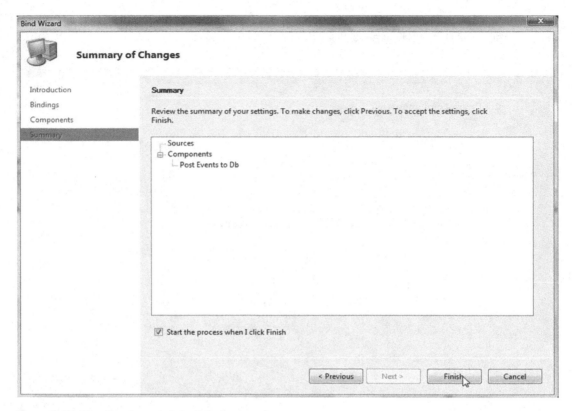

Figure 5-12. *The final step of the Bind wizard*

9. After you have finished creating the process and started it, the process state in RFID Manager will show up as Started (see Figure 5-13).

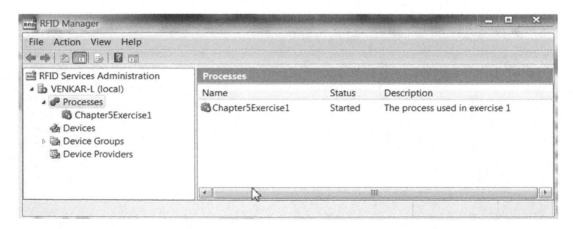

Figure 5-13. *Viewing the status of the running process*

Exercise 5-2. Binding a Logical Device to a Physical Device

In this exercise, you will bind the logical device created in the previous exercise to a physical device. You will use the Contoso physical device in this exercise.

1. Install the Contoso device provider sample by running `%rfidinstalldir%\ Samples\Device Service Provider\Contoso\ContosoEndToEnd\contososetup.cmd`.

2. Run the Contoso device simulator from `ContosoDeviceSimulator\runContososimulator.cmd`. Now you should have a device called ContosoTestDevice (see Figure 5-14).

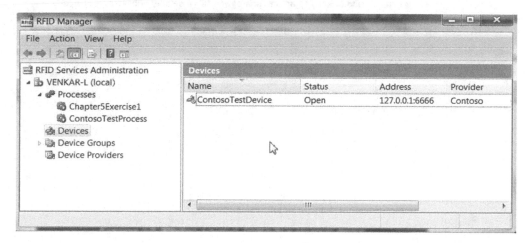

Figure 5-14. *ContosoTestDevice*

3. Browse to the Chapter5Exercise1 process, identify the logical device, and select the Bind option (see Figure 5-15).

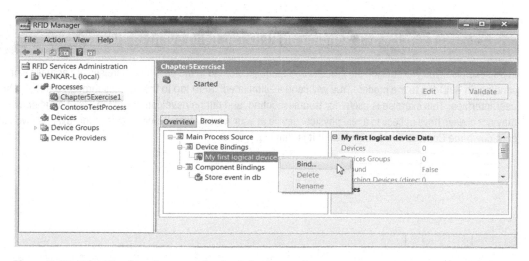

Figure 5-15. *The Bind option on a logical device node*

4. Pick the device that you are going to use in this exercise, and bind it to the process using the device picker (see Figure 5-16). After you finish this step, the device will automatically be opened and used by BizTalk RFID.

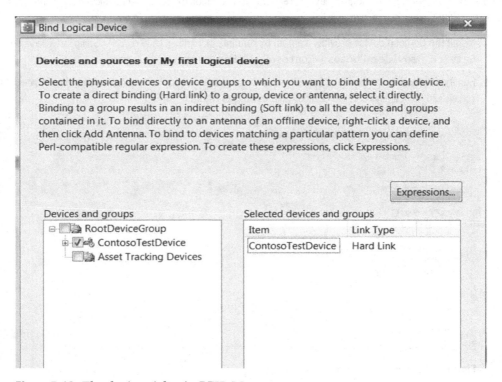

Figure 5-16. *The device picker in RFID Manager*

Exercise 5-3. Sending an RFID Tag Read Event to the Process

In this exercise, you will check if the process and bindings created in the previous exercises are actually working by sending an RFID tag to the process. You will send a "simulated" RFID tag to the process through the RFID Manager user interface. This exercise is useful for troubleshooting, and during development of the event handler, when you may not always have access to a real physical device at your workstation. Before you start this exercise, you should shut down the Contoso device simulator if it is running.

1. Click View Tags on the actions menu for the process to bring up the View Tags dialog (see Figure 5-17).

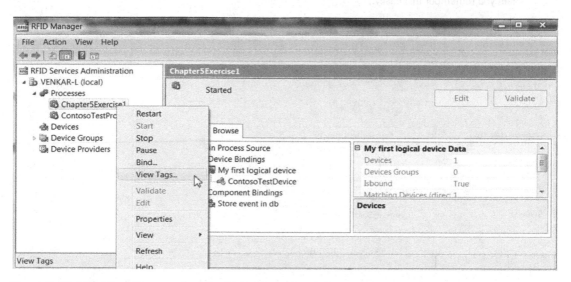

Figure 5-17. *The View Tags option on the actions menu for an RFID process*

2. Click the Send Tags button on the View Tags dialog, as shown in Figure 5-18.

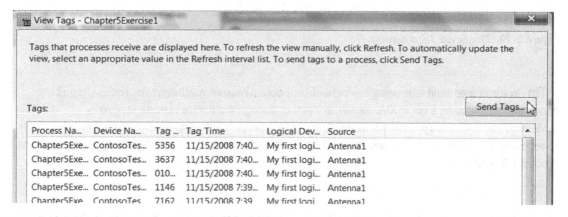

Figure 5-18. *The Send Tags option on the View Tags dialog*

3. Fill out the details, as shown in Figure 5-19. (The tag ID is in hexadecimal format; prepending it with 0x lets you remember this easily.)

Figure 5-19. *The Send Tags dialog*

■**Tip** You can also send tags using the `rfidclientconsole.exe AddEventToProcessPipeline` command, which takes a tag in XML format as input, or through the `ProcessManagerProxy AddEventToProcessPipeline` method call. For great examples of how to use the command-line console to send events, look at the event handler samples that are part of the BizTalk RFID technology samples on the product CD or MSDN.

---

4. Verify that the tags have indeed been delivered to your process by clicking the Refresh button on the View Tags dialog that is shown in Figure 5-20.

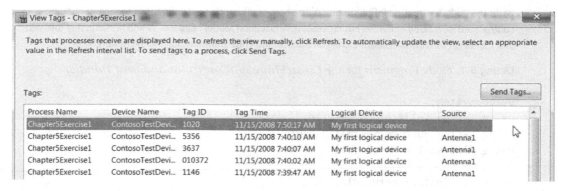

Figure 5-20. *Viewing the new tag in the View Tags dialog*

Exercise 5-4. Creating a Custom Event Handler and Adding It to the Process

In the previous three exercises, you created a process with an existing EventHandler component, bound it to a device, sent tags to the process, and verified that they reached the process, all without writing a single line of code! In this exercise, you are going to write a simple event handler and add it to your process.

1. Create a C# class library project and add references to the BizTalk RFID DLLs by picking the entries from the .NET references tab (shown in Figure 5-21).

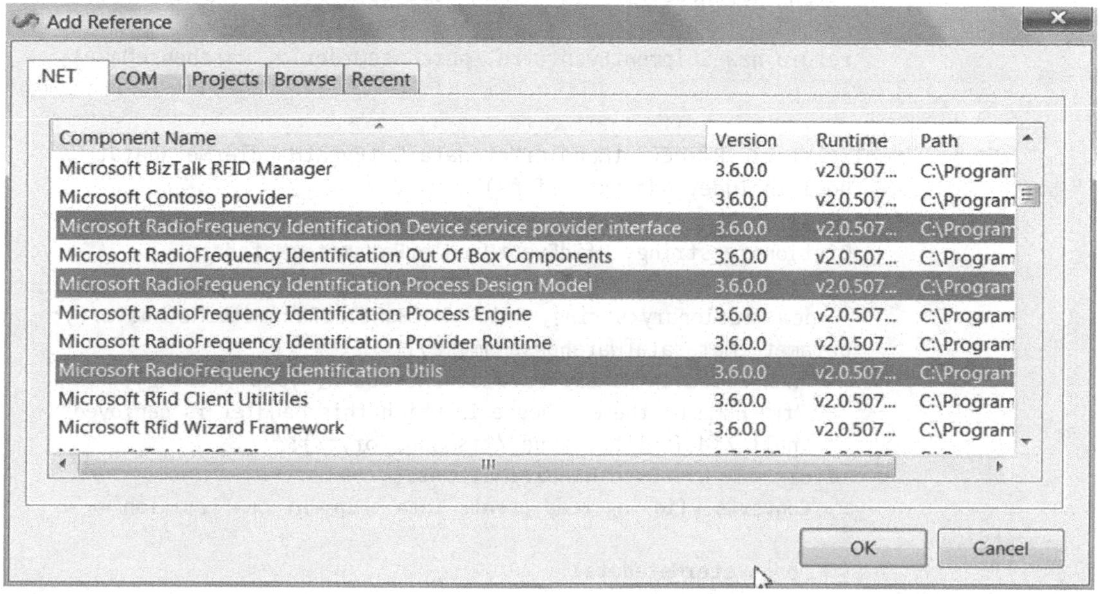

Figure 5-21. *The DLLs most commonly used by BizTalk RFID event handlers*

2. Write the code for the CreateShipmentConfirmation event handler. The details of the event handler contract are described in the "Event Processing Application Model" section, which immediately follows this hands-on exercises section. Listing 5-1 shows the code fragment for the event handler.

Listing 5-1. *Code Fragment for the CreateShipmentConfirmation Event Handler*

```
using System;
using System.Collections.Generic;
using System.Runtime.Serialization;
using Microsoft.SensorServices.Rfid;

namespace CustomEventHandler
{
    public class CreateShipmentConfirmation: RfidEventHandlerBase
    {
        private string warehouseName;
        public override void Init(Dictionary<string, object> parameters,
            RfidProcessContext container)
        {
            warehouseName = (string) parameters[WarehouseNameKey];
        }

        [RfidEventHandlerMethod]
        public ShipmentEvent TransformToShipmentEvent(TagReadEvent tre)
        {
            //to-do: look up local business context to populate it
            string purchaseOrderId = "this will come from the backend";

            return new ShipmentEvent(tre, purchaseOrderId, warehouseName);
        }

        public static RfidEventHandlerMetadata GetEventHandlerMetadata(
            bool includeVendorExtensions)
        {
        Dictionary<string, RfidEventHandlerParameterMetadata>
            parameterMetadata =
          new Dictionary<string, RfidEventHandlerParameterMetadata>();
        parameterMetadata[WarehouseNameKey] =
            new RfidEventHandlerParameterMetadata(typeof(string),
            "the name of the warehouse in which this handler is deployed",
            null /*default*/, true /*isMandatory*/);
        return new RfidEventHandlerMetadata(
            "Converts rfid tag read events into shipment confirmation ➥
events",
                parameterMetadata);
        }
        private const string WarehouseNameKey = "Warehouse Name";
    }
```

```
[DataContract]
public class ShipmentEvent: RfidEventBase
{
    public string PurchaseOrderId
    {
        get { return purchaseOrderId; }
        set { purchaseOrderId = value; }
    }

    public byte[] TagId
    {
        get { return tagId; }
        set { tagId = value; }
    }

    public string OriginationWarehouse
    {
        get { return originationWarehouse; }
        set { originationWarehouse = value; }
    }

    public DateTime CreationTime
    {
        get { return creationTime; }
        set { creationTime = value; }
    }
```

3. Edit the RFID process definition to insert the event handler into the existing RFID process definition. Start off by stopping the process and picking the Edit option on the actions menu (see Figure 5-22).

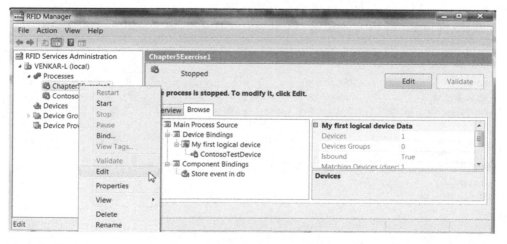

Figure 5-22. *Editing a process from the actions menu on the process in RFID Manager*

4. Add the newly created component from the Component Bindings node (see Figure 5-23).

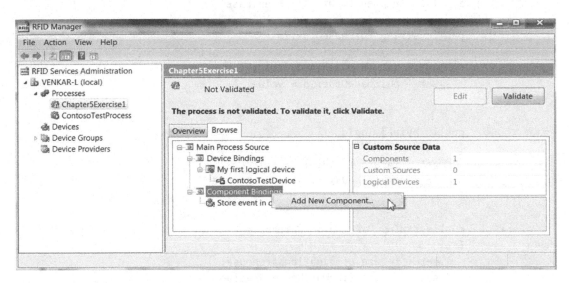

Figure 5-23. *Adding a new component to an editable process*

5. The next step is to register your component with the BizTalk RFID ComponentManager. Click the Register button, as shown in Figure 5-24.

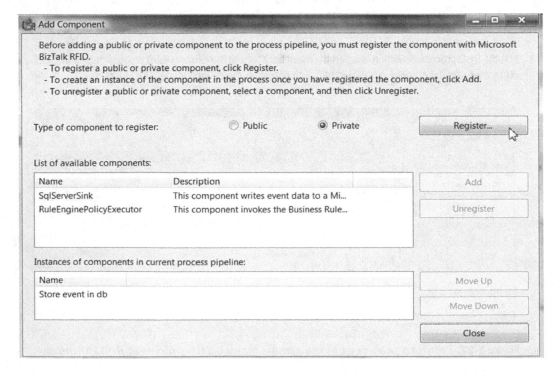

Figure 5-24. *Component registration through RFID Manager*

6. This will bring up a dialog that will allow you to add files. Go to the folder that contains your compiled event handler DLL, and pick the DLL. After component registration succeeds, your event handler should be listed as a new component that is available (see Figure 5-25).

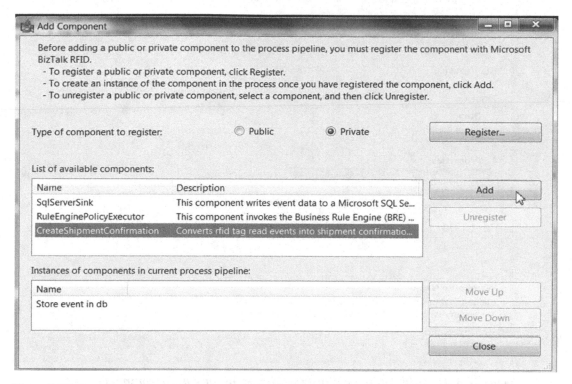

Figure 5-25. *Browse for the new component and add it to your process definition.*

7. Name the new component and fill in the mandatory parameter for the warehouse name (this is a task that the administrator will have to do as part of deployment). Figure 5-26 shows the dialog that pops up when your component is selected. Note that the description for your parameters comes from your event handler metadata.

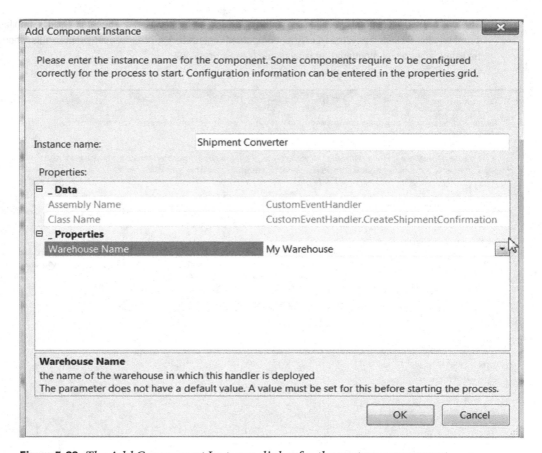

Figure 5-26. *The Add Component Instance dialog for the custom component*

8. Next, ensure that the new event handler is inserted ahead of the `SqlServerSink` event handler (see Figure 5-27 for how your process definition should look when you are done). For a detailed description of how the pipeline of event handlers is validated by BizTalk RFID, refer to the "Strong Typing" section of this chapter.

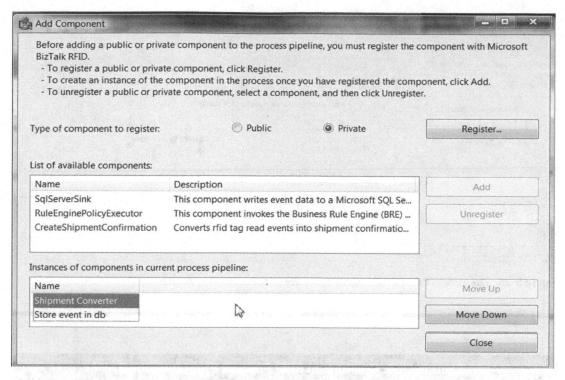

Figure 5-27. *Insert your event handler before the SqlServerSink component.*

9. Validate and start the process by clicking the Validate option on the actions menu, as shown in Figure 5-28. Send an event to the process, and ensure that the event is persisted in the rfidsink SqlServerSink database. Since the pipeline now converts the tag read event into a shipment confirmation event, BizTalk RFID will persist the event in the `GenericEvents` table in SQL Server instead of the `TagEvents` table.

134

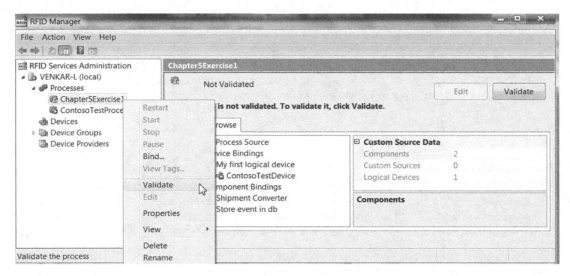

Figure 5-28. *The process validation option on the process actions menu*

Exercise 5-5. Creating an RFID Process Programmatically

In the final exercise of the chapter, you are going to create the same process definition through code, instead of through RFID Manager. Most likely, you will never have to do this, unless you are creating your own processes programmatically, but it is still handy to know. In this exercise, you will walk through the defining of a process in C# by using the following code fragment. You first create an `RfidProcess` object, add a logical source to it, add an event handler definition to it, and then save it.

```
using System;
using System.Collections.Generic;
using System.Text;
using Microsoft.SensorServices.Rfid.Design;
using Microsoft.SensorServices.Rfid.Management;
using Microsoft.SensorServices.Rfid.ProcessComponents;

namespace CustomEventHandler
{
    class ProcessCreator
    {
        public static void CreateProcess()
        {
            //create a new process called Exercise1
            RfidProcess process = new RfidProcess();
            process.Name = "Exercise1";
```

```
        //add a logical device called ExitGateReader
        process.LogicalSource.LogicalDeviceList.Add(
            new LogicalDevice("My first logical device",
            "The device used in exercise 1"));

        //define the SqlServerSink event handler commponent
        string assemblyName = typeof (SqlServerSink).Assembly.FullName;
        string typeName = typeof (SqlServerSink).FullName;
        EventHandlerDefinition postToSqlServer =
            new EventHandlerDefinition("Post to Db", assemblyName, typeName);

        //add the definition to the event processing pipeline for
        //the logical source
        process.LogicalSource.ComponentList.Add(postToSqlServer);

        //save the process
        ProcessManagerProxy pmp = new ProcessManagerProxy();
        pmp.SaveProcess(process);
    }
  }
}
```

Here is the xml definition for the same process:

```
<RfidProcess
  xmlns:i="http://www.w3.org/2001/XMLSchema-instance" ➥
  xmlns="http://schemas.datacontract.org/2004/07/ ➥
  Microsoft.SensorServices.Rfid.Design">
  <description i:nil="true" />
  <logicalSource>
    <componentList>
      <EventHandlerDefinition>
        <componentName>PostToSQL</componentName>
          <eventHandlerInfo>
            <assembly>Microsoft.Rfid.OobComponents, Version=3.6.0.0, ➥
Culture=neutral, PublicKeyToken=31bf3856ad364e35</assembly>
              <className>
  Microsoft.SensorServices.Rfid.ProcessComponents.SqlServerSink
</className>
            <description i:nil="true" />
          </eventHandlerInfo>
        </EventHandlerDefinition>
    </componentList>
    <logicalDeviceList>
      <LogicalDevice>
        <description> The device used in exercise 1</description>
        <name>My first logical device</name>
      </LogicalDevice>
    </logicalDeviceList>
```

```
      <logicalSourceList />
   </logicalSource>
   <messageHandlingReliability>Transactional</messageHandlingReliability>
   <name>Shipping</name>
</RfidProcess>
```

Event Processing Application Model

In this section, we will look in detail into the various components of the event handler contract and the optional behaviors that your event handler can implement, including advanced features such as deployment support.

Initialization

The event handler must derive from the RfidEventHandlerBase class, which has abstract methods for initializing and disposing event handlers. You must override the Init method in your subclass to perform any initialization needed. The signature of the Init method looks like the following:

```
      public override void Init(
Dictionary<string, object> parameters,
RfidProcessContext container)
```

The first argument is the list of parameters that are used by this event handler. (If you're wondering how BizTalk RFID knows what the parameters for your particular event handler are, and how a user can specify them, this is described in the "Design-Time Support" section, which follows.) The last argument is the current RfidProcessContext, which is an application-wide context object. You don't need to hold on to a reference to this context, since it is also always available from the Current property on the RfidProcessContext.

Design-Time Support

Every event handler must implement a static method with this exact signature:

```
      public static RfidEventHandlerMetadata
         GetEventHandlerMetaData(bool includeVendorExtensions)
```

This method returns information about your particular event handler, including the number of parameters, their types, their descriptions, whether they are mandatory, and so on. This information is used in two fundamental ways. The first is when your event handler is in design time (i.e., when a process author is trying to add your component to an RFID process, the metadata is used by the designer to create a property grid for your event handler). The second is internally by the runtime when it has to initialize your component. It uses the metadata to confirm that the bindings for the component are consistent, and ensures that the types are correct and all mandatory properties are specified and present.

■**Tip** You should consider the `includeVendorExtensions` Boolean to determine which scenario is in play: you may have some extra information that is potentially of use to the component configuration experience for the user interface only. For example, if you drop a `RuleEnginePolicyExecutor` event handler into a process definition, you will notice that it has a drop-down of all the available policies in the system, from which you can pick one. This information is useful at design time but not at validation time, and it may potentially be expensive and wasteful to compute and throw away. In such scenarios, use the `includeVendorExtensions` Boolean to determine if the extra information needs to be populated in the metadata dictionary and returned to the caller.

The Actual Event Handler Methods

Your event handler class can contain one or more methods annotated with the `[RfidEventHandlerMethod]` attribute that are used to actually handle the events. Delivery of the events is managed automatically by BizTalk RFID, and your method will be invoked when the event of the appropriate type arrives. A typical event handler method signature will look like this:

```
[RfidEventHandlerMethod]
public ShipmentEvent TransformToShipment(TagReadEvent tre)
```

Details of the semantics of the attribute and the implicit type checking are discussed in the "Strong Typing" section, which follows. For now, keep the annotation in mind, as well as the fact that your method is really one link in the pipeline of event processing. If you want to stop processing the event, there are two possible times to do this: at compile time and at runtime. At compile time, if your method returns `void`, then it is explicit that there can be no downstream event handlers, and your component is the end of the road for that particular event. At runtime, if your method returns `null`, BizTalk RFID assumes that you want to filter the current event, and stops event processing.

A general rule of thumb is to minimize the execution time inside your method, and not perform any long blocking operations within it. Remember, the rest of the RFID process infrastructure is lightweight and low-latency, but once it calls your code, you are holding precious resources that will affect the scalability and performance of the system. If you need to access a database, make every effort to have the database local to the edge server. It is usually a bad idea to hold onto local resources and make a call from the edge to a remote location, since the remote call could take a long time to execute. If your event handler takes a long time to execute, BizTalk RFID will give up on it and treat it as an error condition. (Error handling is covered in detail in the "Error Handling" section.)

Tear-Down and Cleanup

The event handler contract supports the standard .NET `IDisposable` pattern. If your class implements `IDisposable`, the runtime will invoke it when the process is being shut down. To help you implement `IDisposable` correctly, the base class includes an overridable implementation of `Dispose`. We strongly recommend the following pattern for disposing of objects. For excellent discussions on the topic, search for "IDisposable" on MSDN.

```
protected override void Dispose(bool disposing)
{
    try
    {
        //cleanup
    }
    finally
    {
        base.Dispose(disposing);
    }
}
```

Deployment and Undeployment

This part of the contract for an event handler is optional. If your event handler is completely self-contained (e.g., if it is a parser of some encoding), you may not need any installation support for it. On the other hand, most complex real-world event handlers need some level of installation support. For example, the SqlServerSink component that ships with BizTalk RFID needs to create the SQL database and the schema that it needs. If your event handler requires such deployment support, implement the following static method with this exact signature:

```
public static void Deploy (Dictionary<string,Object> parameters)
```

This method will be invoked each time the process containing it is deployed. The parameters dictionary will contain the same parameters that were specified in the metadata for your component.

Tip If you have an event handler that is potentially used in multiple RFID processes (and to be fair, most are), the Deploy method could be called multiple times with the same set of parameters, even concurrently. If you are performing external initialization, such as creating a database using the set of parameter values, ensure that the method will not fail if another invocation has done the initialization already.

The event handler deployment usually runs under the security context of the user running RFID Manager, which is typically a box administrator. This is because most deployment operations (e.g., creating databases) will require extra permissions than those available to the account that is executing the RFID process at runtime. However, during deployment, you may need to access the identity of the runtime user so that you can grant that user the runtime permissions needed. For this reason, the "process runtime user" is passed in as a special key to the Deploy method. You can access the value at this key by using the ProcessRuntimeUserKey property on the ProcessBinding.

If complementary uninstallation must happen when your component is no longer being used, you can implement another static method with the following signature:

```
public static void Undeploy(Dictionary<string, object> parameters)
```

■**Caution** Unlike Windows installers, the Undeploy method does not check whether no other processes are using the same state that this instance is using. You need to be very careful when you throw away state (e.g., when dropping a database) in the Undeploy method. For this reason, there is no support to invoke the undeploy functionality from within RFID Manager. You have to use the rfidclientconsole.exe command-line tool or actually create a small program that you launch directly to do this.

Strong Typing

When users first started creating RFID business processes using beta versions of BizTalk RFID, we noticed a common issue that they ran into: they would compose pipelines of event handlers and run events through them, and nothing would happen. The code in their event handlers never got invoked, and they had a really hard time figuring out why. The problem was, you could have event handlers that wanted to completely handle the event, and would not want to pass them on to the next event handler. The out-of-the-box SqlServerSink event handler is an example of such an event handler, and making it the first component in the pipeline was the usual way that this problem would crop up. Another common issue that users ran into was that no one really knew if an event handler would work until runtime. This was because there was no information available about the kinds of types that the current event handler could consume, nor about the types of events that the previous event handler would produce. Metaphorically speaking, an event handler could return a square peg, and the second would expect a round hole, and you would not be able to tell until the event was delivered to the event handler, by which time it was typically too late.

The strong typing feature in the event processing pipeline robustly addresses both of these common problems in the following way: each event handler in the pipeline describes the types that it consumes and the types that it produces. Given that, the pipeline definition can be "compiled," from a type safety perspective, as part of the deployment of the process into BizTalk RFID. This operation is very similar to the type checking that happens in C#, for example. While introducing this feature, one constraint that had to be supported was the ability to define multiple event handling methods within a single class, and not require the user to define a class for each kind of event they wanted to handle. The solution to this problem was to use a custom attribute to indicate which methods were RFID event handler methods. Consider the following example:

```
public class HelloWorld: RfidEventHandlerBase
{
    [RfidEventHandlerMethod]
    public void DoSomething(TagReadEvent tre)
    {
    }
```

The [RfidEventHandlerMethod] custom attribute is used to indicate the method DoSomething as being special, and capable of being used in an RFID process pipeline. If you have used the [WebMethod] annotation to indicate the methods on a web service, or [OperationContract] to indicate the operations on a WCF service, this is exactly the same kind of pattern, where the custom attribute is used as an out-of-band annotation. Further, the C# signature of the method is used to determine the input and output types for the method. In this case, the method consumes a TagReadEvent, and its return type is void (i.e., it does not return anything). If you try to compose an event handler pipeline where this is the first one in the pipeline and another method comes after it, the validation of the process will fail.

There are a couple of really interesting implications of this model:

- Instead of forcing you to implement a method with a particular signature, it lets you define methods that can have any name that is meaningful to your scenario. For example, instead of calling the method DoSomething, you could call it PostToFile, if that is what the event handler did.

- If you have a custom event that derives from RfidEventBase or one of its subclasses, you could use that in your signature directly instead. This gives you a completely strongly typed experience, with full inheritance support inside Visual Studio.

For example, here is a definition of a custom event called MyCustomEvent:

```
public class MyCustomEvent: RfidEventBase
{
    private string property;
    private string secondProperty;

    public string Property
    {
        get { return property; }
        set { property = value; }
    }

    public string SecondProperty
    {
        get { return secondProperty; }
        set { secondProperty = value; }
    }
}
```

Here is an event handler method that takes a tag read event, does some lookup and transformation, and returns a MyCustomEvent:

```
[RfidEventHandlerMethod]
public MyCustomEvent Transform(TagReadEvent tre)
{
    MyCustomEvent result = new MyCustomEvent();
    //to-do: transform the tag read into a custom event
    return result;
}
```

Next, let's look at how strong typing affects operations during execution time:

- It will implicitly filter events based on the method signature. At execution time, BizTalk RFID will automatically collect the list of types that are understood by your process, and ensure that only events of those types are delivered into your process. All other event types are filtered automatically. This helps avoid an entire class of runtime and type mismatch errors that would otherwise have to be handled by your event handler.

- If your event handler is the *first* event handler in the pipeline, and it takes a TagReadEvent, and a provider raises a TagListEvent, the runtime will automatically "shred" the list into individual events and run them through the pipeline one at a time. However, if the first event handler is actually a TagListEvent, the runtime will not shred the list. The converse is not true—if your pipeline accepts TagListEvents, and a TagReadEvent is posted, the runtime will not convert the single event into a list.

- If one event handler returns an object of the super type—say, RfidEventBase—and the second event handler takes a subtype—say, MyCustomEvent—a runtime cast operator is applied, and the event processing is aborted if the cast fails.

There are many more such interesting rules, and enumerating all of them exhaustively is not something we are trying to do in this section, but we hope you are left with a good idea of what strong typing is and how it benefits you.

Tip BizTalk RFID tries its best to ensure that processes in the store are always in a *validated* state (i.e., they compile successfully). The only exception is intermediate, or "work-in-progress," process definitions created using RFID Manager. In the rare event that you need to implement and validate your own process, you can use the following methods in the ProcessManagerProxy class:

```
ProcessManagerProxy pmp = new ProcessManagerProxy();
RfidProcess process = pmp.GetProcess("MyProcess");
pmp.SaveProcessWithoutValidation(process);
pmp.ValidateProcessAndBinding(process.Name);
```

You can validate a process only if it is not running. Use the GetProcessStatus method on the ProcessManagerProxy object to determine if the process is running, and stop it first if you need to.

Error Handling

BizTalk RFID considers the event handler to have raised an error if any of the following conditions are true:

- The event handler initialization takes more than the permitted time.

- The event handler method itself takes more than the permitted time.

- The event handler method throws an exception.

Each time an event processing sequence ends in an error, the information is accumulated within the runtime. If the number of errors exceeds a specified percentage of the last 100 events processed, the entire RFID process is deemed to be in a faulty state, and is restarted.

The percentage of tolerable errors and the values of the knobs for maximum event processing time are settable on the ProcessBinding object, and also through RFID Manager (see Figure 5-29).

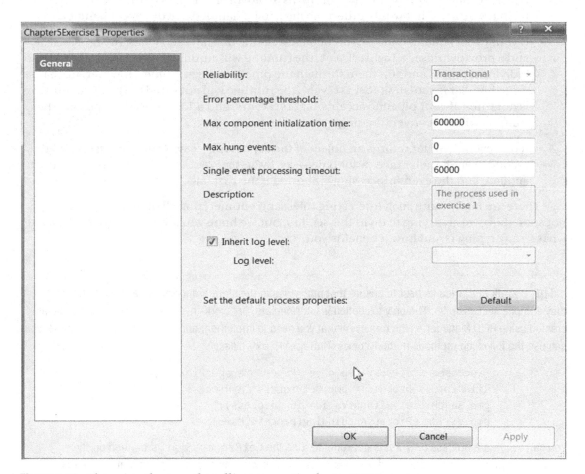

Figure 5-29. *Changing the error handling properties for an RFID process*

■**Tip** The default value for error handling threshold is 0 (i.e., restart on the first error). This could cause the process to restart perpetually when you are developing your event handler and make it hard to debug. Set the value to a high number for development.

You can view the last error encountered by a process on the hub page for the process in RFID Manager. Pay close attention to the time at which the error was reported—there is no way to clear the error information in RFID Manager, and you could be chasing a problem that happened three days ago!

As a rule of thumb, you should handle all "recoverable" errors within your event handler, and take the appropriate actions. If the exception condition is truly exceptional, and the action to be taken is not known, it is best to let the BizTalk RFID runtime handle the exception.

If your event handler creates background threads for any tasks, and you want to plug into the error handling policy infrastructure even for those threads, you can use the ReportError method on the RfidProcessContext object:

```
RfidProcessContext.Current.ReportError("my custom error");
```

Remember, you only need to do this for custom tasks that you schedule through the thread pool yourself, or for threads that you create and manage. For all exceptions on the event handler method itself, this extra step is not needed.

At first glance, this sounds like a lot of machinery to handle an error, but it is actually quite flexible once you get used to it. It lets you create very flexible policies that let you keep running while in development and debugging, and also decide on a pragmatic policy for production deployments. You don't really want to wake up your system administrator if one event fails processing at 3:00 a.m., but you also don't want a process to be "running" but failing all event processing with an error (e.g., you may not be able to write an event to a database once a day, which could be tolerable, but if no events are getting persisted because the database is down, you may want to page your administrator). This level of control ties in naturally with the monitoring and production deployment guidelines that are covered in Chapter 11.

Binding and Deployment

Now you have created a process, and it contains event handlers and logical devices. In this section, we will walk through the process of binding logical devices to real devices, and assigning valid parameter values to all the event handlers in the process. Both of these pieces of information are collectively referred to as the *process binding*, and the ProcessBinding object is a top-level object in the BizTalk RFID ProcessManager API. Before an RFID process is usable, you must associate a binding for it. Just like authoring RFID processes, binding is best accomplished through RFID Manager, either through the Bind wizard or the right-click Bind menu option on the logical device inside the process. However, you are going to do it the hard way, through the BindingManager API, to ensure you understand all the steps that RFID Manager is taking under the hood.

Binding Logical Devices to Physical Devices

Logical devices are application-level names that have some application semantics that are potentially used in the code of the event handler. For example, a logical device named ExitGateReader can let you write code to say, "Whenever an object is read by the exit gate reader, perform exit checks." You would hate to change your code just because the physical reader name is different in a deployment. This is why it is important to use logical devices wherever possible in your code, and not have references to any deployment artifacts.

When you bind a logical device, you must designate a physical source of events that will be hooked up to it. This physical source could come in one of four ways:

- You could bind a logical device to a particular physical device, using the friendly name of the device.

- You could bind a logical device to a device group, in which case events from all the members of the group (and its subgroups transitively, if any) would be routed to your logical device.

- You could bind an antenna of a physical device to a logical device (i.e., just events from a single source would be delivered to your logical device).

- You could use a regular expression, and all friendly device names that match that regular expression would route events to your logical device.

From the preceding choices, you should notice that a logical device can be less than, exactly the same as, or more than a physical device. This flexibility lets you take a process and deploy it in a number of physical topologies without having to redesign. For example, in a really small warehouse station, the ExitGateReader may just be an antenna. In a large warehouse, it may be a bank of readers aimed at all the doors. You can use the binding step to achieve this flexibility.

Tip Both device groups and regular expression bindings have the flexibility that you are binding not to a particular device, but to a collection of devices. This indirection provides you with the flexibility to change the membership of the collection in an online fashion without stopping the process and redeploying bindings. Changing the group membership will automatically cause devices to get opened and closed depending on the processes that are bound to them. If you explicitly bind to devices or device sources, you don't have this flexibility. You cannot drop or change the device name as long as a process has an explicit reference to it. Look at the hard links concept in the BizTalk RFID documentation for a precise explanation of the semantics of these links.

```
ProcessBinding binding = new ProcessBinding();
binding.DeviceBindings["ExitGateReader"] = new DeviceBinding();

//bind a group, a device, an expression, and a source
//to this logical device
          binding.DeviceBindings["ExitGateReader"].DeviceGroupList.Add("MyGroup");
          binding.DeviceBindings["ExitGateReader"].DeviceList.Add("MyDevice");
          binding.DeviceBindings["ExitGateReader"].RegexCollection.Add(
                    new Regex("exit*"));
          binding.DeviceBindings["ExitGateReader"].SourceBindingList.Add(
                    new SourceBinding("MySpecialDevice", "Antenna1"));

BindingManagerProxy bmp = new BindingManagerProxy();
bmp.SaveBinding(p.Name, binding);
```

Binding Event Handler Properties

Binding event handler properties is relatively much more straightforward than binding logical devices. You use the component name to identify your component and the BindingManager API to actually make the change:

```
ProcessBinding binding = new ProcessBinding();

//bind to the post to SQL component, set its database
//parameter to MyDatabase
binding.ComponentBindings["PostToSQL"] = new Dictionary<string, object>();
binding.ComponentBindings["PostToSQL"]
  [SqlServerSink.DatabaseParameterName] = "MyDatabase";

BindingManagerProxy bmp = new BindingManagerProxy();
bmp.SaveBinding(p.Name, binding);
```

You can update both device and component bindings at the same time. In fact, you must do this if you have components that have required parameter values. This is because BizTalk RFID validates component bindings every time you call the SaveBinding API, and rejects invalid/incomplete bindings. This is great—errors that crop up during saving and deployment are more manageable, since the human who is performing the operation knows something is wrong and needs to be fixed.

■**Tip** If you have an advanced scenario where you need to save invalid bindings (e.g., an intermediate save from a design tool), you can use the SaveBindingWithoutValidation method on the BindingManager API. In that case, you still have to fix up bindings and get them into a valid state before the process can be started.

If you are using source binding, ensure that the physical device has the sources with the names that you are interested in, and ensure that the tags are stamped with the correct source name. If the source name has changed or the tag is not stamped with the source name correctly, the tag will be rejected by BizTalk RFID even before it reaches your process.

Note to provider authors: if you are raising TagListEvents, all the events must be from the same source to ensure that source binding works correctly.

■**Tip** The friendly name of the device is very important in ensuring that events from a device are routed correctly. Make sure that you can change the friendly name of the device only from BizTalk RFID. If you change the name directly from another management tool or API outside BizTalk RFID, the names could get out of sync, leading to errors when BizTalk RFID opens the device later.

Executing RFID Processes

To this point, you have seen how to create processes and bind them to devices. The next step is to actually start execution and process events. This is the step of bringing the model to life, so to speak. The good news is, for an RFID process, the model and the application are one and the same. You can deploy it and start it directly, and have a running application. In this section, you will see how that happens under the hood, what the runtime architecture looks like (see Figure 5-30), and what the artifacts created by the application are.

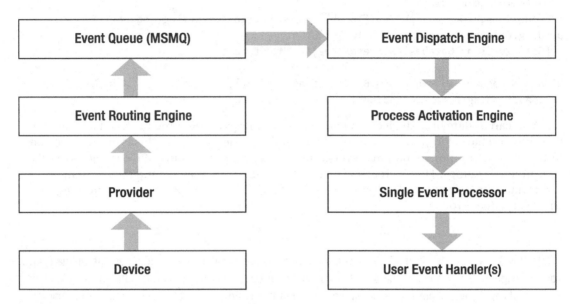

Figure 5-30. *The RFID process runtime architecture*

RFID Process Runtime Architecture

The flow of events starts from the physical device layer and percolates through the provider into a component inside BizTalk RFID that you can best think of as a routing engine. The routing engine has two main functions: for a particular event type from a particular device and source, it determines the processes that are interested in the device. Note that there could be multiple processes interested in the same event. For each such process, there is a separate queue associated with it, called the event queue in Figure 5-30. The routing engine deposits the event in the queue and moves on to the next event. Thus, the queuing of events is completely decoupled from the actual processing of the event.

This store-and-forward capability is at the heart of the event processing runtime. Once an event is available in the queue to be processed, the event dispatch engine dispatches the event to an activated RFID process. The activated RFID process includes live instances of the event handler classes that are glued together by the runtime, so that events from the previous event handler are conveyed to the next appropriate event handler. During the processing of the event, if any of the intermediate event handlers returns a null value, the event is assumed to have been filtered and is rejected.

BizTalk RFID also creates a queue for holding the "rejects," or events that could not be processed successfully. This is in keeping with the philosophy of at-most-once processing of events, and addresses scenarios where a single badly formed event could cause event processing to stall: the problem event is smartly moved to the suspended queue, and event processing continues as usual. BizTalk RFID has management APIs for retrieving and clearing the suspended queue.

Activation and Hosting

At process startup, the runtime creates singleton instances of all the event handler classes, and creates event routing paths for each event type. You can think of this routing path as the call-path in a C# program: the type of the event determines the exact methods that will be invoked and the sequence they will be invoked in. To guarantee process isolation, each RFID process is activated within its own .NET application domain. From an execution efficiency perspective, all the boxes on the right in the preceding runtime architecture diagram are activated in one application domain, and all the boxes on the left are activated in another application domain. There is no cross-application domain call for event processing, but events are transmitted through the event queue. This usage of application domains gives a certain amount of robustness and reliability to the runtime architecture.

After the process pipeline activation happens, the user code in the event handler class will be ready to consume events. BizTalk RFID schedules events as they become available, using the .NET thread pool. Multiple events can be concurrently processed at the same time, so if you have any state in your event handler classes, you must take care of the synchronization of access to such state. You should also not make any assumptions regarding the order in which events are processed. It is quite possible that events will be observed by the reader and delivered in one order, but consumed by the event handler in a different order.

If a process has a problem, the application domain can be torn down and a new one can be created without impacting other processes, up to a point. However, if they share the same Win32 process, there are certain operations where the activities of one process or provider will impact another, including but not limited to stack overflows, out-of-memory errors, memory leaks, and unmanaged access errors. This is where the hosting feature comes in. On Windows Server 2003 and Windows Server 2003 R2, BizTalk RFID hosts each RFID process and provider out of process from the BizTalk RFID server itself, using IIS as the application host.

BizTalk RFID Hosting Model for Windows Server

IIS 6.0, which ships with Windows Server 2003, has a lot of support for hosting applications. This includes the concept of an application pool, which determines the properties of the Win32 process used to host the application. Under Windows Server, each RFID process and provider gets its own web application and application pool. Other than that, all the aspects of the programming model remain exactly the same. You should think of the architecture from Figure 5-30 as having a Win32 process boundary at the queue layer. From a performance perspective, other than the overhead of having a few additional Win32 processes, you should not see significant deviations in the latency of event processing, since no new interprocess calls are introduced between the path where an event is raised and where it is consumed. The event consumption still goes directly through MSMQ, which is the same as in the nonhosted scenario. However, from a deployment and management perspective, the introduction of IIS is a significant moving part, and you should have a handle on the interprocess communication that is happening, which will let you interpret and troubleshoot issues. Figure 5-31 illustrates the process boundaries where interprocess communication through WCF is happening under the covers. Table 5-1 summarizes the differences between the two deployment platforms.

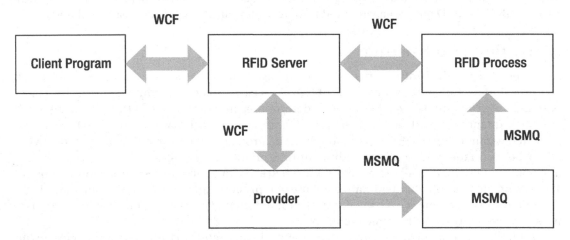

Figure 5-31. *BizTalk RFID hosting architecture on Windows Server 2003*

Table 5-1. *Summary of Hosting Differences on the Desktop and Server Operating Systems*

Item	Windows Vista/XP	Windows Server 2003/2008
Host	BizTalk RFID NT Service (rfidservices.exe)	IIS worker process (w3wp.exe)
Isolation	Application domain isolation only	Win32 process isolation
Process identity	RFID service account	RFID process account (can change)
Config file	Web.config	Web.config
Communication	Uses cross-application domain calls	Uses WCF
Event Collection	Yes	Yes

Transactionality

There are three supported modes for the "message handling reliability" of RFID processes. Basically, they govern the guarantees that BizTalk RFID gives to your application from a reliability perspective. As a colleague once told a room full of trainees, all those who want unreliable messaging, please put up your hand. Seriously, this mode essentially represents the trade-off between reliability and performance. Also, based on your scenario, you may not have any transactional component in your pipeline, in which case it would be unfair to impose the overhead of transactionality on your application. Here is a brief description of the knobs and how you might use them:

Transactional: This is the default level. For each event, the runtime creates a new transaction, which is available as the ambient transaction (`Transaction.Current` for those of you familiar with `System.Transactions` from .NET 2.0). Within this transaction, it dequeues a single event from the event queue. It invokes each event handler method within this same transaction. If the event handler writes the event to SQL Server, for example, it will enlist in this same ambient transaction by default. At the end of the event processing, the system will attempt to commit the global transaction. If the commit succeeds, all is well. If not, the system will roll back the current transaction, start a smaller transaction to dequeue from the event queue, and write the event to the suspended queue. The implications are that you get fully transactional, reliable event processing, which is great for enterprise applications. You also get clean, all-or-nothing semantics, where either the work done by all event handlers is committed, or the work done by none of them is committed. The downside is that you incur the overhead of a distributed transaction for each event that you process, and effectively, you are running at the speed at which synchronous writes can be made to the transactional logging subsystem. On most modern hardware, this means you can process a few hundred events per second, at best.

Reliable: In this mode, the queue is configured to use reliable storage. When an event is successfully posted to the queue, it guarantees that the event can be retrieved later. However, there is no explicit transaction created for each event. The queuing subsystem is free to optimize the batching of sends and receives as it feels appropriate from a performance perspective. If you have lots of concurrent activity, this is a great opportunity for the queuing subsystem to batch operations and attain significantly better throughput than transactional event processing. The runtime dequeues the event, and then executes it through the pipeline, without creating an ambient transaction. If you have an event handler that accesses a transactional resource such as a database, it will have to wrap the execution within its own transaction (SQL Server, for example, has an implicit statement-level transaction if you submit operations to it). In this model, if one event handler succeeds, but the other fails, the first event handler's transaction commit will still stay and not roll back. You have more granular control over transactions, and you gain a significant advantage from a performance perspective. Typically, this kind of event processing yields three to four times the throughput of transactional processing, if the throughput was I/O-bound to start with.

Express: One of the developers who heard about this mode in the chalk talks called this "loosey-goosey event processing," and the name stuck. With this mode, the event queue is configured to be "express"—the emphasis is on delivery speed and efficiency, not correctness. In this model, no guarantees are made that an event that was queued can be dequeued. Also, the runtime does not create an ambient transaction; it dequeues the event and has it processed immediately. In this mode of event processing, under some circumstances, the delivery of events from the provider to the event processing pipeline could all be accomplished without a single disk operation; hence, the throughput is significantly higher compared to transactional event processing. However, you get exactly what you paid for: occasionally, you may lose an event. If you can sleep easily at night knowing that most of your events will be processed very quickly, this is the right mode for you. Typically, it makes sense if your event processing is doing a lot of low-level filtering and elimination of duplicates: if you lose an event under such scenarios, it is usually not such a big deal, since the next one will be along a millisecond later.

Conclusion

This chapter covered the new asynchronous event processing model that is part of BizTalk RFID, which is at the heart of building RFID applications. Each asynchronous event processing application is implemented as an RFID business process. We stepped through the design, authoring, configuration, deployment, and execution of RFID business processes. We covered a lot of ground in this chapter, but in a sense, this new event processing model is really at the heart of what is new about BizTalk RFID.

CASE STUDY: TRACKING GUEST ACTIVITIES TO IMPROVE CUSTOMER SERVICE AND GUEST SATISFACTION

Industry: Tourism.

Overview: When boarding a tourist cruise ship, guests are given an RFID-enabled armband that they can wear throughout their stay. This armband provides access to all amenities, including their hotel room, the workout room, events, and access to the ship when at port. Additionally, the armband enables the guest to keep a running tab on purchases and debts, including trips to the bars, restaurants, casinos, and shows. At the end of the trip, their balance due is included on their final bill.

Results: The process not only improves the ease with which a guest can move around and make transactions during their stay, but it also improves customer service. When a guest steps out of their room, housekeeping can be notified, and the room can be cleaned. When a guest enters a casino, they can be greeted and served according to their needs. From a business perspective, tracking this information allows for extensive business intelligence based on the metrics that are created from numerous guest activities.

CHAPTER 6

■ ■ ■

Command Processing

The event handler components of BizTalk RFID provide a method for capturing the stream of information from RFID devices. The ability to execute synchronous commands completes the device interaction story, allowing tags to be commissioned, device properties to be changed on the fly, and lights to be turned on and off via I/O ports. The term *commissioning* in an RFID context refers to the act of preparing an RFID tag (and accompanying label, etc.) for use. This typically involves programming the ID (for UHF tags), writing any user memory, and printing a physical label. The primary goals of this chapter are the following:

- Establishing synchronous connections to a BizTalk RFID server

- Managing devices from .NET applications

- Performing common RFID-related tasks such as tag printing from .NET applications

All of the examples in this chapter will use the following baseline configuration of simulated readers (as shown in Figure 6-1). Exercise 6-1 introduces the setup of this configuration.

- Two RFID readers (Dock Door Portal and Conveyer A)

- One RFID printer (Warehouse A)

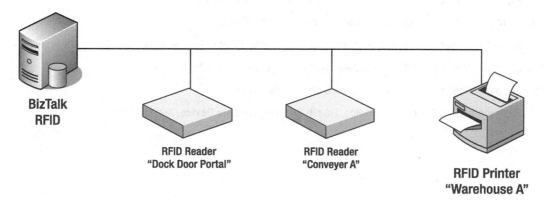

BizTalk RFID

RFID Reader "Dock Door Portal"

RFID Reader "Conveyer A"

RFID Printer "Warehouse A"

Figure 6-1. *Baseline configuration for exercises in Chapter 6*

Exercise 6-1. Setting Up the Baseline Configuration

This exercise will demonstrate how to set up the baseline configuration of two simulated RFID readers and a simulated RFID printer using RFID Manager.

1. Set up the Contoso simulator for two devices, as per Exercise 3-2.

2. Start RFID Manager. Right-click the Devices tab and click New Device.

3. From the Add Device wizard, select Add Single Device and click Next.

4. From the list of available providers, select Simulator and click Next.

5. Select the TCP connection type, with an IP address of 127.0.0.1 and a port of 8001.

6. From the Add Device to a Group page, click Next to accept the default device group.

7. From the Authentication page, click Next to accept the default credentials (no username, no password).

8. When complete, the RFID Manager Devices view should be similar to the one shown in Figure 6-2.

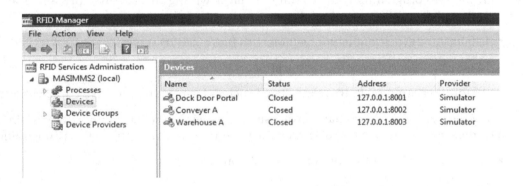

Figure 6-2. *RFID Manager with baseline reader configuration*

9. From RFID Manager, right-click Processes and click New Process.

10. In the New Process window, type in a process name of **Chapter 6 Test**, and click OK.

11. From the "Welcome to the Bind wizard" screen that appears, click Next.

12. From the Bind Process to Logical Devices screen, click New.

13. From the Logical Device Name dialog, type in the name **Sample Device**, and click OK.

14. In the list of logical devices in the Bind Process to Logical Devices dialog, click the check box next to Sample Device, and then click Next.

15. In the "Configure logical device – Sample Device" dialog, click Dock Door Portal and Warehouse A in the "Devices and groups" box (shown in Figure 6-3). Then click Next.

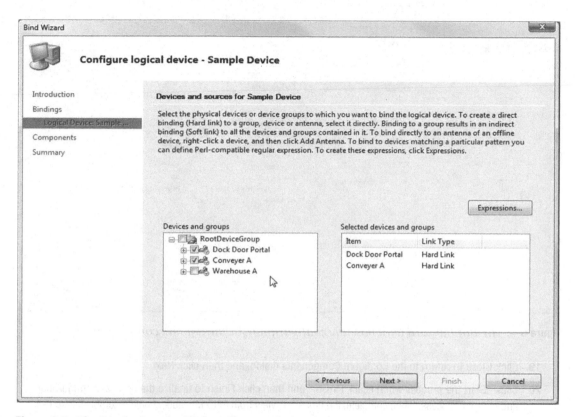

Figure 6-3. *The Bind wizard with baseline configuration*

16. From the Configure Components dialog, click New Component.

17. In the Add Component dialog, click the SqlServerSink component in the list of available components, and then click Add.

18. From the Add Component Instance dialog that appears, type in an instance name of **SqlSink**, and then click OK. The Bind wizard should now look like Figure 6-4.

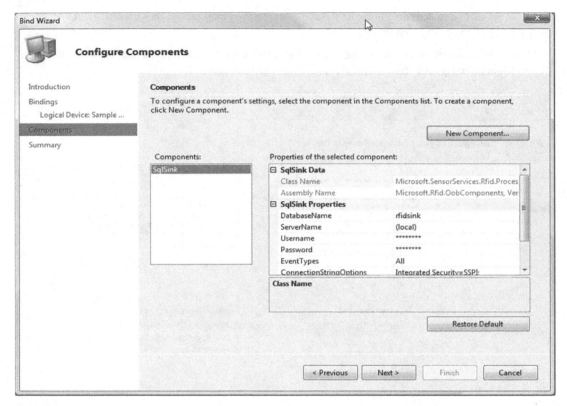

Figure 6-4. *The Bind wizard with baseline configuration for the SqlSink component*

19. Click Close to return to the Configure Components dialog, and then click Next.

20. Click "Start the process when I click Finish," and then click Finish to finalize the process configuration and start the process. When complete, the Processes view from RFID Manager should resemble Figure 6-5.

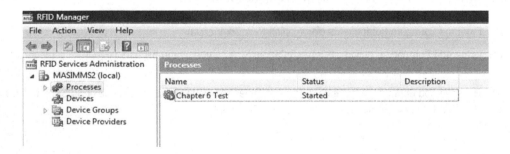

Figure 6-5. *RFID Manager with the Chapter 6 test project configured*

Connecting BizTalk RFID to Your Application

The first step in connecting your application to BizTalk RFID is adding the necessary proxy references and using statements. The ManagementWebServiceProxies assembly exposes all of the synchronous management features provided by BizTalk RFID through a series of proxy objects (shown in Table 6-1).

1. From Visual Studio, create your base project (typically either a Windows Forms or console application).

2. Add the following assembly references to your project (these are typically found in C:\Program Files\Microsoft BizTalk RFID\bin\):

- Microsoft.Rfid.ManagementWebServiceProxies.dll

- Microsoft.Rfid.Design

- Microsoft.Rfid.SpiSdk

Table 6-1. *BizTalk RFID Web Proxy Classes*

Proxy Object	Description	Commonly Used Methods
DeviceManagerProxy	Manages connections to and configuration of RFID devices Allows execution of synchronous commands on RFID devices	GetDevice OpenConnection ExecuteDedicatedCommand GetDevice
ProcessManagerProxy	Manages process creation, configuration, and activation Allows simulation of events	AddEventToProcessPipeline StartProcess StopProcess
ComponentManagerProxy	Manages registration of event handler assemblies	GetEventHandlers RegisterEventHandler
BindingManagerProxy	Manages event handler bindings to processes	GetBinding DeleteBinding SaveBinding
ProviderManagerProxy	Manages provider registration, configuration, and activation	StartProvider StopProvider
ServerManagerProxy	Manages the BizTalk RFID server	GetServerConfiguration

Processes

RFID processes may also be manipulated through the use of synchronous commands (via the ProcessManagerProxy class). These commands allow processes to be registered, started, and stopped. One of the common tasks in external applications relating to RFID processes is retrieving the list of active processes for use in tag simulation. The only "direct" way to push simulated events into a running process is to use the AddEventToProcessPipeline command, which requires a process and a logical device name. The code in Exercise 6-2 uses the ProcessManagerProxy class to obtain the list of processes from the BizTalk RFID server and dump the list of logical devices and event handlers assigned to each.

■Note This exercise requires that the baseline configuration (from Exercise 6-1) is set up and running on the target BizTalk RFID server.

Exercise 6-2. Obtaining a List of Registered Processes

This exercise will demonstrate how to obtain a detailed list of the registered processes on a BizTalk RFID server from a .NET application. It will demonstrate how to retrieve the logical devices and event handlers registered to each process. This application is set to run from the same machine as the BizTalk RFID server, but can run on another machine by changing the hostname in the ProcessManagerProxy constructor.

1. Begin by creating a C# console application in Visual Studio .NET. Name the project SyncSample2.

2. Add the following assemblies as project references:

   Microsoft.RFID.Design

   Microsoft.Rfid.ManagementWebServiceProxies

3. Add the using references as shown in Listing 6-1 to the top of the Program.cs file.

Listing 6-1. *Importing the Required Namespaces*

```
using Microsoft.SensorServices.Rfid.Management;
using Microsoft.SensorServices.Rfid.Design;
```

4. In the Program.cs file, create a new method called DumpProcessList, as shown in Listing 6-2.

Listing 6-2. *Using the ProcessManagerProxy to Obtain a List of Registered RFID Processes*

```
static public void DumpProcessList()
{
 // Create a process manager proxy
 ProcessManagerProxy pmp = new ProcessManagerProxy();

 // Obtain the list of process names
 string[] processNames = pmp.GetAllProcesses();

 foreach (string procName in processNames)
 {
  Console.WriteLine("Process {0}:\r\n-------------------------");

  DumpLogicalDevices(pmp, procName);
  DumpEventHandlers(pmp, procName);
 }
}
```

5. In the `Program.cs` file, create a new method called `DumpLogicalDevices`, as shown in Listing 6-3.

Listing 6-3. *Using the ProcessManagerProxy to Obtain a List of Logical Devices Assigned to a Process*

```
static public void DumpLogicalDevices(ProcessManagerProxy pmp,
    string procName)
{
 // Get detailed information on this process
 RfidProcess process = pmp.GetProcess(procName);

 // Obtain the list of logical devices
 ICollection<LogicalDevice> logicalDevices =
process.GetAllLogicalDevices();

 Console.Write("Logical devices: ");

 foreach (LogicalDevice d in logicalDevices)
  Console.Write(" {0},", d.Name);

 Console.WriteLine("");
}
```

6. In the `Program.cs` file, create a new method called `DumpEventHandlers`, as shown in Listing 6-4.

Listing 6-4. *Using the ProcessManagerProxy to Obtain a List of Event Handler Components Assigned to a Process*

```
static public void DumpEventHandlers(ProcessManagerProxy pmp,
    string procName)
{
 // Get detailed information on this process
 RfidProcess process = pmp.GetProcess(procName);

 // Obtain the list of event handlers
 ICollection<EventHandlerDefinition> eventHandlers =
  process.GetAllEventHandlers();
 Console.Write("Event Handlers: ");

 foreach (EventHandlerDefinition eh in eventHandlers)
  Console.Write(" {0}, ", eh.ComponentName);

 Console.WriteLine("");
}
```

7. In the `Program.cs` file, modify the `main` method as shown in Listing 6-5.

Listing 6-5. *Calling the Method to Dump the Process List*

```
static void Main(string[] args)
{
 DumpProcessList();
}
```

8. From Visual Studio.NET 2008, click Project, then Debug, and then Start Without Debugging. The application will execute and print the following to a command window:

```
Process Testproc:
--------------------------
Logical devices:  Test,
Event Handlers:  sink,
```

Note   You use the Start Without Debugging command to run the application, as it will leave the command window open until a key is pressed.

Devices

The management proxies provide full access to the list of devices configured on a BizTalk RFID server. This allows external applications to inspect the list of provisioned devices, configure devices with specific properties, and add new devices (though this would more commonly be done through RFID Manager, or automated through a PowerShell script or rfidclientconsole.exe command-line tool). One of the common tasks when implementing synchronous commands against BizTalk RFID is obtaining a list of device names (as the BizTalk RFID device name is required to open a connection before issuing commands to RFID devices).

Exercise 6-3 demonstrates how to use the synchronous API to obtain a list of all registered devices.

Exercise 6-3. Obtaining a List of Registered Devices

This exercise will demonstrate how to obtain a list of the names of registered devices on a BizTalk RFID server from a .NET application. Note that this could also be accomplished by using the rfidclientconsole.exe getalldevicestatus command (actually, both the console application and this example are using the same objects in the ManagementWebProxy library to accomplish the same task).

1. Begin by creating a C# console application in Visual Studio .NET. Name the project SyncSample2.

2. Add the following assemblies as project references:

   Microsoft.RFID.Design

   Microsoft.Rfid.ManagementWebServiceProxies

3. Add the using references as shown in Listing 6-6 to the top of the Program.cs file.

Listing 6-6. *Using the ProcessManagerProxy to Obtain a List of Registered RFID Processes*

```
using Microsoft.SensorServices.Rfid.Management;
using Microsoft.SensorServices.Rfid.Design;
```

4. In the Program.cs file, create a new method called DumpDeviceList, as shown in Listing 6-7.

Listing 6-7. *Using the DeviceManagerProxy to Obtain a List of Devices*

```
public void ListDevices()
{
 DeviceManagerProxy dmp = new DeviceManagerProxy();
 DeviceDefinition[] devices = dmp.GetAllDevices();

 foreach (DeviceDefinition device in devices)
 {
  Console.WriteLine("Device {0}: {1}",
  device.Name, device.DeviceInformation);
 }
}
```

5. In the Program.cs file, modify the main method as shown in Listing 6-8.

Listing 6-8. *Using the ProcessManagerProxy to Obtain a List of Event Handler Components Assigned to a Process*

```
static void Main(string[] args)
{
    DumpDeviceList();
}
```

6. From Visual Studio.NET 2008, click Project, then Debug, and then Start Without Debugging. The application will execute, and print the following to a command window:

```
Device Advanced Reader:
<logicalDeviceInformation>
    <deviceInformationBase>
        <connectionInformation>
            <provider>Symbol</provider>
            <transportSettings>
                <tcpTransportSettings>
                    <host>192.168.0.132</host><port>80</port>
                </tcpTransportSettings>
            </transportSettings>
        </connectionInformation>
    </deviceInformationBase>
</logicalDeviceInformation>
```

The rest of the examples in this chapter will assume that a list of physical and logical device names have been obtained from a BizTalk RFID server.

Device Management

The most commonly used synchronous commands relate to controlling and configuring RFID devices as well as printing RFID tags. The two key scenarios are callbacks from an asynchronous command handler and device control from an external application.

Synchronous callbacks are commonly used to implement business logic such as turning on lights or buzzers through I/O ports. From an event handler component, a synchronous callback is made to an RFID device (commonly the device that raised the event, but not always) to perform an I/O change or property update.

Device control from an external application is typically used to implement scenarios such as tag printing, commissioning, or automated configuration. From a .NET application, synchronous commands are issued to an RFID device.

We'll cover how to set up the synchronous command proxies for both .NET applications and event handler components, and manage device connections. Then we'll walk through each of the four core synchronous command types (RFID, configuration, printing, and vendor-specific). For each of these examples, the proxy class used will be the DeviceManagerProxy; however, the same framework code will work for any of the other proxy classes.

Implementing Synchronous Calls from .NET Applications

The most common use of the synchronous commands described in this chapter is creating a stand-alone .NET application (console, GUI, etc.) that can interact with RFID devices. This provides for such functionality as synchronous tag reads, printing tags, and configuring devices.

Implementing Device Callbacks

An alternate scenario for using these commands is when performing a synchronous callback within an event handler. Take the scenario wherein the overall RFID solution must flash a light when an invalid tag read is received (e.g., a tag read indicating a type of product that doesn't belong on the conveyer belt that the RFID reader is monitoring).

In this situation, one of the event handlers would open a connection to the reader from which the event was received and execute a synchronous command to manipulate one of the digital output ports.

Managing Device Connections

Every command issued to an RFID device requires an open device connection (either explicit or implicit). Managing these device connections is crucial to implementing a well-behaved and performant system. Many RFID devices only support a single "administrative" connection for issuing synchronous commands; as such, it is safer to treat RFID device connections like database connections—as a scarce resource. When issuing synchronous commands, follow these guidelines for establishing device connections:

- Only hold the device connection open as long as you're actively issuing commands. Especially in larger installations, keeping a connection open and idle may block another user (such as a system administrator) from connecting to the device.

- If you are issuing a block of commands in close sequence, keep the connection open for the entire set. Rapidly opening and closing connections to issue a set of commands may reduce performance.

- Wrap the DeviceConnection object in a using statement (when developing in C#) to ensure that the object is disposed of properly.

- Use the Open method rather than OpenAdministrationConnection for normal task execution. The OpenAdministrationConnection method should be reserved for use by administrative interfaces as it can interfere with existing connections. Also, there's no guarantee that the OpenAdministrationConnection method will be fully implemented by the device vendor, so mileage may vary.

■**Note** As a developer, you have the choice of either explicitly managing the connection (as per the preceding list) or requesting that BizTalk RFID automatically manage the connection to execute a single command. Think of this as similar to using ADO.NET TableAdapter objects vs. manually opening a DbConnection object. With the TableAdapter, the underlying ADO.NET opens a connection, executes a predetermined command, and closes the connection. BizTalk RFID device connections work the same way. If you want to execute a single command, the ExecuteDedicatedCommand method will handle the device connection. If you want to execute a sequence of commands, it is more efficient to manage the device connection manually.

The baseline code for establishing a device connection and issuing commands is shown in Listing 6-9.

Listing 6-9. *Establishing a Connection to an RFID Device Through the DeviceConnection Class*

```
using (DeviceConnection dc = new DeviceConnection(deviceName))
{
 try
 {
  dc.Open();
  // Do stuff here
  dc.Close();
 }
 catch (Exception ex0)
 {
  // Error handling and reporting
 }
}
```

The deviceName argument should be pulled from the list of registered devices.

Standard Commands

Standard commands are those "baked into" the Device Service Provider Interface (DSPI), and provide functionality that is common across a set of RFID devices. For example, the GetProperty command is implemented by all devices, but the PrintTag command would generally only be supported by RFID printers. The information about which devices support which standard (and extended commands) is available through the provider capability and metadata collections.

It is important to remember that not all device providers (or devices) are created equal. Different providers support different commands, and often implement them in different ways. In some situations, one provider will support multiple devices (such as devices based on the Intel R1000 chip), but not all of the devices will support the feature in question (such as I/O).

Always test your application with physical hardware to ensure that things work the way you expect. Tables 6-2 through 6-6 display the standard commands, along with a description of how they are commonly used.

Table 6-2 describes the general RFID commands, which are general purpose RFID commands that are not specific to a particular protocol or technology (such as HF or EPC Gen 2).

Table 6-2. *General RFID Commands*

Command	Description of Use
GetReadFilter SetReadFilter	These commands are used to manipulate the device's read filter. For those RFID devices that support read filters, this provides a vendor-neutral way of controlling the filtering that occurs directly on the device. This is usually the most efficient way to filter for a particular subset of data.
GetTagData	Retrieves the user data for a particular tag. Note that due to the often large user memories for HF tags (and some newer UHF tags), the use of GetPartialTagData may be more efficient.
GetTagMetadata	Given a particular tag ID, this retrieves the tag metadata. The content of the metadata varies between technologies, but generally provides the tag type, the manufacturer, and sometimes a description of the memory layout on the tag. The tag type/manufacturer codes and memory layout are often used to determine how to invoke commands such as ReadPartialTagData.
GetTags	This command retrieves a list of all of the tags that are currently seen by the target reader (i.e., from all of the available sources/antennae).

Table 6-3 describes the UHF RFID commands. These are standard RFID commands that are more suited to UHF devices and tags.

Table 6-3. *UHF RFID Commands*

Command	Description of Use
Kill	This command is used to permanently disable an EPC UHF tag. Once this command has been issued, it *cannot* be reversed. This is often used in retail scenarios, or other situations with similar privacy concerns, to render an RFID tag inoperative as it leaves the store or other establishment.
LockTag UnlockTag	These commands are used to lock and unlock the data and EPC ID fields of an EPC tag. Once these fields have been locked, they cannot be modified without being unlocked.
WriteId	This command is used to write the EPC ID to *every* EPC UHF tag seen by an antenna, provided that the tags are not locked.
WriteTagData	This command is used to write to the user memory of a specific tag.

Table 6-4 describes the HF RFID commands. These are standard RFID commands that are more suited to HF devices and tags.

Table 6-4. *HF RFID Commands*

Command	Description of Use
GetPartialTagData WritePartialTagData	HF tags often have large user memory areas. The GetPartialTagData and WritePartialTagData commands allow for selective data access and modification. This is used to improve performance and efficiency when you're only interested in a particular segment of data on the tag.
LockPartialTagData UnlockPartialTagData	In conjunction with the large user memory areas, HF tags typically allow segments (or blocks) of data to be individually locked. Note that locking a data block is usually a permanent operation on HF tags. Also note that, depending on the device in question, attempting to lock an area of tag memory that does not line up with the way the tag data is segmented into blocks will usually fail.

Table 6-5 describes the commands that are used to configure and manage devices. All of the device management features provided by RFID Manager can be replicated through the use of the commands in this list. These functions are typically used when automating certain device management scenarios (such as automating the upload of new firmware to a set of devices managed by different BizTalk RFID servers).

Table 6-5. *Device Management Commands*

Command	Description of Use
ApplyPropertyProfile	This command is used to apply a set of properties (i.e., a property profile) to a device. It is often used in performing automated configuration updates across a range of devices, or as a quick method of configuring a reader for a specific scenario from a synchronous application.
GetCurrentPropertyProfile	This command is used to retrieve the set of current properties from a specific device.
GetDefaultPropertyProfile	This command returns the set of default properties as defined by the device vendor. This profile may then be passed back to the device using the ApplyPropertyProfile command to return the device to a known state.
GetProperty SetProperty	These commands are used to access and modify individual properties on a device. A common usage scenario for this is manipulating I/O ports, often through vendor-specific properties.
UpgradeFirmware	This command is used to push updated firmware to a device. The use of this synchronous command (as opposed to performing updates through RFID Manager) is useful for automating updates across a range of devices.

Table 6-6 describes the printing commands. There are a wide range of commands for commissioning and printing RFID tags. Most of these relate to the management of the print templates that are used to generate the physical printing, as well as the sequence of RFID data.

Table 6-6. *Printing Commands*

Command	Description of Use
AddPrintTemplate GetAllPrintTemplateNames GetAllPrintTemplates GetPrintTemplate RemovePrintTemplate	These commands are used to manage the registered printer templates.
GetCurrentPrintTemplateName SetCurrentPrintTemplateName	Use these to manage the active (current) printer template. This is the template passed to the printer whenever a PrintTag command is executed.
GetPrintLabelPreview	This retrieves a preview snapshot (either thumbnail or full-sized image) of the label template. It's extremely useful when developing tag-commissioning applications.
PrintTag	In a single operation, this prints either a label or a sequence of labels and encodes the enclosed RFID tag(s) with the ID and access/kill codes.

Calling any of the standard commands follows the same general pattern:

1. Establish a connection to the target RFID device.

2. Create the appropriate command object (i.e., for a `PrintTag` command, create an instance of the `PrintTagCommand` class).

3. For executing a series of commands in sequence (such as programming a set of device properties), open a connection with `DeviceManagerProxy.OpenConnection` and send commands with the `DeviceManagerProxy.ExecuteCommandForConnection` method.

4. For executing a single command, use the `DeviceManagerProxy.ExecuteDedicatedCommand` method (this automatically opens and closes the required `DeviceConnection`).

5. Parse the command object returned for a valid response object.

■**Note** Each of the command objects returns a specific response object. The response class types for each command are documented in the DSPI reference.

Calling several of the most commonly used standard commands is demonstrated in Exercises 6-4 through 6-7. As not every device supports all of the standard commands (e.g., it makes little sense for a reader to implement support for printing commands), some mechanism is required to determine which commands are supported by a particular device.

Each vendor is responsible for surfacing this information through the `DeviceCapabilities` list. This list can be accessed through the provider metadata, as shown in Exercise 6-4. To find out if a device supports a particular command, check the capabilities list. For example, if a particular device has the `GetTags` entry in the capabilities list, it will support the `GetTags` command.

Exercise 6-4. Obtaining a List of Tags Seen by the Reader (GetTagsCommand)

This exercise will demonstrate how to obtain a list of the tags currently in front of the sources (antennae) for the selected RFID reader.

1. Open the SyncCommands project.

2. Add the `Microsoft.Rfid.Util.dll` assembly.

3. Add a `using` reference to the `Microsoft.SensorServices.Rfid.Utilities` namespace.

4. Add the method as shown in Listing 6-10. This accepts a physical device name (see Exercise 6-3 for information on how to retrieve the list of registered device names) and executes a single `GetTagsCommand` method. The method then prints out the tag ID and source name to the console. Note that the tag ID is a binary array, so a helper method (from the `Microsoft.Rfid.Util` assembly) is used to convert it to a hex string.

Listing 6-10. *Executing the GetTags Command*

```
static public void ExecuteGetTags(string deviceName)
{
 GetTagsCommand cmd = new GetTagsCommand(null);

 DeviceManagerProxy dmp = new DeviceManagerProxy();
 Command c = dmp.ExecuteDedicatedCommand(deviceName, cmd);

 cmd = c as GetTagsCommand;
 if (cmd != null && cmd.Response != null)
 {
  GetTagsResponse response = cmd.Response;
  ReadOnlyCollection<TagReadEvent> tags = response.Tags;

  Console.WriteLine("Tags Read:\r\n----------------");
  foreach (TagReadEvent tre in tags)
  {
   Console.WriteLine("Tag {0} from source {1}",
   HexUtilities.HexEncode(tre.GetId()), tre.Source);
  }
 }
}
```

Note This method does not implement error handling.

5. Modify the main method in the Program.cs file to execute the ExecuteGetTags method, as shown in Listing 6-11.

Listing 6-11. *Calling DumpDeviceList*

```
static void Main(string[] args)
{
    DumpDeviceList();
}
```

Exercise 6-5. Reprogramming an EPC Tag with a New ID (WriteIdCommand)

This exercise demonstrates how to use the `WriteId` command to change the EPC number on a UHF tag.

1. Open the SyncCommands project.

2. Add the method as shown in Listing 6-12. This accepts a byte array (the new tag ID), but leaves the access and kill codes blank.

Listing 6-12. *Executing the GetTags Command*

```
public static void ExecuteWriteId(string readerName, byte[] id)
{
 WriteIdCommand cmd = new WriteIdCommand(null, id, null, null);
 DeviceManagerProxy dmp = new DeviceManagerProxy();
 dmp.ExecuteDedicatedCommand(readerName, cmd);
}
```

3. Modify the `main` method in the `Program.cs` file to execute the `ExecuteGetTags` method, as shown in Listing 6-13.

Listing 6-13. *Calling the ExecuteWriteId Method*

```
static void Main(string[] args)
{
    ExecuteWriteId("Sample Reader", new byte[] { 0x10, 0x20, 0x30, 0x40 }
);
}
```

Exercise 6-6. Changing the Digital Output Port Value

This exercise will demonstrate how to use the `SetProperty` method to manipulate the state of a digital output port on an RFID reader (that supports this feature). Most UHF readers support digital I/O, though the port and source names will differ between each specific model. The examples shown are for using any reader supporting LLRP with at least a digital output port.

1. Open the SyncCommands project.

2. Add the method as shown in Listing 6-14. This accepts a source name and byte value (the digital output port to change and the value to set). Note the use of the `OpenConnection` method to open a dedicated connection to the device. Since the `SetProperty` command can also apply to sources (as opposed to the device), `ExecuteDedicatedCommand` isn't applicable.

Listing 6-14. *Executing the SetProperty Command*

```
static public void SetDigitalPort(string readerName,
    string source, byte[] val)
{
    DeviceManagerProxy dmp = new DeviceManagerProxy();
    Guid connId = Guid.Empty;
    try
    {
        connId = dmp.OpenConnection(readerName);

        EntityProperty prop = new EntityProperty(
            new PropertyKey("Source", "Port Output Value"), val);
        Command mycmd = new SetPropertyCommand(prop);
        Command resp = dmp.ExecuteCommandForConnection(
            readerName, source, connId, mycmd);
    }
    finally
    {
        dmp.CloseConnection(readerName, connId);
    }
}
```

3. Modify the `main` method in the `Program.cs` file to execute the `SetDigitalPort` method, as shown in Listing 6-15. Note that the first digital output port is GPO_1 on LLRP readers, and that a digital LOW value is a byte array with a single byte value of 0.

Listing 6-15. *Calling the SetDigitalPort Method*

```
static void Main(string[] args)
{
    byte[] off = new byte[] { 0 };
    SetDigitalPort("SampleReader", "GPO_1", off);
}
```

Exercise 6-7. Reading the Current Timestamp (GetProperty/Time)

This exercise will demonstrate how to use the GetProperty command to read the timestamp from a device.

■**Note** The list of supported properties can be obtained from the DeviceCapability metadata, as shown later in Exercise 6-8.

---

1. Open the SyncCommands project.

2. Add the method as shown in Listing 6-16. This method uses the GetPropertyCommand method to return the timestamp from the reader, as stored in the General:Time property (*Group:PropertyName* is a common shorthand in BizTalk RFID).

    Listing 6-16. *Executing the SetProperty Command*

    ```
    private static void GetReaderTime(string readerName)
    {
        DeviceManagerProxy dmp = new DeviceManagerProxy();
        PropertyKey key = new PropertyKey("General", "Time");
        Command myCmd = new GetPropertyCommand(key);
        Command resp = dmp.ExecuteDedicatedCommand(readerName, myCmd);
        if (resp != null && resp is GetPropertyCommand)
        {
            GetPropertyResponse response =
                (resp as GetPropertyCommand).Response;
            object respValue = response.Property.PropertyValue;
            DateTime readerTime = (DateTime)respValue;
        }
    }
    ```

3. Modify the main method in the Program.cs file to execute the GetReaderTime method, as shown in Listing 6-17.

    Listing 6-17. *Calling the GetReaderTime Method*

    ```
    static void Main(string[] args)
    {
        byte[] off = new byte[] { 0 };
        GetReaderTime("SampleReader");
    }
    ```

Vendor Commands

Vendor commands and properties are the extensibility points by which the unique capabilities of each hardware device are surfaced by individual vendors. Custom properties are employed to expose the full depth of the configuration experience for a specific device while maintaining a common interface. Custom commands are used to enable functionality that falls outside the standard command set, such as pulsing an I/O port. Understanding how to determine which vendor commands are available and how to invoke them is critical in taking full advantage of the unique capabilities of certain hardware devices.

Exercise 6-8 demonstrates how to retrieve the list of available vendor commands and examine the command metadata. Understanding the metadata is the key to being able to successfully invoke vendor commands, as demonstrated in Exercise 6-9.

Exercise 6-8. Retrieving the List of Vendor Commands (Provider Metadata)

This exercise demonstrates how to retrieve the metadata structure for a specific provider and dump the list of vendor commands supported by that device.

1. This exercise will demonstrate how to obtain a list of the names of registered devices on a BizTalk RFID server from a .NET application. Begin by creating a C# console application in Visual Studio .NET. Name the project SyncSample2.

2. Add the following assemblies as project references:

   Microsoft.RFID.Design

   Microsoft.Rfid.ManagementWebServiceProxies

3. Add the using references as shown in Listing 6-18 to the top of the Program.cs file.

   Listing 6-18. *using Statements for This Exercise*

   ```
   using Microsoft.SensorServices.Rfid.Management;
   using Microsoft.SensorServices.Rfid.Design;
   ```

4. In the Program.cs file, create a new method called DumpProviderCustomCommands, as shown in Listing 6-19.

   Listing 6-19. *Obtaining the List of Vendor Metadata and Dumping the Capability List*

   ```
   static public void DumpProviderCustomCommands(string provider)
   {
    ProviderManagerProxy pmp = new ProviderManagerProxy();
    ProviderMetadata meta = pmp.GetProviderMetadata(provider);
   ```

```
   // Dump the capability list
   Console.WriteLine("Capabilities for provider {0}", provider);
   foreach (ProviderCapability c in meta.ProviderCapabilities)
   {
    Console.WriteLine("Capability: {0}", c);
   }

   // Dump the vendor extensibility info
   DumpVendorInfo(meta.VendorExtensionsEntityMetadata);
}
```

5. In the `Program.cs` file, create a new method called `DumpVendorInfo`, as shown in Listing 6-20. This dumps out the standard command metadata components (name, description, etc.).

Listing 6-20. *Dumping the List of Vendor-Specific Commands*

```
private static void DumpVendorInfo(Dictionary<VendorEntityKey,
    VendorEntityMetadata> dictionary)
{
 foreach (VendorEntityKey k in dictionary.Keys)
 {
  if (k.EntityType == EntityType.Command)
  {
   Console.WriteLine("\r\n---------------------");
   Console.WriteLine("Custom command: {0}", k.Name);
   VendorEntityMetadata meta = dictionary[k];
   Console.WriteLine("Description: {0}", meta.Description);

   // Some commands do not have parameters
   if (meta.SubEntities == null)
   {
    Console.WriteLine("-> No parameters");
    continue;
   }

   foreach (string parm in meta.SubEntities.Keys)
   {
    Console.WriteLine("\r\n=======================");
    Console.WriteLine("Parameter {0}", parm);
    DumpParameterInfo(meta.SubEntities[parm]);
   }
  }
 }
}
```

6. In the `Program.cs` file, create a new method called `DumpVendorInfo`, as shown in Listing 6-21. This dumps out the standard command metadata components (name, description, etc.).

Listing 6-21. *Obtaining the List of Vendor Metadata and Dumping the Capability List*

```
public static void DumpParameterInfo(VendorEntityParameterMetadata meta)
{
// Dump the standard metadata items
Console.WriteLine("Description:\r\n------------");
Console.WriteLine(meta.Description);
Console.WriteLine("\r\nType:        {0}", meta.Type.Name);
Console.WriteLine("Default:     {0}",
meta.DefaultValue == null ? "None" : meta.DefaultValue.ToString());
Console.WriteLine("             {0}, {1}, {2}, {3}",
meta.IsMandatory ? "Mandatory" : "Optional",
meta.IsPersistent ? "Persistent" : "Temporary",
meta.IsWritable ? "Writable" : "Read-only",
meta.RequiresRestart ? "Requires Restart" : "Immediate");

// Dump the validation metadata (ranges, value sets, etc.)
if (meta.Type == typeof(string))
{
 // If the type has a valid set of values, print them
 if (meta.ValueSet != null && meta.ValueSet.Count > 0)
 {
  Console.Write("Valid values: ");
  foreach (object o in meta.ValueSet)
   Console.Write("{0}, ", o.ToString());
 }
 // If the type has a regex validation pattern, print it
 if (meta.ValueExpression != null)
  Console.WriteLine("Valid pat:  {0}", meta.ValueExpression.ToString());
}

if (meta.Type == typeof(int) || meta.Type == typeof(double))
{
 if (meta.HigherRange != double.MaxValue)
  Console.WriteLine("Max value:  {0}", meta.HigherRange);
 if (meta.LowerRange != double.MinValue)
  Console.WriteLine("Min value:  {0}", meta.LowerRange);
}
```

7. In the `Program.cs` file, modify the `main` method to invoke the `DumpProviderCustomCommands` method as shown in Listing 6-22.

Listing 6-22. *Obtaining the List of Vendor Custom Commands*

```
static void Main(string[] args)
{
 DumpProviderCustomCommands("Alien");
}
```

8. Execute the application by selecting Debug, and then Start Without Debugging, in Visual Studio. The sample output shown in Listing 6-23 is a section of the output produced when this application is run against the Alien provider. In Exercise 6-9, you will develop an application to invoke this vendor command.

Listing 6-23. *Sample Output from the Alien Provider*

```
Custom command: PulseOutputCommand
Description: Sending an output impulse to the specified digital output
port of the reader for specified time period.


========================
Parameter Port
Description:
-------------
String representing an Alien digital output port name (e.g.: o1, o3).

Type:         String
Default:      None
              Mandatory, Persistent, Writable, Immediate
Valid values: o0, o1, o2, o3, o4, o5, o6, o7,
========================
Parameter TimeInterval
Description:
-------------
Time interval in milliseconds.

Type:         Int32
Default:      None
              Mandatory, Persistent, Writable, Immediate
Max value:    30000
Min value:    1
```

■**Note** This metadata shows the command `PulseOutputCommand`, which pulses one of the output lines on an Alien reader for a specified period of time (this command is commonly used to flash lights in a light stack). The command has two parameters. The first, `TimeInterval`, takes an integer value between 1 and 30000, and represents the length of time of the pulse. The second, `Port`, represents one of the eight output ports on the Alien device.

Exercise 6-9. Executing a Vendor-Specific Command

This exercise demonstrates how to execute a vendor-specific command. This exercise will build on the results of Exercise 6-8, using the Alien `PulseOutputCommand` as the reference command.

1. Open the SyncSample2 project from the previous exercise.

2. Add the `ExecuteCustomCommand` method as shown in Listing 6-24.

Listing 6-24. *Executing the Vendor Custom Command PulseOutputCommand*

```
public static void ExecuteCustomCommand(string readerName)
{
 VendorSpecificInformation parms = new VendorSpecificInformation();
 parms.Add("Port", "o1");
 parms.Add("TimeInterval", 5000);

 VendorDefinedCommand cmd = new VendorDefinedCommand(
         null, "PulseOutputCommand", null, parms);

 DeviceManagerProxy dmp = new DeviceManagerProxy();
 Command resp = dmp.ExecuteDedicatedCommand(readerName, cmd);
}
```

■**Note** The command and parameter names must match the metadata descriptions *exactly*. For example, attempting to execute the `PulseOutput` command rather than the `PulseOutputCommand` command will fail.

Common Tasks

This section covers two of the common "synchronous" tasks: printing tags (with visual labels) and simulating tag reads (for use in testing or validation).

Simulating Tag Reads

At one point or another, most developers will need to simulate a stream of RFID data in order to test or validate a particular scenario or business process. As alluded to earlier in this chapter, the AddEventToProcessPipeline command allows tag data to be pushed into a running process, providing an ideal entry point for simulated data. This section will demonstrate how to generate simulated single tag and tag list (multiple tags) events and inject them into a running process.

In order to inject simulated RFID data, the following pieces of information are required:

- The event to simulate (such as a TagReadEvent or a TagListEvent). Generating these events is demonstrated next.

- The name of the process into which to inject the event. This may be obtained from the ProcessManagerProxy class.

- The logical reader source from which the event will appear to originate. This may also be obtained from the ProcessManagerProxy class.

Any object deriving from RfidEventBase may be simulated; however, the most useful types will tend to be TagReadEvent and TagListEvent objects. To generate a TagReadEvent, the tag ID (and sometimes tag data) fields are required. Creating the simulated tag data can be a little tricky (especially in scenarios with specific tag IDs or behavior), but the process of actually pushing the tags into a specific process is straightforward in its implementation.

The process of writing an application to simulate tag events is demonstrated in Exercise 6-10.

Exercise 6-10. Writing an Application to Simulate Tag Reads

This exercise demonstrates how to simulate different types of tag events using the AddEventToProcess pipeline command from a WinForms .NET application. It will tie together many of the techniques demonstrated in this chapter, including dynamic lookup of process and logical devices. The exercise will start with laying out the visual elements for the application, and then follow up with filling in the logic.

1. From Visual Studio.NET 2008, create a new Windows Forms application called Exercise6_10, as shown in Figure 6-6.

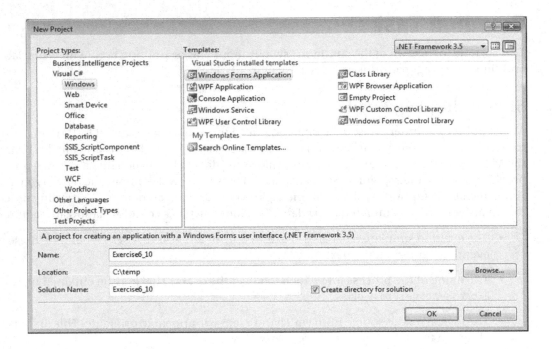

Figure 6-6. *Creating the project*

2. Add the following assemblies as project references:

`Microsoft.Rfid.Design`

`Microsoft.Rfid.SpiSdk`

`Microsoft.Rfid.ManagementWebServices`

3. Open up the code-behind for Form1, and add the following `using` statements:

```
using Microsoft.SensorServices.Rfid.Management;
using System.IO.SensorServices.Rfid.Client;
using Microsoft.SensorServices.Rfid;
```

4. The next step is to add the necessary visuals and logic to allow dynamic selection of the process and logical device lists. Open the form designer for Form1, and do the following:

- Add a GroupBox to the form, and call it Processes and Devices.

- Within that GroupBox, add a label with a text value of Processes.

- Next to the label, add a ComboBox item with a name of cbProcessList.

- Add another label, with a text value of Logical Devices.

- Next to the Logical Devices label, add a ComboBox item with a name of cbLogicalDevices.

- Underneath the Logical Devices label, add a Button control with a name of btnRefresh and a text value of Refresh.

5. In order to configure how the tag event data will be formatted (i.e., event type, number of tags, whether or not to generate user data, etc.), you'll next add the graphical controls shown in Figure 6-7.

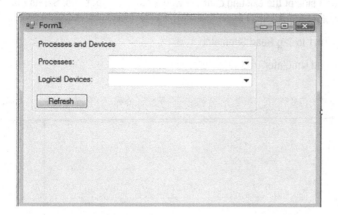

Figure 6-7. *The form after adding the processes and devices*

6. Add another GroupBox to the form, with a text value of Event Details.

7. Within that GroupBox, add a radio button with a name of rbTagList and a value of "Send tags as TagListEvent." Set the Checked property to True.

8. Add another radio button with a name of rbTagRead and a value of "Send tags as TagReadEvent."

9. Add a NumericUpDown control to the Event Details group box with a name of numTagCount. Set its Maximum property to 1000 and its Value property to 1.

10. Add a label next to the numTagCount control with a text value of Number of Tags. Your form should now look like Figure 6-8.

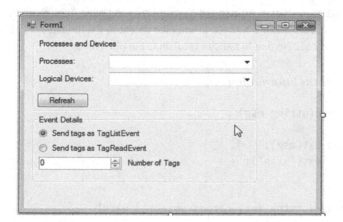

Figure 6-8. *Adding the event details*

11. Add a Button control beneath the Event Details group box with a name of btnSendTags and a value of Send Tags.

12. Add a ContextMenuStrip to Form1 with a name of contextMenuStrip1. Add a single menu item with a name of miClear and a text value of Clear.

13. Add a RichTextBox control to the side of the existing controls with a name of rtbStatus. Set its Context-MenuStrip property to contextMenuStrip1.

14. Change the Text property of Form1 to Tag Read Simulator.

15. Figure 6-9 shows the full tag read simulator.

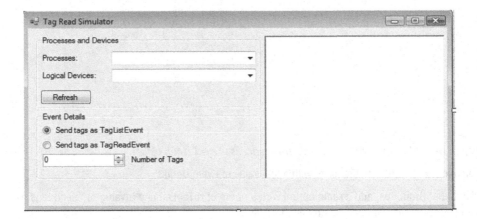

Figure 6-9. *The full tag read simulator*

16. The visual components for your test application are in place. The remaining steps in the exercise deal with implementing the business logic to push simulated tag events to the selected BizTalk RFID process. Add the following variables to the class:

```
private ProcessManagerProxy processProxy;
```

17. Add methods to display status information in the rich text box, as shown in Listing 6-25. Since this example only uses synchronous calls, there is no need to wrap the access to the rtbStatus control in an `Invoke` pattern (using `Control.Invoke` to switch execution to the GUI thread).

Listing 6-25. *Displaying Status Information*

```
private void ShowMessage(string msg)
{
 this.rtbStatus.AppendText(msg);
 this.rtbStatus.AppendText("\r\n");
}

private void ShowMessage(string fmt, params object[] vars)
{
 ShowMessage(string.Format(fmt, vars));
}
```

18. In Form1, add an event handler for the Load event, as shown in Listing 6-26.

Listing 6-26. *Event Handler for the Load Event*

```
private void Form1_Load(object sender, EventArgs e)
{
 // Initialize the proxy objects
 processProxy = new ProcessManagerProxy();

 // Load the initial process and logical device lists
 RefreshProcessLists();
}
```

19. Create an event handler for the Click event of the btnRefresh button, as shown in Listing 6-27.

Listing 6-27. *Event Handler for the Click Event*

```
private void btnRefresh_Click(object sender, EventArgs e)
{
 // Refresh the process and logical device lists
 RefreshProcessLists();
}
```

20. Implement a function to retrieve the list of RFID processes and their related logical devices, as shown in Listing 6-28.

Listing 6-28. *Retrieving the List of RFID Processes*

```
/// <summary>
/// Load a list of currently registered RFID processes along with the
/// logical devices
/// </summary>
private void RefreshProcessLists()
{
 ShowMessage("Retrieving process list..");
 processNames = processProxy.GetAllProcesses();
 if (processNames == null)
  processNames = new string[0];

 ShowMessage("Retrieving logical devices..");
 logicalDevices.Clear();
 foreach (string processName in processNames)
 {
  List<string> devices = new List<string>();
  RfidProcess processInfo = processProxy.GetProcess(processName);
```

```
    foreach (LogicalDevice d in processInfo.GetAllLogicalDevices())
     devices.Add(d.Name);

    logicalDevices.Add(processName, devices);
   }

   // Update the ComboBox control containing the process list
   cbProcessList.Items.Clear();
   cbProcessList.Items.AddRange(processNames);
   cbProcessList.SelectedIndex = -1;

   // Clear the logical device list (this is updated when the selected
   // index changes for the process list)
   cbLogicalDevices.Items.Clear();
  }
```

21. Add a `SelectedIndexChanged` handler to the cbProcessList combo box, as shown in Listing 6-29. This will automatically update the list of available logical devices when the selected process changes.

Listing 6-29. *SelectedIndexChanged Event Handler*

```
private void cbProcessList_SelectedIndexChanged(object sender, EventArgs e)
{
 if (cbProcessList.SelectedIndex > -1)
 {
  string procName = this.cbProcessList.SelectedItem.ToString();
  this.cbLogicalDevices.Items.Clear();
  this.cbLogicalDevices.Items.AddRange(
  this.logicalDevices[procName].ToArray<string>());

  if (cbLogicalDevices.Items.Count > 0)
   this.cbLogicalDevices.SelectedIndex = 0;
 }
}
```

22. All of the work thus far in this exercise has been to set the stage for this step—actually implementing the code to send simulated tag events into a selected process as if coming from a particular logical device. Implement an event handler for the `Click` event of the btnSendTags button, as shown in Listing 6-30. This will either send a tag list or send individual tag read events. The actual content of the tag events will be generated in the `GenerateTagEvents` method, which will be created in the next step.

Listing 6-30. *Event Handler for the Click Event*

```
private void btnSendTags_Click(object sender, EventArgs e)
{
 // Must have a process selected
 if (this.cbProcessList.SelectedIndex == -1)
```

```
{
 ShowMessage("Must select a process before sending tags");
 return;
}
string processName = this.cbProcessList.SelectedItem.ToString();

// Must have a logical device selected
if (this.cbLogicalDevices.SelectedIndex == -1)
{
 ShowMessage("Must select a logical device before sending tags");
 return;
}
string logicalDevice = this.cbLogicalDevices.SelectedItem.ToString();

// Generate a set of tag read events,
List<TagReadEvent> tagEvents =
        GenerateTagEvents((int)this.numTagCount.Value);

// If sending as a tag list, package them up and send to the server
if (rbTagList.Checked)
{
 ShowMessage("Sending {0} events to server as TagListEvent",
 this.numTagCount.Value);
 TagListEvent tle = new TagListEvent(tagEvents, "SIMULATED");
 processProxy.AddEventToProcessPipeline(processName, tle,
   logicalDevice);
 ShowMessage("Event delivered");
}
else
{
 ShowMessage("Sending {0} events to server as TagListEvent",
  this.numTagCount.Value);
 int sent = 0;
 foreach (TagReadEvent tre in tagEvents)
 {
  processProxy.AddEventToProcessPipeline(processName, tre,
   logicalDevice);
  ShowMessage("Sent event {0} of {1}", ++sent,
   this.numTagCount.Value);
 }
}
}
```

23. Implement the GenerateTagList method, as shown in Listing 6-31. This method will generate fake
    EPC (96-bit ID) tag reads, all happening now with no user data.

Listing 6-31. *The GenerateTagList Method*

```
private List<TagReadEvent> GenerateTagEvents(int count)
{
// Generate a set of count TagReadEvent objects, each with a random
// 96-bit tag ID, and a timestamp value of DateTime.Now.
List<TagReadEvent> ret = new List<TagReadEvent>();
System.Random rand = new Random();

for (int i = 0; i < count; i++)
{
 byte[] data = new byte[12]; // 96 bit / 8 bits / byte = 12 bytes
 rand.NextBytes(data);

 TagReadEvent tre = new TagReadEvent(data, TagType.EpcClass1Gen2,
  null, "SIMULATED", DateTime.Now, null, TagDataSelector.All);
 ret.Add(tre);
}
 return ret;
}
```

24. From Visual Studio, click Debug, and then Start without Debugging. The Tag Read Simulator application will appear.

25. In the Processes combo box, select the Test Process process.

26. In the Logical Devices combo box, select the Dock Door Portal logical reader.

27. In the Event Details section, select the "Send tags as TagListEvent" radio button.

28. Select 10 for the number of tags.

29. Click the Send Tags button (see Figure 6-10).

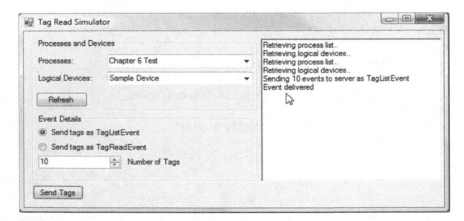

Figure 6-10. *Showing status in the tag read simulator*

30. In order to verify that the tags were received and processed by BizTalk RFID, open SQL Server Management Studio.

31. From the connection screen, select the local database (localhost or .) and click Connect.

32. Click the New Query button, and then select the rfidsink database from the drop-down list.

33. Type in the following query, and then click Execute (or press the F5 key):

```
SELECT * FROM TagEvents WHERE TagSource = 'SIMULATED'
```

34. The results should resemble Figure 6-11, showing ten individual `TagRead` events (the SqlSink event handler component processes the `TagList` event into individual `TagRead` events before posting to the database).

	Id	DeviceName	TagId	TagTy...	TagTypeDescription	TagSource	TagTime	TagD	Sink Time	Pn
1	18	Sample Device	0x26C6BE1F5287E1C856BAA5EA	3	EPC Class 1 - Generation 2 tag	SIMULATED	2008-09-15 16:03:41.750	NULL	2008-09-15 16:03:45.863	Cl
2	19	Sample Device	0x4D04F88221AD5D1886548493	3	EPC Class 1 - Generation 2 tag	SIMULATED	2008-09-15 16:03:41.750	NULL	2008-09-15 16:03:45.863	Cl
3	20	Sample Device	0x8D61133A5FF34602215D38CA	3	EPC Class 1 - Generation 2 tag	SIMULATED	2008-09-15 16:03:41.750	NULL	2008-09-15 16:03:45.863	Cl
4	21	Sample Device	0xD4014C8D562D8B4BADA4E9B8	3	EPC Class 1 - Generation 2 tag	SIMULATED	2008-09-15 16:03:41.750	NULL	2008-09-15 16:03:45.863	Cl
5	22	Sample Device	0x696A39CF7AEA76D2412B92F1	3	EPC Class 1 - Generation 2 tag	SIMULATED	2008-09-15 16:03:41.750	NULL	2008-09-15 16:03:45.880	Cl
6	23	Sample Device	0x73A6696274A2C9F0CC2DAD20	3	EPC Class 1 - Generation 2 tag	SIMULATED	2008-09-15 16:03:41.750	NULL	2008-09-15 16:03:45.880	Cl
7	24	Sample Device	0x61CFC158C939E6E8785BD1F4	3	EPC Class 1 - Generation 2 tag	SIMULATED	2008-09-15 16:03:41.750	NULL	2008-09-15 16:03:45.880	Cl
8	25	Sample Device	0xBA778837E66688A96F5A1AAF	3	EPC Class 1 - Generation 2 tag	SIMULATED	2008-09-15 16:03:41.750	NULL	2008-09-15 16:03:45.880	Cl
9	26	Sample Device	0xC329D70ADAF9EB3CBC186DAB	3	EPC Class 1 - Generation 2 tag	SIMULATED	2008-09-15 16:03:41.750	NULL	2008-09-15 16:03:45.880	Cl
10	27	Sample Device	0x281D080844A97817D574A7FD	3	EPC Class 1 - Generation 2 tag	SIMULATED	2008-09-15 16:03:41.750	NULL	2008-09-15 16:03:45.880	Cl

Figure 6-11. *Results showing ten TagRead events*

35. Switch back to the Tag Read Simulator application.

36. In the Event Details section, select the "Send tags as TagReadEvent" radio button.

37. Select 5 for the number of tags.

38. Click the Send Tags button (see Figure 6-12).

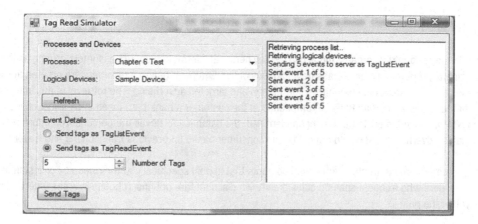

Figure 6-12. *Sent events*

39. Switch back to the SQL Server Management Studio application.

40. Rerun the SELECT query. The results should now resemble Figure 6-13, showing five new TagRead events.

	Id	DeviceName	TagId	TagTy...	TagTypeDescription	TagSource	TagTime	TagD...	SinkTime	Prc
1	18	Sample Device	0x26C6BE1F5287E1C856BAA5EA	3	EPC Class 1 - Generation 2 tag	SIMULATED	2008-09-15 16:03:41.750	NULL	2008-09-15 16:03:45.863	Ch
2	19	Sample Device	0x4D04F88221AD5D1886548493	3	EPC Class 1 - Generation 2 tag	SIMULATED	2008-09-15 16:03:41.750	NULL	2008-09-15 16:03:45.863	Ch
3	20	Sample Device	0x8D61133A5FF34602215D38CA	3	EPC Class 1 - Generation 2 tag	SIMULATED	2008-09-15 16:03:41.750	NULL	2008-09-15 16:03:45.863	Ch
4	21	Sample Device	0xD4014C8D562D8B4BADA4E9B8	3	EPC Class 1 - Generation 2 tag	SIMULATED	2008-09-15 16:03:41.750	NULL	2008-09-15 16:03:45.863	Ch
5	22	Sample Device	0x696A39CF7AEA76D2412B92F1	3	EPC Class 1 - Generation 2 tag	SIMULATED	2008-09-15 16:03:41.750	NULL	2008-09-15 16:03:45.880	Ch
6	23	Sample Device	0x73A6696274A2C9F0CC2DAD20	3	EPC Class 1 - Generation 2 tag	SIMULATED	2008-09-15 16:03:41.750	NULL	2008-09-15 16:03:45.880	Ch
7	24	Sample Device	0x61CFC158C939E6E8785BD1F4	3	EPC Class 1 - Generation 2 tag	SIMULATED	2008-09-15 16:03:41.750	NULL	2008-09-15 16:03:45.880	Ch
8	25	Sample Device	0xBA778837E66688A96F5A1AAF	3	EPC Class 1 - Generation 2 tag	SIMULATED	2008-09-15 16:03:41.750	NULL	2008-09-15 16:03:45.880	Ch
9	26	Sample Device	0xC329D70ADAF9EB3CBC186DAB	3	EPC Class 1 - Generation 2 tag	SIMULATED	2008-09-15 16:03:41.750	NULL	2008-09-15 16:03:45.880	Ch
10	27	Sample Device	0x281D080844A97817D574A7FD	3	EPC Class 1 - Generation 2 tag	SIMULATED	2008-09-15 16:03:41.750	NULL	2008-09-15 16:03:45.880	Ch
11	28	Sample Device	0x54CBEBD43A39AF9770C6F48E	3	EPC Class 1 - Generation 2 tag	SIMULATED	2008-09-15 16:08:50.170	NULL	2008-09-15 16:08:50.523	Ch
12	29	Sample Device	0x70CE80945A49F73D887333BC	3	EPC Class 1 - Generation 2 tag	SIMULATED	2008-09-15 16:08:50.173	NULL	2008-09-15 16:08:52.377	Ch
13	30	Sample Device	0x197C2DE11936EA073E8368A0	3	EPC Class 1 - Generation 2 tag	SIMULATED	2008-09-15 16:08:50.173	NULL	2008-09-15 16:08:58.900	Ch
14	31	Sample Device	0x2ECCF997E7C166936AD1173A	3	EPC Class 1 - Generation 2 tag	SIMULATED	2008-09-15 16:08:50.173	NULL	2008-09-15 16:08:58.917	Ch
15	32	Sample Device	0x871516A07968E4E0972FBABE	3	EPC Class 1 - Generation 2 tag	SIMULATED	2008-09-15 16:08:50.173	NULL	2008-09-15 16:08:58.963	Ch

Figure 6-13. *The five new TagRead events*

Conclusion

The synchronous command functionality in BizTalk RFID is the key method of creating custom applications for configuring devices, printing tags, and controlling I/O. By matching .NET applications with the interface provided by the ManagementWebProxy assembly, any of the functionality provided by RFID Manager or the rfidclientconsole.exe application can be included in your own applications.

CASE STUDY: PERSONALIZING ADVERTISING

Industry: Travel.

Overview: In many countries, organizations can display personal information about consumers as long as they are on company property. In a high-class travel agency of one European nation, customers are greeted at the door by a wall-sized display of personalized information and targeted advertising. The retrieval of this information is initiated by the read of an RFID tag embedded in the customer's bank card (used in all transactions, including ATMs). Once the customer has been identified, the database retrieves the personalized information and calculates advertising that would appeal to this consumer based on previous transactions and travel.

Results: Customers are confronted with advertisements that appeal specifically to their needs. For instance, business travelers who frequent specific cities are shown discount fare options at hotels in areas where they have stayed in the past.

CHAPTER 7

■ ■ ■

BizTalk RFID Mobile

One of the key features in BizTalk Server 2009 is the support for mobile RFID devices running Windows CE Professional 5 (or greater). This support includes a platform for creating applications that run on the CE Professional devices, and out-of-the-box functionality for integrating such devices into your overall application scenario. In this chapter, you will take a quick tour of the various pieces in BizTalk RFID Mobile, and also create your first mobile application that uses this new functionality.

In addition to support for mobile devices, BizTalk Server 2009 also introduces enhanced standards support for Low Level Reader Protocol (LLRP) and Tag Data Translation (TDT). BizTalk Server 2009 uses LLRP to implement communication between mobile devices and the server component, as well as establishing connectivity to LLRP-enabled RFID devices. TDT streamlines the use of global tag data–mapping standards, such as SGTIN, providing various methods and utilities for encoding and decoding tag information.

■**Note** In the rest of this chapter, when we refer to BizTalk RFID Server, Desktop, or just BizTalk RFID, we are referring to the platform that runs on the desktop and server operating systems (i.e., the same version of BizTalk RFID that is covered elsewhere in the book). When we refer to BizTalk RFID Mobile, we are talking specifically about the components that run on the mobile device. To distinguish between the mobile device and its RFID module, whenever we use the word "device" in this chapter, we are talking about the entire device, and when we say "RFID module" or "RF module," we are referring just to the RFID functionality. Phew, with that out of the way, let us dive in!

BizTalk RFID Mobile consists of the following pieces:

DSPI Mobile: This provides a framework for developing device-agnostic applications, in the same fashion as the "server" DSPI implementation. While there are a few minor differences to account for developing on a mobile platform, developers will be able to leverage their existing skill set as the foundation for developing mobile applications.

Application libraries: Analogous to the synchronous commands provided by the server platform, RFID Mobile provides a rich set of classes for performing tasks such as discovering RFID modules, executing tag operations, and configuring settings and properties.

Remote management agent: This is an agent hosted inside of your mobile RFID application that communicates with a BizTalk RFID server using LLRP. This allows the device to be managed and configured from an RFID Manager console. In conjunction with an application, such as Systems Center Operations Manager, this allows both fixed and mobile RFID devices and applications to be managed from a central console.

Store-and-forward agent: This is an agent hosted inside of your mobile RFID application that provides a seamless way to flow events from a mobile application into an RFID process running on a BizTalk RFID server, even when faced with intermittent connectivity.

BizTalk RFID Mobile Architecture

The overall architecture of BizTalk RFID Mobile is consistent with BizTalk RFID Desktop, with a few important differences. Figure 7-1 shows what the architecture picture looks like at the 10,000-foot level. You can contrast that to Figure 2-1 in Chapter 2 for the desktop version of BizTalk RFID.

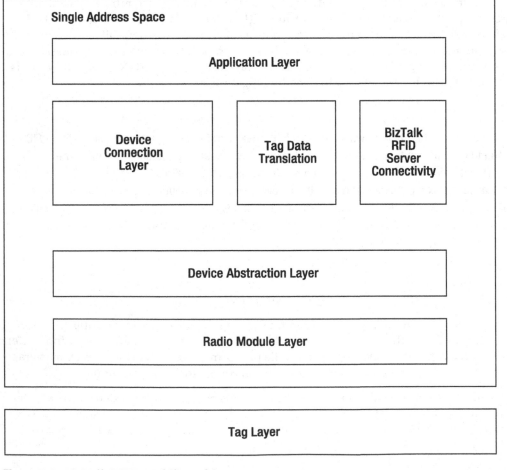

Figure 7-1. *BizTalk RFID Mobile architecture*

The first thing to observe is that the entire BizTalk RFID Mobile platform runs in the same address space as your application, or *in-proc*. There are no Windows services that are hosting your code or the providers, or hidden remote communication that is happening on behalf of your application. Generally, this choice will lead to lower latency in communication between the module and the application, and will consume fewer resources than an out-of-process model. The downside of the in-proc model is reliability; an error in the provider can crash the entire application. As shown in Figure 7-1, the key components of BizTalk RFID Mobile are as follows:

Tag layer: The mobile platform is designed to support a wide variety of RFID frequencies and tag protocols, including LF, HF, and UHF (matching the functionality of the server platform). This provides the capability to connect to RF and bar code modules, both through direct connection (in case of embedded modules) and connectivity options such as Bluetooth, serial, and Wi-Fi. One of the key features specific to the mobile stack is enhanced support for reading and working with bar codes.

Radio module layer: This is the specific implementation of the DSPI for the radio module, which has considerable overlap with the server version (over 90 percent of the API is identical). A provider author can share a significant amount of the command- and property-processing functionality between the server and mobile versions, assuming that the radio interface is similar.

Device abstraction layer: This is a layer hidden from most applications; it provides the necessary glue between the application-facing device connection APIs and the underlying device-specific providers. Rather than a separate asynchronous message stream (i.e., RFID process), the mobile stack provides a method of receiving asynchronous notifications directly in an application through a .NET event handler (note that this functionality is dependent on the specific provider—not all devices will support this).

DeviceConnection APIs: These are the core APIs that every BizTalk RFID Mobile application author will use to access the RF functionality. Again, there is considerable commonality between the desktop and server versions of this API.

Note Since all the APIs are in-proc with the application, the BizTalk RFID Mobile APIs are defined in the following three DLLs: `Microsoft.Rfid.SpiSdk.dll`, `Microsoft.Rfid.Util.dll`, and `Microsoft.Rfid.Design.dll`; and one additional DLL: `Microsoft.Rfid.ObjectModelExtensions.dll`. There is no "ManagementWebServiceProxies" DLL, since there is no web service call between your application and the platform.

Installing BizTalk RFID Mobile

Installing BizTalk RFID Mobile is a fairly reasonable task, but has certain prerequisites:

- A device (or emulator) running Windows Mobile/Windows CE 5 or greater

- Microsoft .NET Compact Framework 2.0 SP2 installed on the device, which can be downloaded from the .NET Framework Developer Center, at http://msdn.microsoft.com/en-us/netframework/aa497273.aspx

- SQL Server Compact 3.5 installed on the device, which can be downloaded from the SQL Server 2008 product page, at www.microsoft.com/sqlserver/2008/en/us/compact.aspx

Please refer to the product documentation for both of these prerequisite applications for installation instructions.

Developing applications for BizTalk RFID Mobile requires Visual Studio 2008 (or Visual Studio 2005) with the Smart Client development feature (which is not available in the Express edition) and the Windows Mobile 5 SDK (available from www.microsoft.com).

After installing the .NET Compact Framework and SQL Server Compact files on the mobile device, the BizTalk RFID Mobile bits may be installed. The BizTalk RFID Mobile installer will install a set of CAB files and DLLs to the Microsoft BizTalk RFID\SDK\Mobile directory under Program Files. Note that the sample applications are not installed automatically, and need to be accessed from the installation directory.

The installation instructions for the BizTalk RFID Mobile CAB files are included in the Installing BizTalk RFID Mobile.htm document included with the installation package. This document also includes step-by-step instructions for installing the prerequisite applications. The basics of installing the necessary CAB files on a mobile device are as follows:

1. On your computer, in the folder containing the BizTalk RFID Mobile installation files, browse to the folder %RFIDInstallDir%\SDK\Mobile\v1.1in\wce500\armv4i.

2. Copy the appropriate installation CAB file to your mobile device, depending on whether it is running Windows Mobile or Windows CE.

   On a computer with Microsoft Sync Center installed (Windows Vista or Windows Server 2008), you should be able to browse the mobile device's file system by clicking Start ➤ Computer, and the mobile device icon.

   a. For a Windows Mobile device, copy the file biztalkrfidmobile.enu.wm.armv4i.cab.

   b. For a Windows CE 5.0 device, copy the file biztalkrfidmobile.enu.wce5.armv4i.cab.

3. Locate the CAB file on your mobile device and tap the file to start the installation process.

When the installation is finished, you should see a BizTalkRfidMobile directory under the Program Files directory, which contains the tools and the default location for the configuration store. You will also see a directory called Logs underneath that. In that directory, you will find the log file for your application, with a format very close to what is produced by the desktop version.

■**Note** The store-and-forward functionality uses the LLRP provider, which has a dependency on having port 5084 available on the BizTalk RFID server host. Ensure that the firewall port is open, either through the MMC administration console, or by executing a `netsh` command such as `netsh advfirewall firewall add rule name="LLRP_Service" dir=in action=allow protocol=TCP localport=5084`.

Creating a BizTalk RFID Mobile Application

In this section, we will write our first RFID Mobile application, for the following scenario. Assume that you are going to track high-value assets in your enterprise, such as laptops. Assume that the laptops already have a bar code tag on them, and the goal is to increase the automatic visibility for such an asset by fixing an RFID tag on the laptop.

Given the kind of sensitive information that resides on most laptops (e.g., official or personal information), this kind of track-and-trace application is actually a very legitimate and popular use case for high-value asset tracking. In this section, we are going to write a small .NET Compact Framework Windows Forms application that reads a bar code and the tag ID from an RFID tag, and then writes the same value back to an RFID tag using the standard BizTalk RFID Mobile device simulator.

The first step is to install the DSPI provider for your device on the handheld reader. Exercise 7-1 demonstrates how to do this using the RFID Manager application that is part of BizTalk RFID Mobile with the default BizTalk RFID Mobile device simulator. Exercise 7-2 builds on this foundation to develop a basic BizTalk RFID Mobile application.

■**Note** If you have an RFID-enabled Windows Mobile device supported by BizTalk RFID Mobile, you may use the vendor's mobile DSPI provider (and physical RFID reader) instead of the simulator.

Exercise 7-1. Installing a Device Provider

This exercise demonstrates how to get the sample DSPI provider installed on the handheld reader, and how to browse the properties of the mobile reader simulator. This exercise will use the Windows Mobile 5.0 Professional emulator and the MyFirstCEProvider sample provider that is part of BizTalk RFID Mobile.

Note that as with the server experience, any task or feature in a provided management application is available through the .NET APIs (this allows applications to include any of the required management or configuration functionality, and not require the use of a separate application).

1. Run the RFID Manager application, which was installed on the device during BizTalk RFID Mobile installation. It may be found in the `\Program Files\BizTalkRfidMobile` directory (the name of the executable file is `ManagementApp`). Figure 7-2 shows you what the initial screen looks like.

Figure 7-2. *The mobile version of RFID Manager*

2. Click Add to browse for provider DLLs. Click the Browse button to bring up the file selection dialog. The `MyFirstCEProvider` DLL should be visible in the dialog, as shown in Figure 7-3. Click the `MyFirstCEProvider` file.

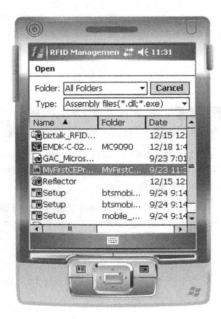

Figure 7-3. *Selecting the MyFirstCEProvider file*

3. The default provider name, MyFirstCEProvider, will be filled in automatically, as shown in Figure 7-4. Click OK to close the file selection dialog and automatically start the provider.

Figure 7-4. *Confirming the provider name*

Note Under Windows Mobile, by default, you can only browse for files under the My Documents root.

---

4. Click OK to close the "Provider started and registered" dialog.

5. As MyFirstCEProvider implements device discovery, the simulated device will be automatically detected. Click the Devices tab to view the list of available devices, and then click MyCEDevice, as shown in Figure 7-5.

Figure 7-5. *Selecting the simulated reader*

6. Click Menu and then Properties to bring up the configuration page for the device, as shown in Figure 7-6.

Figure 7-6. *Properties of the simulated reader*

7. Click the Advanced tab to view the device and source properties. Just as for fixed RFID readers, mobile readers can have properties bound to the device or any sources on the device. Typical sources on a mobile device include RFID (the primary RFID device) and Barcode. Click the drop-down box to expose the list of sources, as shown in Figure 7-7.

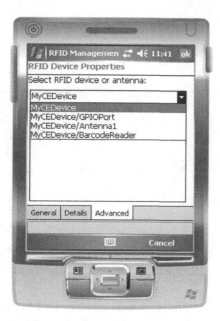

Figure 7-7. *Sources of the simulated reader*

Exercise 7-2. Creating a Simple BizTalk RFID Mobile Application

In this exercise, you will write an application that uses the RF module (and indirectly the provider) installed in Exercise 7-1. The goal is to create a simple application for reading tags using the mobile platform.

1. Start Visual Studio, click File ➤ New Project, and then select the Smart Device category from under the Visual C# node (as shown in Figure 7-8). Select the Smart Device Project type, and then select an appropriate location (such as C:\temp\) and name the project HelloMobileRfid. Click OK to open the Add New Smart Device Project dialog.

2. From the Add New Smart Device Project dialog, select Windows Mobile 5.0 Pocket PC SDK and .NET Compact Framework Version 3.5, as shown in Figure 7-9.

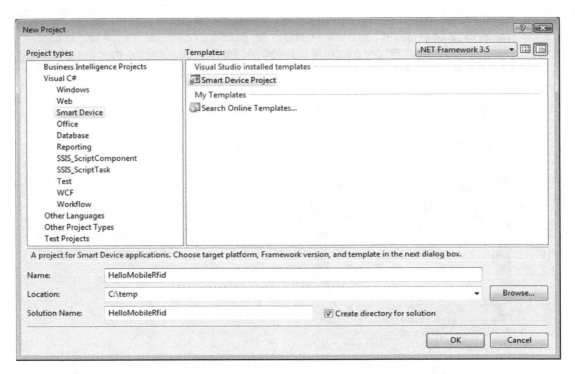

Figure 7-8. *Creating a Smart Device project*

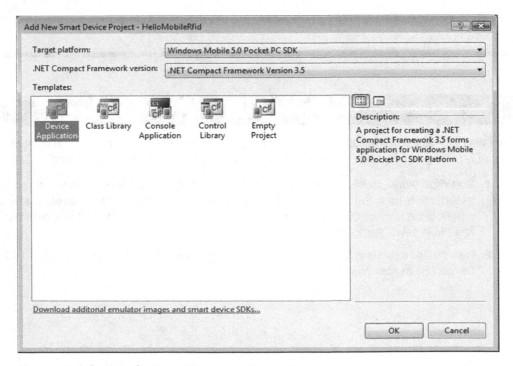

Figure 7-9. *Selecting the Smart Device project type*

3. Click the Device Application project type, and then click OK.

4. The next step will be to add the BizTalk RFID Mobile libraries to the application. Open the Add References dialog and browse to the `Microsoft BizTalk RFID\SDK\Mobile\v1.1\bin` directory. Select the following assemblies, and click OK to add them to the project:

   a. `Microsoft.Rfid.Design.dll`

   b. `Microsoft.Rfid.Llrp.dll`

   c. `Microsoft.Rfid.ObjectModelExtensions.dll`

   d. `Microsoft.Rfid.SpiSdk.dll`

   e. `Microsoft.Rfid.Util.dll`

Note The names of the mobile DLLs are the same as those for the desktop version of BizTalk RFID. Be sure to link with the correct version for your application (i.e., not the DLLs in the `BizTalk RFID\bin` directory).

---

5. Add some basic graphical elements to the form, as shown in Figure 7-10:

   a. Select the Form1 form and change the Text property to Read Tag.

   b. Select the Form1 form and change the MinimizeBox property to False.

   c. Drag a button onto the form, name it btnOpen, and give it a Text property of Open RF.

   d. Drag a button onto the form, name it btnClose, and give it a Text property of Close RF.

   e. Drag a button onto the form, name it btnRead, and give it a Text property of Read Tag.

   f. Drag a text box onto the form and name it tbTag.

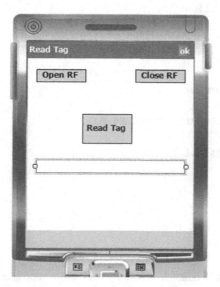

Figure 7-10. *The Read Tag main form*

6. Double-click the Open RF button in the designer to create a `Click` event handler in `Form1.cs`. Fill in the `Click` event handler as shown in Listing 7-1. Note that this code only works because you have previously registered the provider and device in Exercise 7-1.

Listing 7-1. *Using the ProcessManagerProxy to Obtain a List of Registered RFID Processes*

```
// Shared DeviceConnection object - used to communicate with RFID module
private DeviceConnection connection;

private void btnOpen_Click(object sender, EventArgs e)
{
    // Create a device manager proxy to obtain the device list
    DeviceManagerProxy proxy = new DeviceManagerProxy();

    // Obtain the name of the first (usually the only) device
    string deviceName = proxy.GetAllDevices()[0].Name;

    // Establish a connection to that device
    connection = new DeviceConnection(deviceName);
    connection.Open();
}
```

7. Add the `using` statements shown in Listing 7-2 to the top of the `Form1.cs` file.

Listing 7-2. *Adding the Required using Statements*

```
using Microsoft.SensorServices.Rfid.Management;
using System.IO.SensorServices.Rfid.Client;
```

8. From the Form1 designer, double-click the Close RF button to create a `Click` event handler. Fill in the event handler as shown in Listing 7-3.

Listing 7-3. *The Close RF Button Event Handler*

```
private void btnClose_Click(object sender, EventArgs e)
{
    // If an active connection exists, close it
    if (connection != null)
    {
        connection.Close();
        connection = null;
    }
}
```

9. From the Form1 designer, double-click the Read RF button to create a `Click` event handler. Fill in the event handler as shown in Listing 7-4.

Listing 7-4. *The Read RF Button Event Handler*

```
private void btnRead_Click(object sender, EventArgs e)
{
    // Confirm the connection is available
    if (connection != null &&
        connection.ConnectionState == ClientConnectionState.Open)
    {
        // Read tags through the synchronous GetTags function and display
        // in the text box
        foreach (TagReadEvent tre in
connection.GetTags(TagDataSelector.All))
        {
            string hex = HexUtilities.HexEncode(tre.GetId());
            tbTag.Text = hex;
            tbTag.Refresh();
        }
    }
}
```

■**Note** The concepts from Chapter 6, including device connections, synchronous commands, and the TagReadEvent object, are exactly the same on the mobile and server platforms.

10. The application is now ready to deploy to the device or emulator. For this exercise, the application will be deployed to the Windows Mobile 5 device simulator (which was installed with the Windows Mobile 5 SDK). From the drop-down box underneath the File menu, as shown in Figure 7-11, select the USA Windows Mobile 5.0 Pocket PC R2 Emulator option.

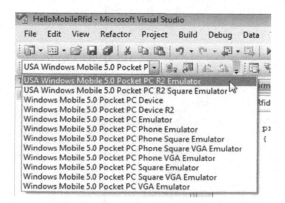

Figure 7-11. *Selecting the deployment device in Visual Studio*

11. In order to ensure that the appropriate libraries are accessible, the next step will be to deploy this application into the BizTalkMobile directory on the mobile device. From Solution Explorer, right-click the HelloMobileRfid project and click Properties. Click the Devices tab to bring up the Deployment Options page.

12. Click the ... button next to the "Output file folder" option to bring up the Output File Folder dialog, as shown in Figure 7-12. Change the subdirectory to BizTalkRfidMobile, and click OK.

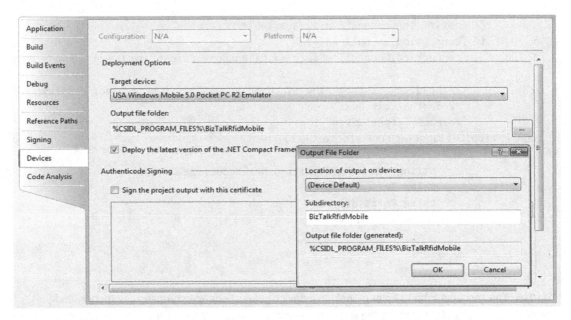

Figure 7-12. *Changing the output directory*

13. Click Debug ➤ Start without Debugging to deploy the application to the emulator. This may bring up the Deploy dialog, as shown in Figure 7-13. If so, select the USA Windows Mobile 5.0 Pocket PC R2 Emulator, and click Deploy.

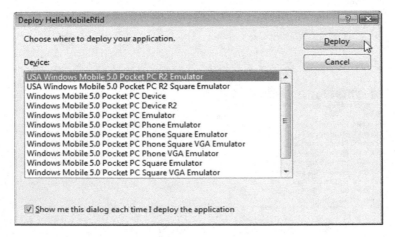

Figure 7-13. *Selecting the deployment target in Visual Studio*

14. After the emulator starts up and the application is deployed and launched, test out your first mobile RFID application. Click the Open RF button and then the Read Tag button. A simple tag ID should appear in the text box, as shown in Figure 7-14.

Figure 7-14. *Reading your first tag with BizTalk RFID Mobile*

In the following sections, we are going to look at some of the features that are unique to the BizTalk RFID Mobile platform that make it easy for you to build mobile applications.

Asynchronous Event Notification

If your application requires you to receive events continuously from an RFID reader, instead of "on demand," you can use the new NotificationEvent .NET event on the DeviceConnection object (provided this feature is supported by the mobile provider and RFID hardware). Using the NotificationEvent provides asynchronous notification functionality similar to an RFID process in the BizTalk RFID server world.

The code fragment in Listing 7-5 shows you a small example of how to do this.

Listing 7-5. *Using the NotificationEvent in the DeviceConnection Object*

```
static void HandleTagReadEvent(object sender, NotificationEventArgs args)
{
 TagReadEvent tre = args.Notification.Event as TagReadEvent;
 if (tre != null)
 {
```

```
 string hex = HexUtilities.HexEncode(tre.GetId());
 MessageBox.Show("Read tag " + hex);
 }
}
```

You can hook the `NotificationEvent` up to the `DeviceConnection` class as follows:

```
connection.NotificationEvent += HandleTagReadEvent;
```

and when you are done, you should unregister your callback as follows:

```
connection.NotificationEvent -= HandleTagReadEvent;
```

Note that the C# delegate simply provides a channel for receiving events as the underlying RF module raises them. For the module to actually start reading (and raising asynchronous events), typically you have to do one of two things:

- Set the `Source:ContinuousRead` property on the device connection to `True`. Setting this tells the RF module to continuously poll for tags.

- Use triggers to control the read operation. The use of triggers is covered in the next section.

■**Caution** Polling for tags is usually a very power-intensive operation; if you are going to use continuous read, you should have a way to enable and disable it, either by user input, triggers, or timers from your application. If you don't have these controls, you can quickly drain the battery on the device. In addition to this, if a Windows Mobile device enters its hibernation or power-saving state with an active RFID connection, the connection state may not automatically reset.

Using Triggers to Control Asynchronous Notifications

Most handheld RFID and bar code scanners come with triggers, or simple pull-release mechanisms for the operator to interact with the application on the device. In a warehouse or plant floor environment, triggers tend to be used heavily for user input, as compared to other methods such as typing with the keyboard or tapping with the stylus on the screen.

Since the most common operations in an RFID application will involve enabling RF to read tags and then turning it off, BizTalk RFID has some pretty nifty functionality to enable this set of scenarios with very few lines of code (provided the device and RFID module support triggers—it's an optional feature in the DSPI).

```
connection.SetProperty(StandardDevicePropertyGroups.Notification,
                                NotificationPropertyGroup.OnTriggerPull,
                        TriggerAction.ScanRfid);
```

The permissible values for trigger action include whether you want to scan RFID tags, bar code tags, both, or none.

BizTalk RFID Mobile also recommends that the device expose trigger events as keypress events, so if you want to use the trigger for some other part of the application, you should use the ScanNone option and handle the keypress event in the application.

Combining the trigger with the notification event delegate gives you a very convenient way to get asynchronous event notification, with the RF module actually coming on exactly when the user presses the trigger, so it is power efficient and works with a minimal amount of code on your part. If your handheld device supports triggers, this is the best way to read tags from a device.

Scanning Bar Codes from Your BizTalk RFID Mobile Application

BizTalk RFID Mobile preserves the concept of a source in the same way that the desktop platform does. You should check with your hardware provider for details on the number of sources. Typically, there should be two sources on a handheld, supporting both RFID and bar code scanning, and the bar code scanner source should be disabled by default (since the platform assumes that RFID is the primary scenario for BizTalk RFID Mobile).

If you need to access the bar code scanner engine, enable the bar code source, and then set the OnTriggerPull property to the appropriate value. Once you do that, bar code events will also be delivered up through the same notification event mechanism. The code snippet in Listing 7-6 illustrates how you would enable bar code functionality (assuming the source on your device is called "Barcode").

Listing 7-6. *Enabling Bar Code Functionality*

```
void EnableBarcodeScan(DeviceConnection connection)
{
    // Enable the Barcode reader (source) by setting its Enabled property to True
    connection.SetProperty("Barcode",
        StandardDevicePropertyGroups.Source,
        SourcePropertyGroup.Enabled, true, null);

    // Set the asynchronous notifications to raise events from the "Barcode" source
    // not the RFID source
connection.SetProperty(StandardDevicePropertyGroups.Notification,
        NotificationPropertyGroup.OnTriggerPull,
        TriggerAction.ScanBarcode);

    // Capture asynchronous notifications from the device in the HandleTagReadEvent
    // method
    connection.NotificationEvent += HandleTagReadEvent;
}
```

Within your event handler, you can check if the event is from the bar code scanner by using the TagType property. If it is a bar code scan, the additional properties shown in Listing 7-7 are available to decode the bar code symbology and the human-readable text for the bar code.

Listing 7-7. *Handling Bar Code Events*

```
static void ProcessBarcodeScan(TagReadEvent tre)
{
    // Determine if the TagReadEvent is a bar code
    bool isBarcodeScan = tre.Type == TagType.Barcode;
    if (isBarcodeScan) {
        // Obtain the bar code binary ID
        byte[] binaryId = tre.GetId();

        // Obtain the data label from the bar code (i.e. the data)
        string textualBarcode = (string)
            tre.VendorSpecificData[BarcodeConstants.ScanDataLabel];

        // Obtain the encoding type of the bar code
        string symbology = (string)
            tre.VendorSpecificData[BarcodeConstants.ScanDataType];

        // Display the information to the user
        MessageBox.Show("Read barcode scan " + textualBarcode +
            "with symbology " + symbology);
    }
}
```

Note Check whether your hardware provider vendor supports decoding bar code scans and the supported symbologies.

Integration with BizTalk RFID Server

BizTalk RFID Mobile was designed from the beginning to be tightly integrated with BizTalk RFID Server. It includes a component called the RfidServerConnector, which can be used to send events from the mobile device to BizTalk RFID. The API for using the RfidServerConnector is very straightforward, but you should understand how it works from a troubleshooting perspective.

The RfidServerConnector is a stand-alone agent that can take a tag read event from any application and post it to BizTalk RFID. Since connectivity between the device and the server could be intermittent, especially if you are using Wi-Fi or Bluetooth to establish the connection, the component supports an out-of-the-box notion of *store-and-forward.* If the connection is up, the event is sent immediately. If the attempt to send the event fails, the event is persisted to local storage and sent whenever the connection is reestablished.

By default, the RfidServerConnector will retry the connection every 60 seconds. However, this value is configurable in your application. Depending on the amount of RFID data that will be ready and the time between pushing the tag events to a central store, it may be a best practice to store the local SqlCe database on a storage card.

```
using (RfidServerConnector connector = new RfidServerConnector(defaultActiveSyncIp,
defaultPort))
{
    connector.Initialize();
    connector.Post(new RfidEventBase[] {tre});
}
```

Under the covers, the platform does a fair bit of work to implement the connector. It actually establishes a transport connection that uses LLRP to transmit the events over to the BizTalk RFID server, which must have the LLRP provider running. Here are the prerequisites for using the store-and-forward feature:

- You must have the BizTalk RFID standards pack installed on the desktop machine, with port 5084 allowed through the firewall.

- The LLRP provider must be running.

- The device must be discovered and configured.

- You must have an RFID process that is interested in events from the mobile device.

Remote Management Support

In the previous section, you saw how BizTalk RFID Server could receive events from the mobile device. That is actually just one half of the story. The other half is remote manageability. Yes, you can manage the RF functionality on your mobile device, using the familiar desktop RFID Manager. There are two ways to enable remote manageability; one is through the RfidServerConnector API described previously, and the other is through the RFID Manager application that is on the handheld device.

The default autoconfiguration IP for ActiveSync (or Windows Mobile Device Center) connections is 169.254.1.2, as shown in Figure 7-15 (a snapshot of the Manage tab in the RFID Manger mobile application). If you are not using ActiveSync (e.g., Wi-Fi), ensure that you have provided the correct IP address for the server.

Note This remote management still requires some interaction from your handheld user—either the RFID Manager application on the handheld device must be running or some application must be using an initialized RfidServerConnector.

Figure 7-15. *Enabling remote management with RFID Manager (mobile)*

Once the remote managemement functionality is enabled, you can browse properties, change settings, and apply them. The best reasons to do this are to enforce a standard set of property profiles on all your mobile readers (using the device template feature), and to centrally track changes to property settings.

The device management feature implicitly manages the first RF module on the device. This is controllable through the HKLM\Software\Microsoft\Rfid\AgentModuleName registry setting on the device. Each source on the RF module is exposed as a source in RFID Manager, with the name Antenna_<source number>. Using this, you can change common properties such as power level, if the provider supports it.

■**Tip** If you look at the Custom tab for the device from the desktop RFID Manager, you will see a number of LLRP properties. These are really intended for LLRP devices, and are not truly applicable to mobile devices. Scroll past them, and near the end you will see a category called RFID Mobile, which contains the custom settings that are valid for BizTalk RFID Mobile devices.

Storing Events Locally in a SQL Server CE Database

Just like the desktop version of BizTalk RFID has out-of-the-box support for storing events in a SQL Server database, BizTalk RFID Mobile has out-of-the-box support for storing events in a SQL Server Compact Edition (SQL Server CE) database. It has support for the standard TagRead and TagList events, including the vendor extensions on the TagReadEvent object. The core class for storing events is NotificationStorage.

By default, the object creates a SQL Server CE database called sink.mdf at the root directory of your device. You can customize the location using the connection string property. The
following code fragment shows you how to post an event to the SQL Server CE database:

```
using (NotificationStorage storage = new NotificationStorage())
{
 storage.Post(tagReadEvent);
}
```

Tag Data Encoding and Translation

One of the new standards conformance features in BizTalk RFID Mobile is the TDT API. This
includes a set of classes and helper utilities for translating between the serialized binary tag
representation and the various standard encoding schemes, such as GTIN, GID, SSCC, SGLN,
and so on. There exist two flavors of the encodings, one for 64-bit tags and another for 96-bit tags.

■**Note** The TDT API is an implementation of the EPCglobal Tag Data Standard (TDS) version 1.1,
revision 1.27 of the spec.

You can use the classes to translate binary quantities to the specific encoding formats, and
back to strings. Listing 7-8 outlines how to convert a raw value into an EPC.

Listing 7-8. *Converting a Raw Value into an EPC*

```
static void Translate(byte[] rawValue)
{
 IdentityEncoding decodedValue;
 if (IdentityEncoding.TryParse(rawValue, out decodedValue))
 {
  EpcEncoding epc = decodedValue as EpcEncoding;
  if (epc != null)
  {
   string uriEncodedString = epc.ToString();
  }
 }
}
```

The preceding TryParse pattern lets you translate values where you don't know ahead of
time if the tag is going to follow a particular encoding scheme or not. There are four important
use cases for the TDT library:

Cross-enterprise scenario: If the tags in your scenario are going to be placed in one company and read in another company, as is the case in most global supply chain visibility scenarios, using a standard serialization makes your solution more open and interoperable. A corollary to this scenario is, if there are tags from other scenarios and companies floating around in your environment, being able to identify "your" tags in an easy and straightforward manner is valuable.

Pallet-case-item tagging and filtering: If you are going to tag items at multiple levels of granularity, and different scenarios require you to focus on different groups of tags, using the EPC encoding with its `Filter` property is both convenient and performant. In many cases, the `Filter` property can be expressed at the air protocol level or on the reader, thus reducing the event processing load on your application server.

Hierarchical item representation: If your products have a set of common attributes, you can model them using the `ItemClass` construct in the TDS.

Self-describing tags: This is an interesting scenario with some benefits, but also the potential for overuse. If you think of the classical way to use RFID tags, they represent an opaque identifier, or a license plate (think GUID in Microsoft terminology). Any interpretation would require a local database lookup of some kind before processing. With TDT, you can parse the information contained in the tags to potentially extract some business context directly without doing a database lookup. This could be extremely useful in the mobile context, where it would be impractical to have a database of RFID tags for product classes, for example. However, if you encode too much information in the tag, you run the risk of an inflexible solution, where changes to the information that you encode require rewriting a large number of tags, some of which may have figuratively, and literally, left the building.

Conclusion

In this chapter, we took a tour of the BizTalk RFID Mobile platform. We started with the overall architecture and installation, followed by a simple mobile application for reading tags. Finally, we looked at some of the new services that make it easier to write applications that need to interoperate between the mobile and desktop platforms. The key concepts to remember are as follows:

- BizTalk RFID Mobile extends the reach of the BizTalk platform's RFID capability to a wide range of Windows Mobile devices.

- The mobile API is virtually identical to the server API, allowing developers to quickly ramp up on developing mobile RFID applications.

- The mobile API includes support for automatically storing and forwarding RFID events into a server-side RFID process.

- The TDT library can be leveraged both on the mobile and server platforms for managing tag data formatting in a standard format, such as SGTIN.

Building on the foundation of developing server-side applications (both synchronous and asynchronous), the next step will explore integrating the flow of RFID data with back-end business applications and systems.

CASE STUDY: MANAGING BURIED UTILITIES THROUGH MOBILE RFID

Industry: Utilities.

Overview: A firm that works with damage prevention and asset management has integrated mobile RFID into its infrastructure to enable the rapid location of buried utilities. In one scenario, RFID transmitters are embedded on buried pipelines at specific intervals. Information about the pipeline, including content (oil/gas/other), make (plastic/concrete/other), and metadata (such as date of placement) is added to the chip that is embedded. Once the pipeline has been buried, a mobile device can be used to locate the buried utilities and retrieve information.

Results: Rather than relying on the current methods of manually tracing utilities (using above-surface technologies), this approach ensures accurate locating of buried utilities. If successful, the company projects that damages resulting from poor utility management will be drastically reduced. Mobile RFID ensures accuracy and maintainability of data that does not exist in the utility industry today.

CHAPTER 8

■ ■ ■

Integrating with BizTalk Server

BizTalk RFID and BizTalk Server are applications completely separate from one another. Because of this, integrating with the core BizTalk Server engine (including the MessageBox, ports, orchestrations, and other components) from BizTalk RFID is similar to integrating with any other external system or application. There is generally a handoff that must occur between the two—due to BizTalk Server's adapter framework, there are a large variety of messaging protocols available, including File, FTP, SQL, and WCF. Though similar to other integration efforts, there are a number of aspects to integrating between BizTalk Server and BizTalk RFID that are extremely easy to implement, especially when it comes to formatting data in XML and working with the Business Rules Engine (BRE). The primary topics covered in this chapter are as follows:

- Publishing data to BizTalk Server using MSMQ

- Publishing data to BizTalk Server using SQL Server

- Calling the BRE

- Calling a BizTalk RFID Web Service Proxy

The first two sections in this chapter will outline how to publish events to BizTalk Server using different event handlers; the first describes a custom approach and the second uses components that ship with the BizTalk RFID installation. The third section introduces the basics of working with the BRE, while the last section explains how certain web proxies are available for integration back to BizTalk RFID from BizTalk Server orchestrations. After reading these sections, you will have the building blocks necessary to be able to implement your own custom publishing scenarios.

Publishing Events to BizTalk Server

The intent of this discussion is to walk through the steps needed in publishing an event from BizTalk RFID to an orchestration in BizTalk Server using an MSMQ as the delivery mechanism. By walking through a full demonstration of the entire cycle, from the creation of an event handler and the configuration of a process, through the reception of the event in the BizTalk MessageBox and beyond, you will have a complete picture of how all of the pieces interact with one another. Where knowledge is lacking, you will be able to turn to other chapters in this book to get more information.

Publishing to BizTalk Server Using MSMQ

To introduce the process of publishing RFID information to BizTalk Server, a detailed example of working with MSMQ will be outlined. Using MSMQ as the publishing mechanism requires that a custom event handler be used. By working with a custom event handler, all aspects of configuring and developing the full process can be introduced. The full life cycle of the publication of the data using this approach is shown in Figure 8-1.

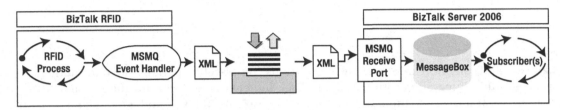

Figure 8-1. *Publishing an event to BizTalk Server using MSMQ*

The key ideas that will be discussed are

- How to create and deploy a custom event handler that posts to MSMQ

- How to configure and create all components needed in publishing events from BizTalk RFID to an MSMQ

- How to subscribe to the published event using an MSMQ adapter and orchestration

The MSMQ Event Handler

Event handlers were introduced and discussed in detail in Chapter 5. Here, we'll discuss the specifics of how to create and use an MSMQ event handler. An MSMQ event handler must receive an event, transform it to XML, and post it to a queue. Using the MSMQ event handler that accompanies this book, the key factors of importance in the code are referencing the RFID libraries and serializing and posting the tag read event. It is also worth outlining how to debug an event handler in code.

■**Note** The full code for the MSMQ event handler can be found in the code download for the book, available from the Source Code section of the Apress web site (www.apress.com/). The event handler code is located in the files associated with Chapter 8.

From a code perspective, event handlers are nothing more than class libraries that are deployed to the global assembly cache (GAC) (or local to the process via the privateprobing path) and called by BizTalk RFID processes. The steps in Exercise 8-1 outline how to use the MSMQ event handler to publish data to BizTalk Server. Before the exercise can be completed, the event handler must be deployed. Using the MSMQ event handler code that accompanies this book, take the following steps to enable it to be referenced by a BizTalk RFID process:

1. Using Visual Studio, build the event handler assembly.

2. Deploy the event handler assembly to the GAC. This can be done by opening the Microsoft .NET Configuration Framework console from Administrative Tools.

3. If the assembly is being redeployed, restart the Microsoft BizTalk RFID service. This will ensure that the most recent assembly is executed when a process runs.

Referencing the BizTalk RFID Libraries

The MSMQ event handler, like all event handlers, inherits from the RfidEventHandlerBase class and requires several BizTalk RFID–specific assemblies to be referenced. These required assemblies are Microsoft.RFID.Design, Microsoft.RFID.SpiSDK, and Microsoft.RFID.Util, all of which are in the bin folder of the installation directory of Program Files\Microsoft BizTalk RFID. Once these assemblies have been referenced, the using directive in the event handler should appear as shown in Listing 8-1.

Listing 8-1. *Event Handler using Directive*

```
using System;
using System.Collections.Generic;
using System.Text;
using Microsoft.SensorServices.Rfid;
using Microsoft.SensorServices.Rfid.Utilities;
using Microsoft.SensorServices.Rfid.Dspi;
using System.Messaging;
using System.Globalization;
using System.Xml;
using System.Runtime.Serialization;
```

Serializing and Posting the Event to MSMQ

At the heart of the MSMQ event handler is the conversion from an RFID event to an XML document, and the posting of that XML to MSMQ. The conversion is very simple, taking the data within the RFIDEventBase evt handler and placing it into an XML document, as shown in Listing 8-2.

Listing 8-2. *Posting the Serialized Event*

```
// the call to post to the transactional queue
destQ.Send(SerializeEvent(evt), MessageQueueTransactionType.Single);

// the conversion of the event to XML
private object SerializeEvent(RfidEventBase evt)
{
 if (evt == null)
  return null;
```

```
XmlDocument xml = new XmlDocument();
xml.LoadXml(evt.ToString());
return xml;
}
```

■**Note** Remember that an event handler can be debugged in Visual Studio by attaching it to the
RfidService.exe service.

Exercise 8-1. Publishing to an MSMQ Using BizTalk RFID

This exercise will demonstrate how to build and deploy all of the components necessary to publish messages from
BizTalk RFID to an MSMQ. It will demonstrate the first half of the steps in publishing events to BizTalk Server using MSMQ.

■**Note** This exercise requires that a device has already been added and configured in BizTalk RFID Manager.

1. Begin by creating a message queue to which an event can be published. This can be done by taking
   these steps:

   a. From Administrative Tools, open Computer Management and expand the Message Queuing header.
      If message queuing is not available, you can add it through Add Windows Components.

   b. Right-click Private Queues and create a new queue named publishtobiztalk. Ensure that the
      queue is transactional (as shown in Figure 8-2) and click OK.

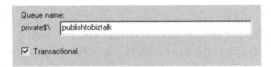

Figure 8-2. *Creating a private transactional queue*

2. Using BizTalk RFID Manager, create a new process by right-clicking Processes from the main window
   and selecting New Process.

3. In the window that opens, enter an appropriate name for the process (as shown in Figure 8-3). Set the
   "Tag processing mode" property to Transactional and enter a description. Make sure that the Start Bind
   Wizard check box is checked, and click OK.

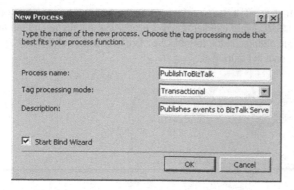

Figure 8-3. *Adding a new process*

4. In the Bind wizard, on the Bind Processes to Logical Devices screen, click the New button. This will allow for the creation of a new device.

   a. Give the device a valid name and select the device. Click Next.

   b. On the "Configure logical device" screen, select a device that has been set up. If no devices are available, a new device will need to be created. This exercise will use the ContosoTestDevice provided with the BizTalk RFID SDK. Once you've selected the device, click Next.

5. Add the MSMQ event handler on the Configure Components screen of the Bind wizard. Take the following substeps to reference this event handler (you must deploy the assembly to the GAC prior to taking these steps):

   a. Click the New Component button. This will open the Add Component dialog box.

   b. Select Public as the type of component to register, and then click the Register button. This will enable the selection of the MSMQ event handler DLL that was deployed to the GAC.

   c. In the window that opens, select MSMQEventHandler from the list and click the Register button (as shown in Figure 8-4).

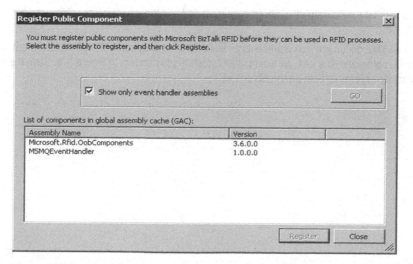

Figure 8-4. *Registering the MSMQ event handler*

d. Once the event handler has been registered, it can be added. Click the Add button and configure the event handler properties. The MSMQ event handler has two properties: the name and the queue address. You should enter the queue address in the format `.\private$\publishtobiztalk`. The fully configured event handler is shown in Figure 8-5.

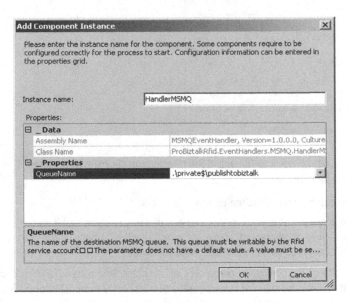

Figure 8-5. *Configuring the MSMQ event handler*

e. Complete and exit the Bind wizard once everything has been configured successfully.

6. Right-click the PublishToBizTalk process and select Start.

7. To test that the process has been configured properly, you can publish an event. One way to do this is to use the RFID client command-line tool. The steps to test the process using this tool are as follows:

a. Make sure that the PublishToBizTalk process is started and the device being referenced by this process is enabled.

b. Create an XML document that represents an event that is being submitted. This document will be sent using the command-line tool. An example of a document is shown in Figure 8-6. Save the document to an easily accessible path on the hard drive.

```
- <RfidEventBase xmlns:i="http://www.w3.org/2001/XMLSchema-instance" i:type="TagReadEvent"
  xmlns="http://schemas.datacontract.org/2004/07/Microsoft.SensorServices.Rfid">
  <m_lockObject />
  - <vendorSpecificData
    xmlns:d2p1="http://schemas.datacontract.org/2004/07/System.IO.SensorServices.Rfid.Client">
    - <d2p1:dictionary xmlns:d3p1="http://schemas.microsoft.com/2003/10/Serialization/Arrays">
      - <d3p1:KeyValueOfstringanyType>
        <d3p1:Key>ItemID</d3p1:Key>
        <d3p1:Value xmlns:d5p1="http://www.w3.org/2001/XMLSchema"
        i:type="d5p1:string">1234</d3p1:Value>
      </d3p1:KeyValueOfstringanyType>
      - <d3p1:KeyValueOfstringanyType>
        <d3p1:Key>PONumber</d3p1:Key>
        <d3p1:Value xmlns:d5p1="http://www.w3.org/2001/XMLSchema"
        i:type="d5p1:string">PO123456</d3p1:Value>
      </d3p1:KeyValueOfstringanyType>
    </d2p1:dictionary>
  </vendorSpecificData>
  <m_deviceName>MyDevice</m_deviceName>
  <m_sourceName>Antenna 1</m_sourceName>
  <m_time>2007-06-22T11:37:10.5218784+05:30</m_time>
  <data>QgBpAHoAVABhAGwAawAgAFIARgBJAEQA</data>
  - <dataSelector
    xmlns:d2p1="http://schemas.datacontract.org/2004/07/System.IO.SensorServices.Rfid.Client">
    <d2p1:dataSelector>123</d2p1:dataSelector>
  </dataSelector>
  <id>AQEBAQ==</id>
  <numberingSystemIdentifier i:nil="true" />
  - <type
    xmlns:d2p1="http://schemas.datacontract.org/2004/07/System.IO.SensorServices.Rfid.Client">
    <d2p1:description>EPC Class 0 tag</d2p1:description>
    <d2p1:enumValue>1</d2p1:enumValue>
  </type>
</RfidEventBase>
```

Figure 8-6. *Sample event XML*

c. Using a Visual Studio command prompt, execute the following command-line statement. This statement tells the RFID client utility to publish the event in the XML document to a specific logical device
within a specified process.

```
rfidclientconsole -m localhost AddEventToProcessPipeline
PublishToBizTalk rfidsample.xml MSMQDemoDevice
```

d. After the event has been sent, you need to check several items:

  i. Check the event viewer for any errors. If an exception occurs during processing of the event, it will be
  logged to the Windows Event Viewer.

  ii. Check the target MSMQ. If the event made it, the message body will be available on the queue in the
  message queuing section of Computer Management (in Administrative Tools).

  iii. In BizTalk RFID Manager, right-click the PublishToBizTalk process and select View Tags. Events that
  have been submitted will be listed in the window that opens (as shown in Figure 8-7).

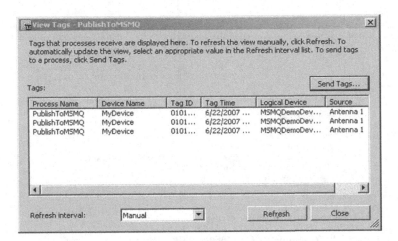

Figure 8-7. *Viewing all submitted tags in RFID Manager*

Once an event has been published to the queue, it can be consumed by BizTalk Server using an MSMQ adapter. The configuration of the adapter and the receive port is very simple, and is outlined in Exercise 8-2. The pipeline that is used is the PassThruReceive pipeline, which does no document validation on the incoming XML. This is fine for illustration, but it is important to note that BizTalk Server requires the use of schemas if any type of content-based routing is required. For example, if a field in the RFID event needs to be used in the logic within an orchestration, that field must be promoted. To promote the field, the schema must be defined and the XMLReceive pipeline must be used.

■**Note**   There are several ways to create a schema (XSD) for use with the RFID event's XML. The easiest approach would be to follow the steps in Exercise 8-2 and write out an instance of the XML to a file drop using the PassThru pipeline. Once a sample instance is available, a schema can be created using either the XSD.exe command-line tool or the Add Generated Items option from the Visual Studio BizTalk project.

Exercise 8-2. Subscribing to an MSMQ in BizTalk Server

This exercise will demonstrate how to subscribe to the events that are published to the MSMQ, as outlined in Exercise 8-1. The components created will consist of an MSMQ receive port and a file send port. The file send port will write out an XML file that represents exactly what was on the MSMQ.

1. Using the BizTalk Administration Console, create a new MSMQ receive port and perform the following substeps:

    a. Name the receive port ReceiveFromBizTalkRFID.

    b. Set the receive pipeline as PassThruReceive. (The document will be picked up without inspection.)

   c. Set the queue address to `FORMATNAME:DIRECT=OS:LOCALHOST\PRIVATE$\PUBLISHTOBIZTALK`.

   d. Set the remainder of the properties as shown in Figure 8-8.

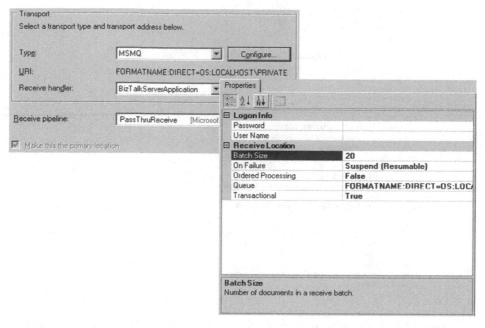

Figure 8-8. *Configuring the MSMQ receive port*

2. Once the receive port has been successfully created, add a new file send port. This send port will subscribe to the receive port created in step 1, and will write out a file to a file directory. Perform the following substeps:

   a. Name the send port OutputRFIDEvent.

   b. Set the send pipeline to `PassThruTransmit`.

   c. For the file path, set the file to output to a valid location.

   d. Set a filter to subscribe directly to the receive port by entering the values shown in Figure 8-9.

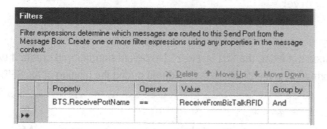

Figure 8-9. *Setting a filter on the send port*

3. Start the send port and enable the receive port. If an event has previously been published to the queue, it should be immediately picked up and written out to the specified file location. If no event is on the queue, use the steps in Exercise 8-1 to publish a new event. An example of the format of an XML document that could be written out is shown in Figure 8-10.

```xml
<?xml version="1.0" ?>
- <tag>
  - <rfidEventBase>
    - <VendorSpecificInformation>
      - <properties>
        - <property>
            <vendorKey>ItemID</vendorKey>
            <value>1234</value>
          </property>
        - <property>
            <vendorKey>PONumber</vendorKey>
            <value>PO123456</value>
          </property>
        </properties>
      </VendorSpecificInformation>
    </rfidEventBase>
  - <observation>
      <time>6/22/2007 12:07:10 AM</time>
      <sourceName>Antenna 1</sourceName>
      <deviceName>MyDevice</deviceName>
    </observation>
    <tagId>AQEBAQ==</tagId>
    <tagType>EPC Class 0 tag</tagType>
    <tagData>QgBpAHoAVABhAGwAawAgAFIARgBJAEQA</tagData>
    <tagSource>Antenna 1</tagSource>
    <tagTime>6/22/2007 12:07:10 AM</tagTime>
  - <dataSelector>
    - <tagDataSelector>
        <isId>True</isId>
        <isData>True</isData>
        <isType>True</isType>
        <isTime>True</isTime>
        <isNumberingSystemIdentifier>True</isNumberingSystemIdentifier>
      </tagDataSelector>
    </dataSelector>
  </tag>
```

Figure 8-10. *Sample output XML*

Publishing to BizTalk Server Using SqlServerSink

The SqlServerSink event handler is deployed with the base installation of BizTalk RFID, and provides an interface to push RFID events to a SQL Server database. The event handler saves data to tables within the rfidsink database. This section will outline how to use the prepackaged SqlServerSink event handler, and how to process messages from the rfidsink database using a SQL adapter in BizTalk Server.

■**Note** If the rfidsink database does not exist, the SqlServerSink event handler will create it when an event is received. All connection information to the database is configured during the binding of the RFID process.

In the previous section, a process was created that published events to an MSMQ. In Exercise 8-3, the process will be extended to also publish events to SQL Server. The flow of this exercise is shown in Figure 8-11.

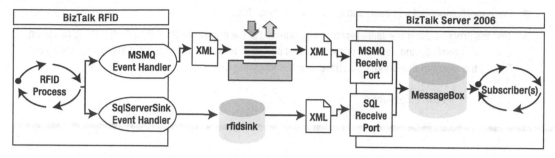

Figure 8-11. *Extending the PublishToBizTalk RFID process with SQLServerSink*

Exercise 8-3. Publishing an Event Using the SqlServerSink Event Handler

This exercise will introduce the use of the `SqlServerSink` event handler. Note that you must complete the steps in Exercise 8-1 prior to beginning this exercise.

1. Stop the PublishToBizTalk process in BizTalk RFID Manager if it is running. Once it has been stopped, right-click the process and select Edit.

2. Right-click Component Bindings and select Add New Component. Add the `SqlServerSink` event handler so that it appears in order after the MSMQ event handler, as shown in Figure 8-12. When the event handler is added, a dialog box containing the configuration settings will open. Assuming that the database is on the local machine, the default settings can be retained.

■**Note** The MSMQ event handler is designed to be the first component in a list. The `SqlServerSink` event handler can be added at any point. An event handler must be designed to listen for an event if another event handler appears before it in the component list.

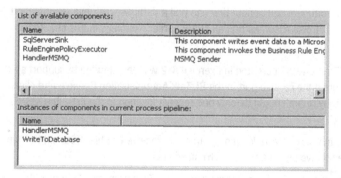

Figure 8-12. *Adding the SqlServerSink event handler to the process*

3. Once the component has been added, start the PublishToBizTalk process.

4. Test the process using the same technique as outlined at the end of Exercise 8-1. If everything has been configured correctly and no errors occur, the event should arrive on the MSMQ and in the rfidsink database. To find the event in the rfidsink database, run the following query:

```
select * from tagevents
```

The GetAndDeleteEventsForBizTalk Stored Procedure

Included with the rfidsink database are a number of stored procedures. One of these stored procedures is designed to be used by a SQL adapter in BizTalk Server to retrieve the data from the TagEvents table and delete it once it has been successfully accessed. It is a very simple stored procedure, with two basic statements. The first statement is the selection of data based on the name of the RFID process, and the second statement is the deletion of all the records retrieved. The selection of data is retrieved in XML. The pertinent code for this stored procedure is shown in Listing 8-3.

Listing 8-3. *Original GetAndDeleteEventsForBizTalk Query*

```
select * from TagEvents WITH (UPDLOCK) where ProcessName = @ProcessName for xml auto

delete from TagEvents where ProcessName = @ProcessName
```

The use of this stored procedure in the retrieval of RFID data is outlined in Exercise 8-4. This exercise will demonstrate how to configure the SQL adapter to call the GetAndDeleteEventsForBizTalk stored procedure that is installed with the rfidsink database.

Exercise 8-4. Subscribing to the SqlServerSink Database Using a SQL Adapter

The BizTalk SQL adapter is an easy-to-configure component that can poll a database, retrieve records, and deliver them to the BizTalk MessageBox. This exercise assumes that all of the earlier exercises in this chapter have been completed successfully.

1. The ReceiveFromBizTalkRFID receive port created in Exercise 8-2 will be extended to support a SQL receive location. To do this, open the receive port in the BizTalk Administration Console and click the Receive Locations tab. Currently, there should be only one receive location in the list—the MSMQ receive location.

2. Click the New button to create a new receive location. Name this receive location SQL, set the Type property to SQL, and set the receive pipeline to PassThruReceive.

3. To configure the SQL adapter, click the Configure button next to the Type property. Set the configuration information as shown in the following substeps (see Figure 8-13 for a fully configured adapter):

   a. For the Connection String property, click the ... button and connect to the rfidsink database using the appropriate credentials (generally, Windows NT Integrated security will work). Click the Test Connection button to validate that the information is correct, and then click OK to save the settings.

   b. For the Document Root Element Name property, enter a value such as Results. This will be the root node that wraps all of the results that will be returned.

   c. Set the Document Target Namespace to any valid namespace—for example, `http://PublishToBizTalk`.

   d. The SQL Command property is what will call the stored procedure and get back results. Set the value to exec `GetAndDeleteEventsForBizTalk 'PublishToBizTalk'`. The parameter represents the name of the RFID process to return results for.

   e. Leave the URI property at the default value, which will be something like `SQL://localhost/rfidsink`.

Receive Configuration	
Poll While Data Found	False
Polling Interval	30
Polling Unit of Measure	Seconds
SQL Configuration	
Connection String	Provider=SQLOLEDB.1;Integra...
Document Root Element Name	Results
Document Target Namespace	http://PublishToBizTalk
SQL Command	exec GetAndDeleteEventsForBizT
URI	SQL://localhost/rfidsink/

Figure 8-13. *Configuring the SQL adapter*

4. Once you've entered the configuration settings, save the receive location by clicking OK.

5. Enable the receive location. The steps in Exercise 8-2 worked through creating a file send port that subscribed to all data coming in on the PublishToBizTalk receive port. Since this new receive location was added to the PublishToBizTalk port, all documents will be automatically written out by the send port. When the receive location is enabled, check the output directory of the OutputRFIDEvent port. If events existed in the rfidsink database, a new file should be written. If no events existed, publish one or more test events to the rfidsink database; these should be automatically picked up and written out by BizTalk Server. The output should look similar to that shown in Figure 8-14.

```
<?xml version="1.0" encoding="utf-16" ?>
- <Results xmlns="https://PublishToBizTalk">
    <TagEvents Id="7" DeviceName="MyDevice" TagId="dbobject/TagEvents[@Id='7']/@TagId"
    TagType="1" TagTypeDescription="EPC Class 0 tag" TagSource="Antenna 1" TagTime="2007-06-
    22T00:07:10.523" TagData="dbobject/TagEvents[@Id='7']/@TagData" SinkTime="2008-09-
    11T08:06:07.013" ProcessName="PublishToBizTalk" ExtData="<VendorSpecificInformation
    xmlns:i="http://www.w3.org/2001/XMLSchema-instance"
    xmlns="http://schemas.datacontract.org/2004/07/System.IO.SensorServices.Rfid.Client">
    <dictionary xmlns:d2p1="http://schemas.microsoft.com/2003/10/Serialization/Arrays">
    <d2p1:KeyValueOfstringanyType> <d2p1:Key>ItemID</d2p1:Key> <d2p1:Value
    xmlns:d4p1="http://www.w3.org/2001/XMLSchema"
    i:type="d4p1:string">1234</d2p1:Value> </d2p1:KeyValueOfstringanyType>
    <d2p1:KeyValueOfstringanyType> <d2p1:Key>PONumber</d2p1:Key> <d2p1:Value
    xmlns:d4p1="http://www.w3.org/2001/XMLSchema"
    i:type="d4p1:string">PO123456</d2p1:Value> </d2p1:KeyValueOfstringanyType>
    </dictionary> </VendorSpecificInformation>" LogicalDeviceName="MSMQDemoDevice"
    TagIdAsHex="0x01010101"
    TagDataAsHex="0x420069007a00540061006c006b0020005200460049004400" />
```

Figure 8-14. *An example of the GetAndDeleteEventsForBizTalk standard formatting*

Extending the Flexibility of Event Retrieval

There are some obvious limitations to the out-of-the-box functionality of the GetAndDeleteEventsForBizTalk stored procedure, and no developer should feel forced to use this (or any other prepackaged component) if it does not fit the need. One of the limitations is in how the XML is structured when returned by the stored procedure. By using the For Xml Auto directive, SQL Server automatically structures the result set in a specific format. Notice how some of the attribute data contains information that is irrelevant or unusable. Especially prominent is the ExtData attribute (shown in Listing 8-4), which contains a string representation of the XML data that is stored in the database. All of the XML characters have been escaped, and the string is virtually worthless to components in BizTalk Server.

Listing 8-4. *The Default ExtData Attribute with String Representation of XML*

```
ExtData="&lt;VendorSpecificInformation
xmlns:i=&quot;http://www.w3.org/2001/XMLSchema-instance&quot;
xmlns=&quot;http://schemas.datacontract.org/2004/07/
System.IO.SensorServices.Rfid.Client&quot;&gt;
 &lt;dictionary xmlns:d2p1=&quot;http://schemas.microsoft.com/2003/10/
 Serialization/Arr
ays&quot;&gt;
  &lt;d2p1:KeyValueOfstringanyType&gt;
   &lt;d2p1:Key&gt;ItemID&lt;/d2p1:Key&gt;
   &lt;d2p1:Value
 xmlns:d4p1=&quot;http://www.w3.org/2001/XMLSchema&quot;
i:type=&quot;d4p1:string&quot;&gt;1234&lt;/d2p1:Value&gt;
  &lt;/d2p1:KeyValueOfstringanyType&gt;
  &lt;d2p1:KeyValueOfstringanyType&gt;
   &lt;d2p1:Key&gt;PONumber&lt;/d2p1:Key&gt;
   &lt;d2p1:Value xmlns:d4p1=&quot;http://www.w3.org/2001/XMLSchema&quot;
i:type=&quot;d4p1:string&quot;&gt;PO123456&lt;/d2p1:Value&gt;
  &lt;/d2p1:KeyValueOfstringanyType&gt;
 &lt;/dictionary&gt;
&lt;/VendorSpecificInformation&gt;"
```

Far more useful than a string representation of the vendor information would be to enable BizTalk to receive this data in true XML, so that once it has been received, the information can be promoted, used in content-based routing, or used in orchestration and business rule logic. This can be done in several ways, but one approach is to alter how the XML is formed when it is first queried. Rather than the simplistic directive of For Xml Auto, a developer can give explicit instructions on how the data should be formatted.

To illustrate this, the GetAndDeleteEventsForBizTalk stored procedure will be modified. Modifying the SELECT statement with For Xml Explicit and ordering the results allows for much greater flexibility in the result set. The code shown in Listing 8-5 will produce the results shown in Figure 8-15. The output of the ExtData field is now formatted in true XML, and can be used in field promotion, content-based routing, and other core BizTalk Server activities.

Listing 8-5. *Revised GetAndDeleteEventsForBizTalk Query*

```
-- This is only a partial retrieval of all available fields in table
SELECT Id AS "Id"
 ,DeviceName AS "DeviceName"
 ,TagId AS "TagId"
 ,CAST(CAST(ExtData as nvarchar(max)) AS xml) As "ExtData"
FROM TagEvents
WITH (UPDLOCK)
WHERE ProcessName = @ProcessName
FOR XML PATH('TagEvent'), BINARY BASE64, TYPE

delete from TagEvents where ProcessName = @ProcessName
```

```
- <TagEvent>
    <Id>23</Id>
    <DeviceName>MyDevice</DeviceName>
    <TagId>AQEBAQ==</TagId>
  - <ExtData>
    - <VendorSpecificInformation xmlns:i="http://www.w3.org/2001/XMLSchema-instance"
        xmlns="http://schemas.datacontract.org/2004/07/System.IO.SensorServices.Rfid.Client">
      - <dictionary
          xmlns:d2p1="http://schemas.microsoft.com/2003/10/Serialization/Arrays">
        - <d2p1:KeyValueOfstringanyType>
            <d2p1:Key>ItemID</d2p1:Key>
            <d2p1:Value xmlns:d4p1="http://www.w3.org/2001/XMLSchema"
             i:type="d4p1:string">1234</d2p1:Value>
          </d2p1:KeyValueOfstringanyType>
        - <d2p1:KeyValueOfstringanyType>
            <d2p1:Key>PONumber</d2p1:Key>
            <d2p1:Value xmlns:d4p1="http://www.w3.org/2001/XMLSchema"
             i:type="d4p1:string">PO123456</d2p1:Value>
          </d2p1:KeyValueOfstringanyType>
        </dictionary>
      </VendorSpecificInformation>
    </ExtData>
  </TagEvent>
```

Figure 8-15. *The revised results of GetAndDeleteEventsForBizTalk using explicit XML*

Calling the BizTalk BRE

BizTalk RFID is designed to be able to interact directly with the BizTalk BRE through the use of an event handler. This event handler is fairly robust, in that it allows not only for the calling of policies, but for the creation of facts used in policy instantiation. This section will give a general overview of how to call a set of rules from the RulesEnginePolicyExecutor event handler.

Logging Using the BRE

One of the methods on the RFIDRuleEngineContext class available within the BRE is LogMessage. This method allows for information to be logged. Log files are written for each device or process that is being logged from. For example, if the LogMessage method in a business rule policy is called from the PublishToBizTalk RFID process, information will be logged to %\Program Files\ Microsoft BizTalk RFID\Processes\PublishToBizTalk\PublishToBizTalk.log. Figure 8-16 illustrates the full architecture for logging, as demonstrated in Exercise 8-5.

■**Note** The last modified date does not always get updated when writing to log files. Make sure to open the file and look for the entries based on a timestamp.

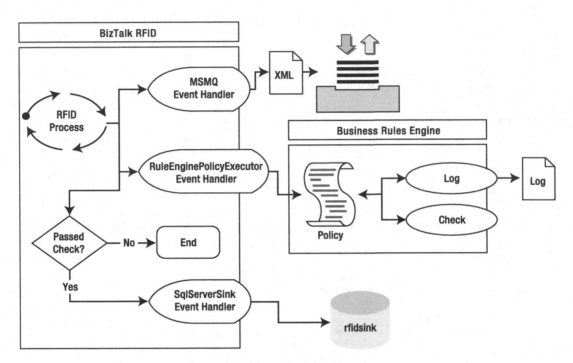

Figure 8-16. *Extending the PublishToBizTalk RFID process with business rules*

Exercise 8-5. Calling the BRE

This exercise will build upon the work completed in Exercise 8-3 by adding a call to the BizTalk BRE after the MSMQ event handler, but prior to the SqlServerSink event handler.

1. Begin by opening the Business Rule Composer. This will be used to create a policy with two rules.

2. Add a new policy and call it LogAndCheck. This will create a new policy set to version 1.0.

3. Right-click the version number and select Add New Rule. This first rule can be named Log, and will write an entry to the log file.

4. Next, you will create the IF conditional logic. Use the following substeps to complete this task:

    a. The logging should occur every time the rule is called. Therefore, in the IF conditions, a rule will be created that always returns true. The easiest way to do this is to drag the Equal vocabulary from the Vocabularies Predicates list and drop it on the IF logic. The result is shown in Figure 8-17.

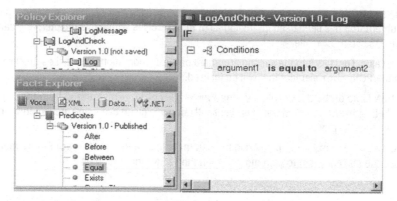

Figure 8-17. *Adding the Equal vocabulary predicate to the log rule*

    b. Set both arguments in the new condition to 1. The result will be a condition that states "If 1 is equal to 1." This will always evaluate to `true`, and will cause the THEN logic to execute.

5. The THEN logic will now be created. This logic will call the `LogEvent` method in the `RFIDRuleEngineContext` library. Use the following substeps to complete this task:

    a. In the Facts Explorer, click the .NET tab. Right-click the .NET Assemblies folder and select Browse. In the window that opens, find the `Microsoft.RFID.OobComponents` assembly and add it.

    b. With the `Microsoft.RFID.OobComponents` assembly available in the .NET tab, expand the `RFIDRuleEngineContext` class and click the `LogMessage` method. Drag and drop this method in the THEN logic of the rule.

    c. The method requires two arguments. The first argument can be manually entered, and should read `BRE Event Logged {0}`.

    d. The second argument should be the `get_CurrentTagReadEvent` method. It can be dragged from the `RFIDRuleEngineContext` and dropped on the rule. The completed THEN logic is shown in Figure 8-18.

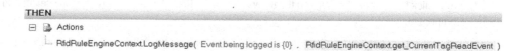

Figure 8-18. *The THEN logic to log an event*

6. Create a new rule and call it Check. This rule will check whether the PONumber of the incoming event is equal to a test value, and if it is, it will remove the event from the process, which will keep it from being published to the `SqlServerSink` event handler and rifdsink database. Take the following substeps to complete this task (the full logic for this rule is shown in Figure 8-19):

    a. In the IF conditional logic, add the `Equal` operator from the Predicates list.

    b. Drag and drop the `GetVendorSpecificData` method from the `RfidRuleEngineContext` class onto the first argument. This will look at the content of the incoming event. The specific field that will be checked is PONumber.

c. Enter the text **PONumber** for the parameter in the GetVendorSpecificData method. This field is in the document that has been used for testing all of the exercises within this chapter, and can be found in the RFIDSample.xml file.

d. Enter the value **Test123** into the second argument of the IF conditional logic. Test123 represents a value in the PONumber element that will be ignored.

e. In the THEN logic of the Check rule, add the RemoveOutputEvent method from the RfidRuleEngineContext class. This event will remove a given event and prevent further execution of it within an RFID process.

f. Drop the get_CurrentEvent method in the parameter of the RemoveOutputEvent method. This will cause the current event to be removed when the THEN logic executes.

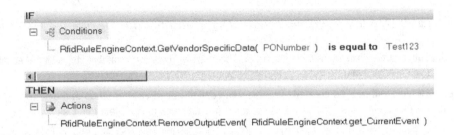

Figure 8-19. *The logic for the Check rule*

7. The policy is now complete. Save it.

8. Once the policy has been saved, right-click it and select Deploy.

9. After the policy has been deployed, right-click and select Publish. The policy will now be available to call from the RFID process.

10. Open RFID Manager. The PublishToBizTalk process will now be modified to include the call to the BRE. Stop the process, and then right-click it and select Edit.

11. Right-click Component Bindings on the Browse tab of the PublishToBizTalk process and select Add New Component.

12. Select the RuleEnginePolicyExecutor event handler from the list and add it to the process pipeline.

13. In the window that opens, the event handler will be configured to call the new policy in the BRE. Set the instance name to LogAndCheck and then follow these substeps to complete this task:

a. Next to the Rules Configuration property, click the ... button next to Configure. This will open a new window where the call to the policy will be made.

b. Select the LogAndCheck policy from the drop-down menu, as shown in Figure 8-20. Click OK to save the settings and return to the main Add Component screen.

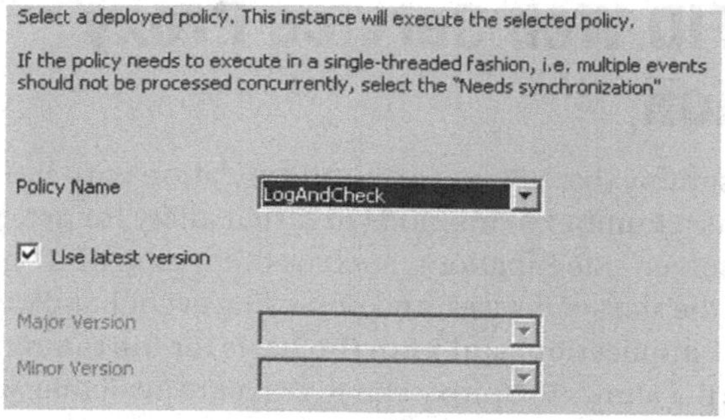

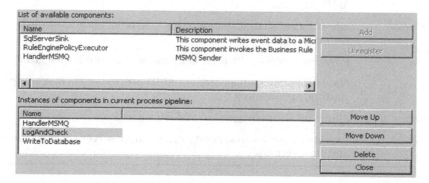

Figure 8-20. *Referencing the policy in the RuleEnginePolicyExecutor event handler*

14. The `RuleEnginePolicyExecutor` event handler should be placed between the existing `HandlerMSMQ` and `SqlServerSink` event handlers, as shown in Figure 8-21. Use the Move Up and Move Down buttons to reorder the events in the process pipeline.

Figure 8-21. *Adding LogAndCheck as the second item in the process pipeline*

15. Once completed, validate the PublishToBizTalk process by clicking the Validate button in RFID Manager.

16. Once the process has been validated, start it.

17. When the process is started, it can be tested. Begin by testing using the same method outlined in Exercise 8-1. An event should be logged to the MSMQ and to the rfidsink database. The execution of the rules engine will log an entry to the `PublishToBizTalk.log` file.

18. Now test that the Check rule operates correctly. Open the `RFIDSample.xml` file in a text editor and change the value of the PONumber node to Test123. Retest using this modified file. This time, an event should be logged to the MSMQ, and the `PublishToBizTalk.log` file should be written to, but no event will be added to the rfidsink database.

Calling a BizTalk RFID Web Service Proxy from an Orchestration

Packaged with BizTalk RFID is an assembly that allows for communication with the RFID server components. The assembly has a number of methods in it that allow for external applications to perform a wide variety of server-side functions, such as managing RFID processes, performing binding functions, setting the state of devices, and deploying event handlers. These methods can be called from any .NET application, and form the basis for the functionality behind BizTalk RFID Manager. Table 8-1 shows the proxy classes that are available, with a brief description of each.

Table 8-1. *BizTalk RFID Web Proxy Classes*

Class Name	Description
BindingManagerProxy	Provides methods that allow for component and device binding to RFID processes
ComponentManagerProxy	Allows for registering, unregistering, and other basic tasks associated with event handlers
DeviceManagerProxy	Provides functionality for managing devices and device groups
ProcessManagerProxy	Allows for state management of RFID processes, such as stopping, starting, and deleting
ProviderManagerProxy	Allows for the management of device providers
ServerManagerProxy	Provides methods to set and retrieve some server configurations and state settings

Calling the majority of the classes and methods shown in Table 8-1 from an orchestration in BizTalk Server has limited real-world applicability. There is rarely a time that the deployment of an event handler, for example, will need to be automated. So, too, it is unlikely that the server will need to be configured in a workflow or devices will need to be bound or unbound. The ProcessManagerProxy class, however, has a number of methods that may be useful in workflow automation and orchestration development. The methods in this class allow for such functionality as starting, stopping, and instantiating BizTalk RFID processes. Several of the most important methods are described in Table 8-2. All of these should look extremely familiar to anyone who has used RFID Manager to work with processes.

Table 8-2. *ProcessManagerProxy Methods*

Method Name	Description
AddEventToProcessPipeline	Sends an event to instantiate a process. Notice that this is the same method called for testing from the RFID client command-line tool (see Exercise 8-1).
DeleteProcess	Deletes a specified process.
GetProcess	Gets a specific process. This could be used to determine if a process is deployed.

Table 8-2. *ProcessManagerProxy Methods*

Method Name	Description
GetProcessStatus	Returns the status of all processes in the input array. This method, like several others, uses arrays as parameters and result sets. Due to the complex data types, it would be easiest to add these to .NET class assemblies that could be called from orchestrations, rather than call them directly from an expression shape.
StartProcess	Starts a specified process.
StopProcess	Stops a specified process.
ValidateProcessAndBinding	Ensures that all of the components associated with the process are valid.

One example of the use of the ProcessManagerProxy methods in an orchestration would be the automation of the state of RFID processes. For example, assume that it was discovered that processes were stopping unexpectedly due to connectivity issues or faulty components, and that the desired solution was to ensure that the processes were always restarted. To solve this, an orchestration could be built and deployed that would execute on a timed basis and call a .NET assembly to check the status of one or more processes. If it was found that a process was not started, the StartProcess method could be called. This would eliminate the need for manual actions to be taken by an administrator and ensure that the processes were constantly restarted. The orchestration would look similar to that shown in Figure 8-22.

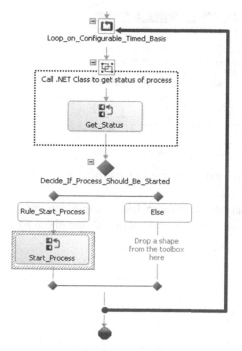

Figure 8-22. *An orchestration loop to automate process state*

To illustrate how a proxy method is called from an orchestration, refer to Exercise 8-6. Since the proxies are all in .NET assemblies, all that is required is to create a variable of the proxy class type and to call the method from an expression shape. Remember you can most easily call complex types associated with these proxy methods (such as arrays) through the use of a referenced .NET helper class, rather than directly from an orchestration. The .NET helper assembly can then be referenced by the orchestration.

Exercise 8-6. Calling a BizTalk RFID Web Service Proxy

Referencing and calling a BizTalk RFID web service proxy method within an orchestration will be outlined in this exercise. It is assumed that an orchestration already exists.

1. Begin by creating an orchestration variable that is of the `ProcessManagerProxy` type. This will allow the methods on the class to be called from an orchestration shape. Take the following actions to do this:

   a. On the Orchestration View tab of the orchestration, right-click the Variables folder and create a new variable named `processManager`.

   b. For the Type property of this variable, select the .NET Class option and browse to the `Microsoft. SensorServices.Rfid.Management.ProcessManagerProxy` assembly, as shown in Figure 8-23.

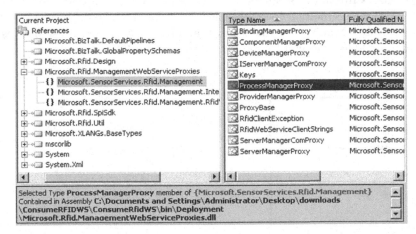

Figure 8-23. *Selecting the ProcessManagerProxy assembly as a variable type*

2. Once the variable has been created, it can be used in an expression shape. Drop an expression shape into the orchestration and type in the variable name, `processManager`. All of the public methods will be available to call, as shown in Figure 8-24.

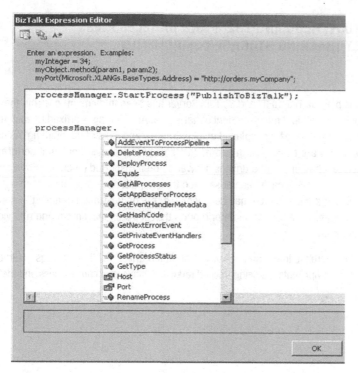

Figure 8-24. *Calling a proxy method within an expression shape*

Conclusion

Using BizTalk Server to process and route information from BizTalk RFID to external systems and applications has a number of benefits. These include prebuilt transmission protocols (in the form of adapters); robust functionality for workflow process (in the form of orchestrations); a configurable BRE; and extensive error handling, tracking, and reporting (through the BizTalk Administration Console and other tools). Rather than having to write complex code into RFID components or middle-tier objects, BizTalk Server enables developers to rapidly develop and deploy architectures to support data transmission and mapping. Given the variety of uses and advantages of BizTalk Server, it is important that you be familiar with a number of aspects of incorporating it into your BizTalk RFID solutions.

CASE STUDY: REDUCING THEFT AND CARELESSNESS BY TRACKING STORAGE COMPONENTS

Industry: Financial.

Overview: A solution using both BizTalk RFID and BizTalk Server has been implemented within the banking industry to reduce the theft and misplacement of hardware. An RFID tag is affixed to each hard drive within an organization. An RFID reader is placed at all entrances and exits of the building. As hard drives pass by the readers, they are tracked, with information posted to orchestrations that perform business rules. Rules include whether or not a drive is allowed to be transported (such as within an employee's laptop) and whether drives have been absent too long (e.g., a drive may have been out of the office for several weeks). If a business rule has been violated, the orchestration notifies the appropriate administrative party. Administrators can monitor reports that show all movement and rule violations of all tracked components.

Results: There is a sizeable decrease in the number of lost or stolen drives. While RFID tags could be removed, the knowledge that components are being tracked reduces instances of carelessness and theft.

■ ■ ■

CHAPTER 9

Direct Communication with Enterprise Applications

Chapter 8 detailed how to communicate with BizTalk RFID by using BizTalk Server as the integration broker. Often, it is unnecessary to have orchestrations and ports sitting between BizTalk RFID and external applications, and the purpose of this chapter is to illustrate how to effectively implement more direct patterns of communication. This chapter uses two primary discussions to illustrate how to interact directly with BizTalk RFID throughout the enterprise. The first discussion centers on SQL Server Reporting Services, and making the BizTalk RFID SQL data accessible to external platforms and applications. The second discussion centers around calling BizTalk RFID from a SharePoint 2007 web part. By reading these discussions and working through the exercises, you will come to understand how to interact with BizTalk RFID across networks and platforms, and you should be able to apply this understanding to whatever distributed application model is needed.

Key ideas that will be introduced are the following:

- Querying BizTalk RFID databases and making the information available in SQL Server Reporting Services

- Building basic reports in Reporting Services

- Calling BizTalk RFID from machines across different network configurations

- Interacting with BizTalk RFID from a SharePoint 2007 web part

- Deciding when to use a custom web service vs. the BizTalk RFID web service proxy assemblies

Integrating with SQL Server Reporting Services

The purpose of this section is to outline how data within BizTalk RFID's databases can be made available to end users with SQL Server Reporting Services. There are a wide variety of metrics and data that would be useful to display in web-based reports and dashboards. This section will illustrate a subset of these by concentrating on devices and related TagRead events held in two databases: RFIDSTORE and rfidsink. The discussion will center on how to extract relevant data from these two databases and display it in web-based reports. The key ideas that will be introduced are as follows:

- Creating several stored procedures to query devices and related tag events

- Creating several Reporting Services reports that call the stored procedures and display the returned data

The architecture of this section is shown in Figure 9-1. It shows the databases, the two stored procedures, and the Reporting Services reports, which are rendered as ASPX pages.

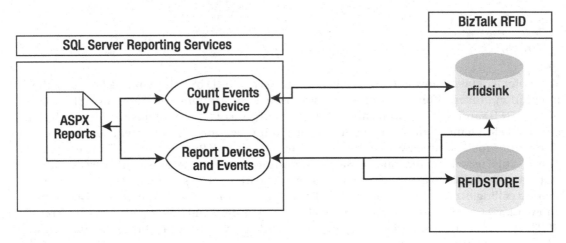

Figure 9-1. *SQL Server report architecture*

Querying the BizTalk RFID Databases

The databases that lie beneath BizTalk RFID are relatively simple. Much of the information that defines devices and events is stored in XML strings within ntext fields. There are a number of preexisting stored procedures that provide certain data. In many cases, however, custom queries will need to be written to access the desired information. The discussions in this section will outline how to access information in the XML and how to create certain metrics across multiple databases.

Querying Devices and Related Events

The first stored procedure that will be outlined (shown in Listing 9-1) concerns retrieving all tag events related to devices. This procedure will demonstrate how to work with the device information stored in XML and retrieve data from both databases. It includes a single input parameter, vchDeviceStatus, which will determine what devices to return based on their connection status. You begin the procedure by placing all of the device information into a temporary table, converting the runtimeDeviceInfo field from ntext to XML in the process. This allows for easy access to the connection status information in the next portion of the procedure, which returns the information from the two tables.

■**Note** The stored procedure shown in Listing 9-1 would be deployed on a custom database used primarily for reports in Reporting Services. It is not intended to be placed on any of the preexisting BizTalk RFID databases.

Listing 9-1. *The Report Devices and Events Stored Procedure*

```
-- ============================================
-- Sample Implementation:
-- EXEC spReportDevicesAndEvents 'ConnectionEstablished'
-- ============================================
CREATE PROCEDURE [dbo].[spReportDevicesAndEvents]
(
@vchDeviceStatus varchar(50) = 'All'
)
AS
BEGIN
 -- loading into a temporary table allows for easy conversion
 -- from ntext to XML
 SELECT name, CAST(runtimeDeviceInfo as XML) As runtimeDeviceInfo
 INTO #temporary
 FROM RFIDSTORE.dbo.devices

 -- join the two databases together to get information
 SELECT d.name, t.sinktime
 FROM #temporary d
 LEFT JOIN rfidsink.dbo.TagEvents t ON t.DeviceName
 COLLATE DATABASE_DEFAULT = d.name COLLATE DATABASE_DEFAULT
 WHERE (@vchDeviceStatus = 'All' OR
  CAST(d.runtimeDeviceInfo.query(
   'declare namespace
s="http://schemas.datacontract.org/2004/07/MS.Internal.Rfid.Service.Devices";
data(//s:m_connectionStatus)') As varchar(50)) = @vchDeviceStatus
  )
END
```

There are two important items to point out in this query: collation and the XML query.

First, the RFIDSTORE and the rfidsink databases are, by default, created with different collation. Trying to join one table to another in a query will result in the error that states the following:

```
Cannot resolve the collation conflict between "SQL_Latin1_General_CP437_BIN"
and "SQL_Latin1_General_CP1_CI_AS" in the equal to operation.
```

Adding the COLLATE DATABASE DEFAULT directive will force both tables to temporarily adhere to the default collation of SQL Server, and will allow the query to execute without error.

Second, querying the XML to get the connection status can be a little challenging. As stated before, the runtimeDeviceInfo field is an XML string stored in an ntext field. Once the field is converted to an XML data type, the node that contains the connection status can be queried using XQuery. However, an extra level of complexity is added due to the namespace stored in the root element of the document (see Figure 9-2). This namespace must be declared in the XQuery statement to successfully retrieve the value of the connection status node; without the namespace declaration, no value will be returned.

```
<DeviceRuntimeInformation
    xmlns:i="http://www.w3.org/2001/XMLSchema-instance"
    xmlns="http://schemas.datacontract.org/2004/07/MS.Internal.Rfid.Service.Devices">
  <m_CheckpointDeviceOnConnect>true</m_CheckpointDeviceOnConnect>
  <m_connectionStatus>NotConnected</m_connectionStatus>
  <m_deviceId i:nil="true" />
</DeviceRuntimeInformation>
```

Figure 9-2. *Example of the runtimeDeviceInfo XML*

Querying Count Events by Device

The second stored procedure is very simple. There is nothing that needs to be pointed out about the procedure, beyond the code listing shown in Listing 9-2. The purpose of including this procedure in the discussion is to illustrate how a chart can be used in Reporting Services to display BizTalk RFID metrics in a visually appealing way.

Listing 9-2. *spCountEventsByDevice*

```
-- ================================================
-- Sample Implementation:
-- EXEC spCountEventsByDevice
-- ================================================
CREATE PROCEDURE [dbo].[spCountEventsByDevice]
AS
BEGIN
  SELECT DISTINCT DeviceName
    ,(SELECT COUNT(*)
      FROM rfidsink.dbo.TagEvents child
      WHERE child.DeviceName = parent.DeviceName) As EventCount
FROM rfidsink.dbo.TagEvents parent
END
```

Writing the SQL Server Reporting Services Reports

With the stored procedures defined, the accompanying web reports can now be created in Reporting Services. This section will walk through how to build a report for each of the procedures outlined in the previous section. Before looking at creating the reports, Exercise 9-1 will introduce you to creating a Reporting Services project, in case you're unfamiliar. After the project has been created, you will add two individual reports to it.

Exercise 9-1. Creating a SQL Server Reporting Services Project

This exercise will outline the steps necessary to create a Reporting Services project.

1. Open SQL Server Business Intelligence Development Studio. This can be found at Start ➤ All Programs ➤ Microsoft SQL Server. This is an add-on to Visual Studio, and enables the creation of SQL Server–related projects such as Reporting Services, Analysis Services, and Integration Services.

2. Create a new Report Server project, available under the Business Intelligence Projects heading (as shown in Figure 9-3).

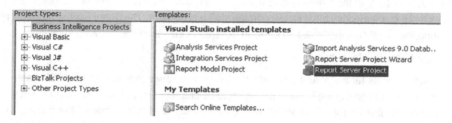

Figure 9-3. *New Report Server project*

3. Once the project has been named and created, the next task is to create a data source. Right-click the Shared Data Sources folder in the Solution Explorer window and select Add New Data Source. Connect to the database where the RFIDSTORE and rfidsink databases reside (this assumes that both databases are on the same SQL server).

Creating the Report for Devices and Related Events

The first report interacts with the stored procedure defined in Listing 9-1. It will allow a user to determine what devices to query (those that are connected, disconnected, or both) through the use of a drop-down box, and will display a report similar to that shown in Figure 9-4. To show you how to get to this result, Exercise 9-2 will walk through connecting a new dynamic report with the stored procedure.

vchDeviceStatus	Disconnected ▼	View Report

Dynamic Devices And Events

Device Name	Sink Time
ContosoTestDevice	9/5/2008 11:14:44 AM
ContosoTestDevice	9/5/2008 11:14:44 AM
ContosoTestDevice	9/5/2008 11:14:44 AM

Figure 9-4. *The Dynamic Devices and Events report with the user-controlled drop-down*

Exercise 9-2. Building the Dynamic Devices and Events Report

This exercise will walk through the creation of a new SQL Server report that is tied to the stored procedure outlined in Listing 9-1. It assumes a project has already been created (see Exercise 9-1).

1. Add a new report to the SQL Server Reporting Services project. The Report wizard will open.

2. Begin by connecting to the appropriate data source in the Report wizard and move on to the Query Builder screen.

3. The Report wizard requires that a SQL statement be entered in the Query Builder. Generally, with stored procedures, this fails. In the case of the spReportDevicesAndEvents stored procedure, it will fail because there is a temporary table included in the stored procedure. The Query Builder has a problem generating the result set and throws an error. To get around this, take the following substeps:

   a. Click the Query Builder button.

   b. Enter **Select 'a' as temp, 'b' as temp2** into the Query Builder window. Any generic SQL statement will work, with the goal being to allow the report to be created. The reason this specific statement is helpful is that it will set up the report with two columns, which is what the result set that is returned by the stored procedure contains.

   c. Click OK, and then move on to the Report Type screen.

4. Set the Report Type to Tabular and go to the next screen.

5. Click the Finish button (you don't need to add the temp field to the Displayed fields—just ignore and move on).

6. On the final screen, give the report an appropriate name and exit the Report wizard.

7. The initial version of the report will appear, looking somewhat similar to that shown in Figure 9-5.

Figure 9-5. *Temporary report (before the query has been corrected)*

8. The first task is to get the appropriate result set (instead of the temporary result added in step 3). You do this by clicking the Data tab and taking the following substeps:

   a. Set the Command Type drop-down to Stored Procedure.

   b. Enter the name of the stored procedure in the query window: **spReportDevicesAndEvents**.

c. Click the exclamation mark (!) to run the query. A small window should pop up that requests the value of the stored procedure parameter (see Figure 9-6). You can set this to All.

Figure 9-6. *Entering the value for the device status parameter*

d. Click OK to run the query. A list of results will be returned (assuming there are values in the databases—if not, post some events).

9. With the stored procedure returning valid results, update the report's dataset. You can do this by clicking the Data tab, right-clicking the Report Datasets heading, and selecting Refresh. The refreshed dataset should look like that shown in Figure 9-7.

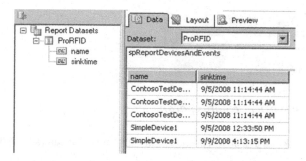

Figure 9-7. *The corrected dataset with parameters returned from the query*

10. Next, update the report grid by clicking the Layout tab. Drag the "name" field from the dataset and drop it in the first column. Drag the "sinktime" field and drop it into the second column.

11. Rename both of the column headers to an appropriate value and resize the report grid so that the data has plenty of room to display (see Figure 9-8).

Figure 9-8. *The updated Layout tab*

12. With the data structured properly, the final tasks involve enabling a dynamic parameter to be passed in. Click the Report menu option and select Report Parameters. This opens a window where the device status parameter used by the stored procedure can be worked with.

13. In the "Available values" window, enter three nonqueried values, as shown in Figure 9-9. The values correspond to the three values that are stored in the XML string in the RFIDSTORE database's device table, and that are queried in the stored procedure. The labels are simply what appear to the end user in the drop-down. In addition to these values, set the Non-queried default value to All. Once all of these are entered, click OK to continue.

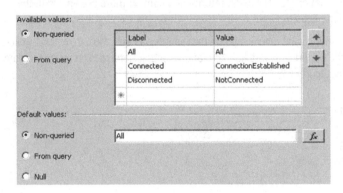

Figure 9-9. *Setting values for the vchDeviceStatus parameter*

14. The report is complete, and should look like that shown previously in Figure 9-4. You can validate this by clicking the Preview tab.

■**Note** The report is complete within the Visual Studio project, and it can now be deployed. Once a report has been deployed, it is moved to a virtual directory in IIS, and can be referenced via a URL and embedded into a standard ASPX page.

Creating the Count Events by Device Report

The goal of the Count Events by Device report is to show how to create a chart report that is tied to BizTalk RFID metrics. The steps to creating a chart are slightly different than they are with a standard report, and therefore need some additional explanation. It is also important to highlight that some information from BizTalk RFID is of greater value in a well-structured, visually appealing chart than it would be in a text-based presentation. The chart that will be created in Exercise 9-3 is shown in Figure 9-10.

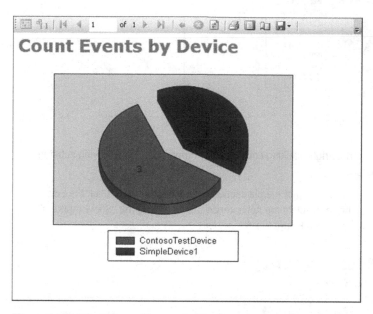

Figure 9-10. *The Count Events by Device pie chart*

Exercise 9-3. Building the Count Events by Device Pie Chart

This exercise will walk through the creation of a new SQL Server report that is tied to the stored procedure outlined in Listing 9-2. It assumes a project has already been created (see Exercise 9-1).

1. Create a new report and add the appropriate data source.

2. The dataset should be the results returned by the spCountEventsByDevice stored procedure. Use the detailed steps in Exercise 9-2 to complete this step.

3. Set the initial state of the report to Tabular. Once the report is in designer mode, the table should be deleted to make room for the chart.

4. On the Toolbox tab, select the chart, drag it, and drop it onto the design surface. It will default to a bar graph.

5. Right-click the bar graph and select Chart Type. Set the type to an exploded pie chart.

6. Drop the EventCount field from the dataset onto the "Drop data fields here" section, and drop the DeviceName field onto the "Drop series fields here," as shown in Figure 9-11.

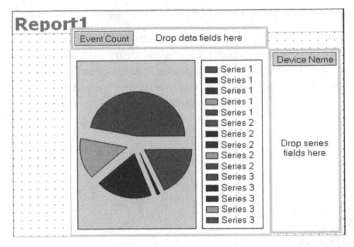

Figure 9-11. *Creating the pie chart*

7. Next, set the properties of the chart by right-clicking and selecting Properties. The following substeps will be helpful in creating the chart:

   a. To get the number of events to show on top of the pie sections, click the Data tab. Click the Edit button to the right of the Values box and select the Appearance tab. Selecting the "Show markers" check box will enable this to happen (see Figure 9-12).

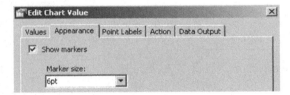

Figure 9-12. *Enabling the markers prints the count on the pie slice.*

   b. To give the device names plenty of room to display, click the Legend tab and set the properties so that the legend displays at the bottom center (see Figure 9-13).

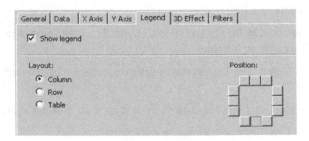

Figure 9-13. *Setting the placement of the legend*

8. The report, once completed, should look similar to that shown in Figure 9-10. You can verify this by clicking the Preview tab.

Connecting to BizTalk RFID via Remote Machines

The discussion will now turn to an important digression: introducing how to connect from a remote machine to the BizTalk RFID server. There are a variety of methods of interaction with BizTalk RFID, the most common of which is through the use of the proxy web service assemblies. These assemblies can be referenced on any machine, regardless of where BizTalk RFID is hosted. To be able to connect to the RFID server, the user under which the code is executing must be a member of the RFID_USER group on the host machine. If a user without permissions tries to connect to BizTalk RFID, an error stating "The server has rejected the credentials" will be returned to the application, and an error similar to that shown in Figure 9-14 will be logged to the Windows Event Viewer on the host machine.

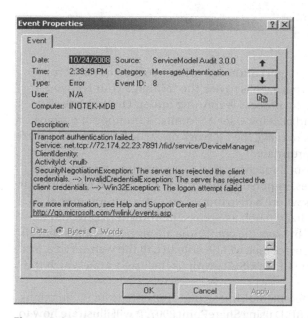

Figure 9-14. *An error indicating that the calling user is not a member of the RFID_USER group*

Note The default port that the BizTalk RFID web services operate under is 7891.

The solution to this issue is fairly simple when connecting to a host machine that is in the same domain (or a trusted domain) of the calling machine. All that must be done is to add the user to the RFID_USER group. There should be no issues in adding the user, as the user will be accessible to be added either via the local computer groups or Active Directory (see Figure 9-15).

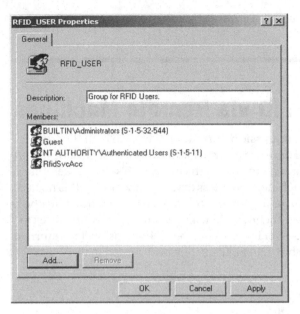

Figure 9-15. *The RFID_USER group*

For incidents where NTLM (NT LAN Manager) authentication needs to occur across machines on different domains, the easiest approach is to use the "Manage your Network Password" options on the user account that the process is running under. On Windows XP, you can do this by opening Control Panel and clicking User Accounts. A number of options are available for each user, one of which is to manage the network password. Set the password information for the domain/machine as appropriate.

However, if you're trying to connect from a machine that is not on the network, these approaches won't be an option. In some cases, impersonation could be used, but even that has limitations (such as over the Web). In cases where a distributed communication model is necessary and credentials can't be standardized (such as across the Internet), it would be most appropriate to create a web service that brokers the communications between the BizTalk RFID host and the calling machines. Calling machines will be able to call the web service, and the only user that will need to be added to the RFID_USER group is the user under which the web service executes (e.g., ASP.NET).

The BizTalk proxy web services are extremely helpful, but are not appropriate for all situations. The next section covers connecting to BizTalk RFID using SharePoint 2007. It will illustrate how to connect using the web proxies, and, separately, how to use a web service to broker the calls. Once you understand both approaches, you will be able to determine when and how to use them in your own implementations.

■**Note** The BizTalk RFID proxy web service classes should only be used by applications that are on the same network as the BizTalk RFID service. Applications outside of the network should depend on a custom web service to expose the needed methods.

Integrating with SharePoint 2007

This section will give an overview of several paths to integrating BizTalk RFID–related information with SharePoint 2007. Administration of BizTalk RFID is generally done through the RFID Manager, which is fine for development, but is limiting in a production environment. Frequently, users who should not have access to the production BizTalk RFID server (where the RFID Manager and other client tools are installed) need the ability to view data and perform administrative tasks. There are several ways to solve this, but the most appropriate is to implement an enterprise-wide solution, which would allow controlled access within a known environment. SharePoint 2007 is being widely adopted and implemented as the enterprise portal of choice, enabling extensive permission handling, interoperability with existing applications and code bases, and rapid web-based application development and deployment, and therefore will be the focus of this section.

The exercises in this section are intended to aid you in understanding how BizTalk RFID can be made available to the wider organization. The text will look at how to interact with BizTalk RFID through a SharePoint web part. The rendered web part is very simple, displaying a drop-down list of available devices, but you should be able to extend the ideas behind this to enable any type of administration needed in a web part. Anything that can be handled through the BizTalk RFID web proxy classes can be made available to users in external applications.

As outlined in the earlier discussion about connecting to BizTalk RFID from remote machines, there are two possible approaches to take. The first is to connect directly to BizTalk RFID using the web service proxy assemblies. The second is to use an intermediary web service to enable the call. The BizTalk RFID web service proxy assemblies are useful when the calling system is on the same network as BizTalk RFID. These assemblies can be added to a project and called with little effort. The architecture and components related to this approach are illustrated in Figure 9-16, and will be implemented later in Exercise 9-5.

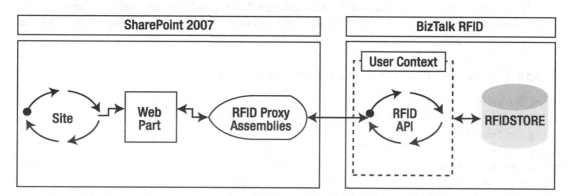

Figure 9-16. *SharePoint component architecture using BizTalk RFID proxy assemblies*

In many cases, the calling application will not be on the same network as the BizTalk RFID service, or will not have permissions to interact directly with BizTalk RFID using the proxy assemblies. In cases such as this, it is more appropriate to use a custom web service to broker external requests (calling parties not on the network) from the internal systems (BizTalk RFID). The web service would reference the proxy assemblies and call the methods, exposing public web methods to the external clients. All permissions are handled by IIS, and a decoupled, easily maintainable solution is created. The architecture and components related to this approach are illustrated in Figure 9-17, and will be implemented later in Exercise 9-6.

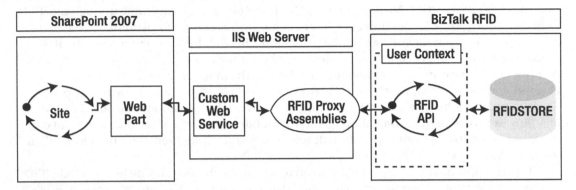

Figure 9-17. *SharePoint component architecture using a custom web service*

Developing the SharePoint Web Part Foundation

Before moving on to the details of how to implement the different approaches to calling BizTalk RFID, it will be useful to first put together the foundation by building the SharePoint web part. If you're unfamiliar with SharePoint web part development, you'll benefit greatly by looking at the steps needed to add a custom web part to a SharePoint site. Once the foundation of the web part has been laid out, it will be extended first to call the BizTalk RFID web service proxy assemblies directly, and second to call an intermediary web service.

Exercise 9-4 details the steps needed to create and deploy a web part to SharePoint 2007. This will form the base for the remaining SharePoint-related exercises in the section. The full code for the web part framework is shown in Listing 9-3. This code sets up a single configurable field to define the BizTalk RFID host IP, and creates all of the necessary methods to render data to the user interface.

Listing 9-3. *SharePoint BizTalk RFID Administration Web Part*

```
using System;
using System.Collections.Generic;
using System.Text;
using System.Web;
using System.Web.UI;
using System.Web.UI.WebControls;
using System.Web.UI.WebControls.WebParts;
using Microsoft.SharePoint.WebPartPages;

namespace SharePointBizTalkRFIDWebParts
{
 public class AdministrativeFunctions :
 Microsoft.SharePoint.WebPartPages.WebPart
 {
  // default value of the variable.  Overridden by configurable field.
```

```csharp
private String rfidProxyHost = "192.168.0.175";
// user-configurable field declaration
[WebBrowsable(true), Personalizable(PersonalizationScope.Shared),
WebDisplayName("RFID Proxy Host Server"),
SPWebCategoryName("Administrative Function Settings")]

public String RFIDProxyHost
{
 get { return rfidProxyHost; }
 set { rfidProxyHost = value; }
}

protected override void CreateChildControls()
{
 base.CreateChildControls();

 // label to give name
 Label tableDescription = new Label();
 tableDescription.Text = "Devices Available: ";

 // add label to control for rendering
 this.Controls.Add(tableDescription);
}

protected override void RenderWebPart(HtmlTextWriter output)
{
 base.RenderWebPart(output);
 }
 }
}
```

Exercise 9-4. Building and Deploying a Web Part

This exercise will demonstrate how to create a SharePoint 2007 web part that will be able to call BizTalk RFID and perform several administrative functions. The steps introduce the full development life cycle of a web part, from the build through deployment.

1. Create a new C# class library project in Visual Studio. This will be the framework of the web part. Give it an appropriate name (this exercise will refer to it as AdminstrativeFunctions).

2. Add the web part code shown in Listing 9-3. This includes the class declaration and web part inheritance, and a single configurable field for the BizTalk RFID host URL (used when connecting through the proxy or through a web service).

3. Add an entry in the SharePoint Web.config file under the <SafeControls> node. The entry should look similar to the following:

```
<SafeControl Assembly="SharePointBizTalkRFIDWebParts, Version = 12.0.0.0,
Culture=neutral" namespace = "SharePointBizTalkRFIDWebParts" TypeName="*"
Safe="True" />
```

4. Copy the `SharePointBizTalkRFIDWebParts.dll` assembly to the following directory:

   `$\Inetpub\wwwroot\wss\VirtualDirectories\80\bin`

5. Now the web part can be added to the SharePoint gallery. Open SharePoint Server in a web browser, click the Home tab, and take the following substeps:

   a. Click Site Action ➤ Site Settings ➤ Modify All Site Settings.

   b. Under Galleries, click Web Parts. A list of all available web parts will be shown.

   c. Click the New button. In the window that opens, find the entry for SharePointBizTalkWebParts and set the check box next to it. Once checked, click the Populate Gallery button.

   d. Validate that the web part appears, as shown in Figure 9-18.

Figure 9-18. *The web part has been added to the gallery.*

6. Determine what SharePoint site to add the web part to. To create a site, take the following substeps:

   a. From the Home tab, click Site Actions and select Create Site.

   b. Set the title and description of the site, and give a valid URL. An example of this is shown in Figure 9-19.

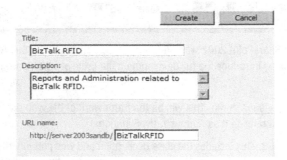

Figure 9-19. *Creating the site*

   c. The remainder of the properties relate to the look and feel of the site and where it sits in relation to other SharePoint entities. Once you have entered the values, click the Create button.

7. Next, add the web part to the site. Click a site and take the following steps:

   a. Click Site Actions ➤ Edit Page.

   b. Click the Add Web Part button in the editable area.

   c. Under the Miscellaneous heading, the AdministrativeFunctions web part will be available. Click the check box next to it, and then click the Add button. The outcome should look similar to that shown in Figure 9-20.

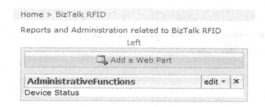

Figure 9-20. *Adding the web part to a site*

   d. Once the web part has been added, click the Exit Edit Mode link to return to the site's root.

8. With the web part deployed, you can modify the value of the configurable field (the IP—or namespace—of the BizTalk RFID host) by clicking the drop-down arrow on the right-hand side of the web part and selecting Modify Shared Web Part. The modification of the configurable field occurs in the properties of the web part, as shown in Figure 9-21.

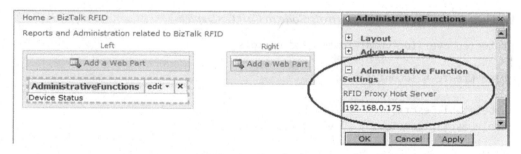

Figure 9-21. *Modifying the configurable host value*

9. The creation and deployment of the web part is complete. You can make updates to the web part and redeploy the assembly by copying to the same `bin` directory as before (`$\Inetpub\wwwroot\wss\VirtualDirectories\80\bin`) and refreshing the web page.

Extending the Web Part to Use the RFID Web Service Proxies

Now that the web part has been defined, it can be extended to call BizTalk RFID using the web service proxy assemblies. These assemblies can be added to the Visual Studio project and the methods can be called directly from the web part. The assemblies that need to be added are shown in Exercise 9-5. The code shown in Listing 9-4 contains a method that can be added to the web part code to return a list of devices that are available from BizTalk RFID.

Listing 9-4. *The GetDevices Method*

```
// returns a list of device names in a sorted ArrayList
public ArrayList GetDevices()
{
 ArrayList results = new ArrayList();
 DeviceManagerProxy proxy = new DeviceManagerProxy(rfidProxyHost);
 DeviceDefinition[] devices = proxy.GetAllDevices();

 for(int x=0; x<devices.Length; x++)
 {
  results.Add(devices[x].Name);
 }

 results.Sort();
 return results;
}
```

The GetDevices method can be called from CreateChildControls in the web part, and the results can be rendered in a drop-down. The code for this is shown in Listing 9-5.

Listing 9-5. *The CreateChildControls Code to Call GetDevices*

```
protected override void CreateChildControls()
{
 base.CreateChildControls();

 Label tableDescription = new Label();
 tableDescription.Text = "Devices Available: ";

 DropDownList deviceDropDown = new DropDownList();

 deviceDropDown.DataSource = GetDevices();
 deviceDropDown.DataBind();

 this.Controls.Add(tableDescription);
 this.Controls.Add(deviceDropDown);
}
```

Exercise 9-5. Using the BizTalk RFID Proxy Assemblies in a Web Part

This exercise demonstrates the steps needed to reference the BizTalk RFID web proxy assemblies and call them from the SharePoint web part built in Exercise 9-4.

1. Open the Visual Studio project created in Exercise 9-4.

2. In the project, add the following assemblies as references (see Figure 9-22). All of these are available in `$:\Program Files\Microsoft BizTalk RFID\bin`.

   a. `Microsoft.SharePoint.dll`: This assembly gives access to all of the SharePoint classes needed for a basic web part.

   b. `System.Web.dll`: This assembly will enable the inclusion of a configurable field in the web part settings within the SharePoint user environment.

   c. `Microsoft.RFID.Design.dll`: This assembly contains the classes that will be used in the administrative functions within the web part.

   d. `Microsoft.RFID.ManagementWebServiceProxies.dll`: This assembly allows for the remote interaction with the BizTalk RFID API.

   e. `Microsoft.RFID.SpiSdk.dll`: This assembly has a number of base classes needed by the other RFID assemblies.

   f. `Microsoft.RFID.Utl.dll`: This assembly has a number of base classes needed by the other RFID assemblies.

Figure 9-22. *Referencing the proxy assemblies in the web part project*

■**Note** Make sure all of the referenced `Microsoft.RFID` assemblies are deployed to the global assembly cache (GAC) or copied to the SharePoint `bin` folder. The web part will not execute properly if the assemblies cannot be found during runtime.

---

3. Add the following using directives to the web part for access to the proxy functionality:

    a. using Microsoft.SensorServices.Rfid.Management;

    b. using Microsoft.SensorServices.Rfid.Runtime;

    c. using System.IO.SensorServices.Rfid.Client;

    d. using Microsoft.SensorServices.Rfid;

    e. using Microsoft.SensorServices.Rfid.Design;

    f. using Microsoft.SensorServices.Rfid.Dspi;

4. To get a list of devices, add the method shown in Listing 9-4. To call this method, update the CreateChildControls method with the code shown in Listing 9-5.

5. Recompile and redeploy the web part assembly. The outcome should look like that shown in Figure 9-23.

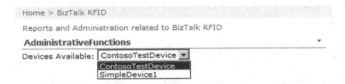

Figure 9-23. *The GetDevice result shown in the SharePoint web part*

Extending the Web Part to Use a Custom Web Service

With the assumption that the BizTalk RFID web service proxy classes are not an option for interacting with the host machine, the discussion will now turn to implementing an intermediary web service that will broker the calls. This allows all permissions to be handled by IIS, and the functionality of the RFID API to be available across distributed clients. This section will demonstrate how to create the web service and call the web service from the SharePoint web part created earlier in this chapter.

The code shown in Listing 9-6 is the complete code for the web service. It takes little more than referencing the BizTalk RFID assemblies and adding a web method to allow for the functionality needed. The steps in Exercise 9-6 outline how to call the web service from the SharePoint web part, instead of using the web service proxy assemblies.

Listing 9-6. *The Intermediary Web Service*

```
using System;
using System.Web;
using System.Web.Services;
using System.Web.Services.Protocols;
using System.Collections;
```

```
using Microsoft.SensorServices.Rfid.Management;
using Microsoft.SensorServices.Rfid.Runtime;
using System.IO.SensorServices.Rfid.Client;
using Microsoft.SensorServices.Rfid;
using Microsoft.SensorServices.Rfid.Design;
using Microsoft.SensorServices.Rfid.Dspi;

[WebService(Namespace = "http://tempuri.org/")]
[WebServiceBinding(ConformsTo = WsiProfiles.BasicProfile1_1)]
public class Service : System.Web.Services.WebService
{
 public Service () {}

 [WebMethod]
 public ArrayList GetDevices()
 {
  ArrayList results = new ArrayList();
  DeviceManagerProxy proxy = new DeviceManagerProxy("localhost");
  DeviceDefinition[] devices = proxy.GetAllDevices();

  for(int x=0; x<devices.Length; x++)
  {
   results.Add(devices[x].Name);
  }

  results.Sort();
  return results;
 }
}
```

Exercise 9-6. Calling a Custom RFID Web Service from the Web Part

This exercise demonstrates the steps needed to create a web service that references the BizTalk RFID web proxy assemblies and call this web service from the SharePoint web part built in Exercise 9-4.

1. Begin by creating a new web service project in Visual Studio.

2. Add the BizTalk RFID assembly references to the web service project as outlined in step 2 of Exercise 9-5.

3. Set the code of the web service to that shown in Listing 9-6.

4. Build the web service project and make sure that it can be accessed as a web service from IIS. This can most easily be done by opening IIS from Administrative Tools and configuring the directory to be an application (see Figure 9-24).

5. With the web service deployed, a reference can be made to it in the SharePoint web part project. To do this, right-click the References folder in Solution Explorer and select Add Web Reference. Add a reference to the new web service. The web service should appear as shown in Figure 9-25.

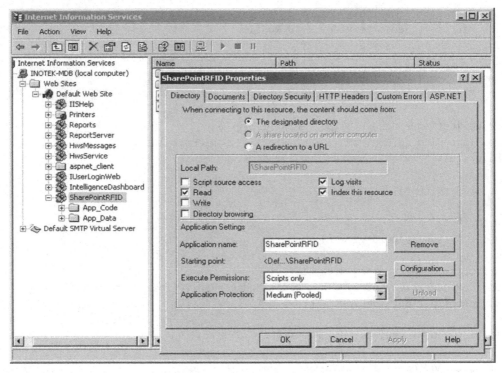

Figure 9-24. *Setting the web service properties in IIS*

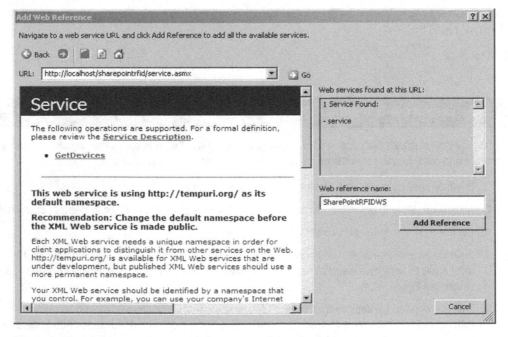

Figure 9-25. *Adding a reference to the new web method*

6. Update the code in the `CreateChildControls` method to call the web service. The code should look like that shown in Listing 9-7.

Listing 9-7. *The CreateChildControls Code to Call GetDevices in the Web Service*

```
protected override void CreateChildControls()
{
base.CreateChildControls();

Label tableDescription = new Label();
tableDescription.Text = "Devices Available: ";

DropDownList deviceDropDown = new DropDownList();

// instantiate the web service
SharePointRFIDWS.Service ws = new SharePointRFIDWS.Service();
ArrayList devices = new ArrayList(ws.GetDevices());

deviceDropDown.DataSource = devices;
deviceDropDown.DataBind();

this.Controls.Add(tableDescription);
this.Controls.Add(deviceDropDown);
}
```

7. Redeploy the web part and refresh the SharePoint web site. The drop-down should appear (exactly as it did before) as shown in Figure 9-23.

Conclusion

There are numerous ways to integrate systems throughout the enterprise and across networks. The intent of this chapter was to introduce two core approaches that would illustrate many of these methods. While SharePoint 2007 is a popular portal, and will likely be used in a number of BizTalk RFID implementations, we hope that you'll be able to extend the concepts to apply to your own situations. The most important concept to leave this chapter with is how to connect from remote systems to access the data needed. Some data is most easily accessed directly from SQL Server (especially in read-only types of implementations). Other information is better accessed via the BizTalk RFID API using the proxy assemblies (especially when enabling administrative read-write capabilities).

Remember that the initially obvious approach to integration is not always the most appropriate. Take time to think through the architecture and requirements, and make sure that the implementation being built today matches the short- and long-term needs of the solution at hand.

CASE STUDY: MONITORING INVENTORY THROUGH SHAREPOINT SERVER

Industry: Retail.

Overview: For one large retail music vendor, it was becoming apparent that CDs were being lost for a variety of reasons, including lost shipments from the warehouse, poor inventory management, and theft. By tagging each CD case with an RFID tag, inventory could be more closely monitored. The retailer then wanted to let specific retail outlets monitor their own merchandise. The data was being captured by BizTalk RFID and stored on a centralized server. The retailer moved to implement SharePoint 2007 to quickly deploy a solution that allowed different retailers access to view information that specifically related to them. This information included times of shipment, total number of items shipped, current expected inventory, and other appropriate metrics.

Results: The organization as a whole increased visibility into the entire inventory control process, and was better able to monitor what occurred during shipments. The different retail outlets were given far more insight into their expected inventory, and were better able to control costs around inventory management.

CHAPTER 10

■ ■ ■

Diagnostics and Troubleshooting

This chapter will cover the platform capabilities around diagnostics and troubleshooting, including performance monitor counters, Windows event logs, the logging infrastructure, and exception handling patterns. It will also cover best practices for logging from within your application code, as well as tips and tricks for troubleshooting common problems.

Setting the Stage: Tools and Techniques

Many of the diagnostic techniques described in this chapter require analyzing log files and Windows instrumentation. In order to efficiently access and analyze this information, appropriate tools are required. To set the stage for these efforts, several key tools, including PowerShell, Microsoft's new .NET-based scripting language, will be introduced and their basic operations explained.

Introducing PowerShell

Microsoft Windows PowerShell is Microsoft's next-generation command-line shell and scripting language, designed to help IT professionals streamline their lives. Based on .NET technology, PowerShell has become the de facto automation framework for Exchange Server 2007, and is poised become the go-to tooling for a host of other Windows server technologies (including IIS).

This section is not intended to make you an expert on PowerShell, but provide a gentle introduction to some canned commands that can simplify certain key diagnostic tasks. For more information on PowerShell and its capabilities, refer to *Pro Windows PowerShell*, by Hristo Deshev (Apress, 2008), and www.microsoft.com/windowsserver2003/technologies/management/powershell/default.mspx.

Downloading and Installing

To install PowerShell, follow these steps:

1. Browse to the PowerShell download URL, www.microsoft.com/windowsserver2003/technologies/management/powershell/download.mspx.

2. Download the appropriate installation file for your operating system (XP/Vista/Server 2003, and 32/64 bit).

3. Run the installation package.

Optionally, download and install the open source PowerShell GUI tool, PowerGUI, from http://powergui.org/index.jspa.

■**Note** PowerShell is included with Windows Server 2008 as an optional feature. To install PowerShell on Windows Server 2008, open the Server Manager (under Administrative Tools), click the Features node, and then click Add Features. From the Add Features Wizard, click the check box next to Windows PowerShell.

The Basics

PowerShell is sufficiently large and powerful to need its own series of books; the scope of Power-Shell content in this book is a simple introduction to performing some core tasks related to BizTalk RFID and to provide a starting point for your own exploration of using PowerShell for management tasks.

To start a PowerShell console, navigate to the Start menu (All Programs on Vista) ➤ Windows PowerShell 1.0, and click Windows PowerShell. This will open up what appears to be a familiar command-line prompt. Many of the familiar command-line operations, such as cd (change directory) and dir (list directory), work in a similar fashion in this new environment. Some of the key cmdlets (specialized classes in PowerShell that implement a particular operation) to get started with are shown in Table 10-1.

Table 10-1. *Using Basic PowerShell Cmdlets*

Command	Description	Example
cd	Changes directory; same effect as in cmd.exe	PS C:\> cd 'C:\Program Files\Microsoft BizTalk RFID' PS C:\Program Files\Microsoft BizTalk RFID>
dir	Lists directory contents; same effect as in cmd.exe	PS C:\> dir
type	Lists file contents; same effect as in cmd.exe	PS C:\Program Files\Microsoft BizTalk RFID\Logs> type RfidServices.log
more	Paginates contents of pipeline; same effect as in cmd.exe	PS C:\Program Files\Microsoft BizTalk RFID\Logs> type RfidServices.log | more
get-help	Prints out detailed help on any PowerShell command	PS C:\> get-help cd | more

Filtering Log Files

The primary use of PowerShell in these examples will be to capture, filter, and analyze information in the various log files. As detailed in a later section, the BizTalk RFID log files consist of data records in columns separated by | characters. The standard columns are thread ID, log level, timestamp, description, and component.

While basic text filtering is reasonably effective for extracting error information, tasks such as extracting all of the commands executed in a single thread require more finesse. Exercise 10-1 provides a walkthrough of using PowerShell to perform basic filtering on a log file, while Exercise 10-2 demonstrates how to use PowerShell to browse Windows Management Instrumentation (WMI) data.

Exercise 10-1. Filtering a Log File Using PowerShell

This exercise will demonstrate how to filter text from a log file using PowerShell, specifically extracting all of the error lines from a log file.

1. Start a PowerShell console by clicking Start ➤ All Programs ➤ Windows PowerShell 1.0 ➤ Windows PowerShell.

2. Change the working directory to the BizTalk RFID Services log file directory by entering the cd command shown here:

    ```
    PS C:\> cd 'C:\Program Files\Microsoft BizTalk RFID\Logs'
    PS C:\Program Files\Microsoft BizTalk RFID\Logs>
    ```

3. Type the following command into the PowerShell console. This will use the gc (an alias for Get-Content) cmdlet to pipe the contents of the RfidServices file into the Select-String cmdlet. The Select-String cmdlet will filter out any entries not containing the string Error.

    ```
    PS C:\Program Files\Microsoft BizTalk RFID\Logs> gc RfidServices.log |
        select-string "Error"
        11|   Error|110208 16:17:19|Unable to load provider - Symbol
    |[ProviderManager]
        11|   Error|110208 16:17:19| Unknown Exception Failed to start HTTP server.
    The requested context
    ```

■**Note** The sample output shown will look different on your machine, depending on the number of error records in the file. Other useful search strings are Info and Warning.

Browsing WMI

So far, there probably hasn't been any "wow" factor for the use of PowerShell. Browsing directories, listing the contents of files, and filtering text are reasonably basic operations with many different options for tools.

One of the key advantages to using PowerShell, as opposed to data source–specific tools, is its concept of *providers* (not to be confused with RFID device providers). In PowerShell, a provider is a browsable data source, such as the file system provider in the log filtering examples, or the WMI provider. The same filtering and sorting techniques used on the stream of text from a file may be used to manage WMI-related data.

This paradigm allows the WMI data store to be browsed and queried using the same commands and patterns. Compared to the arcane interface provided by some of the native WMI tools (such as WMIC—see http://msdn.microsoft.com/en-us/library/aa394531.aspx for more details), PowerShell provides an accessible path to the rich information contained within the WMI store.

WMI is arranged as a hierarchy of namespaces that contain a set of classes (which are typically either information sources or events). The scope of information available through WMI is staggering, and beyond the scope of this book.

Exercise 10-2. Browsing a WMI Namespace

This exercise will demonstrate how to list all of the available classes in the RFID WMI namespace using PowerShell.

1. Start a PowerShell console by clicking Start ➤ All Programs ➤ Windows PowerShell 1.0 ➤ Windows PowerShell.

2. Type the following command into the PowerShell console. This will use the Get-WmiObject command to retrieve the list of all classes under the root\Microsoft\Rfid namespace (the namespace where all of the RFID-related WMI classes and events live) and assign it to the $rfidClasses variable.

   ```
   PS C:\> $rfidClasses = Get-WmiObject -List -Namespace "root\Microsoft\Rfid"
   ```

3. Check the number of classes available in the RFID namespace by executing the following command; as shown in the output from the command, there are 110 items in the namespace.

   ```
   PS C:\> $rfidClasses.Count
   110
   ```

4. To see the complete list of available events, execute the following command. Note that the complete output from this command is not displayed.

   ```
   PS C:\> $rfidClasses
   ManagementEvent                           ServerManagementEvent
   ServerProviderManagementEvent         ProviderStartedEvent
   ProviderStoppedEvent                      ProcessManagementEvent
   ProcessDefinitionModifiedEvent        ProcessStoppedEvent
   ProcessBindingModifiedEvent            ExceptionInEventQueuerEvent
   ```

Capturing WMI Events

The previous section demonstrated how to enumerate the list of available events in the RFID WMI namespace. However, without a way to monitor and capture events, this rich source of diagnostic information cannot be leveraged.

There are a number of ways to accomplish this task, including .NET applications (well suited to formal monitoring applications) and PowerShell (more suited to ad hoc and exploratory work, as is common when tracking down issues). Exercise 10-3 demonstrates how to capture and display WMI events using a .NET console application.

Exercise 10-3. Capturing WMI Events Using a .NET Application

This exercise will demonstrate how to capture all of the RFID-related events from the WMI namespace using a .NET console application.

1. Start Visual Studio.NET 2008, and create a new C# console application named WmiListener.

2. Add the System.Management assembly to the reference list.

3. Add System.Management to the using list.

4. Add the code in Listing 10-1 to the Main function.

Listing 10-1. *Creating a WMI Query and Listening for WMI Events*

```
static void Main(string[] args)
{
    // Create an event query to capture all ManagementEvent events
    WqlEventQuery query = new WqlEventQuery(
        "SELECT * from ManagementEvent");

    // Within the root\Microsoft\Rfid namespace
    ManagementScope scope = new ManagementScope(
        @"root\Microsoft\Rfid");

    // Watch every 1 ms in this query and scope
    ManagementEventWatcher watcher = new ManagementEventWatcher(
        scope, query);
    EventWatcherOptions options = new EventWatcherOptions();
    options.Timeout = new TimeSpan(0, 0, 0, 0, 1);
    watcher.Options = options;

    // Route events to the watcher_EventArrived method
    watcher.EventArrived += new EventArrivedEventHandler(
        watcher_EventArrived);

    // Start listening for events
    watcher.Start();
```

```
        // Loop until the <Enter> key is pressed
        Console.WriteLine("Press the [Enter] key to exit the application");
        Console.ReadLine();

        watcher.Stop();
    }
```

5. Create a new method called `watcher_EventArrived` with the code shown in Listing 10-2.

Listing 10-2. *Processing WMI Events*

```
static void watcher_EventArrived(object sender,
    EventArrivedEventArgs e)
{
    Console.WriteLine("Event is " + e.NewEvent.ToString());
    Console.WriteLine("Event type is " +
        e.NewEvent.ClassPath.ToString());
    foreach (PropertyData o in e.NewEvent.SystemProperties)
    {
        Console.WriteLine("{0}:{1} ({2})", o.Name, o.Value, o.Type);
    }

    foreach (PropertyData o in e.NewEvent.Properties)
    {
        Console.WriteLine("{0}:{1} ({2})", o.Name, o.Value, o.Type);
    }
}
```

6. Run the application (press F5).

7. From RFID Manager, perform an operation that will trigger a management event (such as stopping a process). Listing 10-3 shows the output from this application when a `ProcessStoppedEvent` is received. Note the `ProcessName` property, which contains the information about which process was the source of the event.

Listing 10-3. *Result of Capturing and Displaying a ProcessStoppedEvent*

```
Press the [Enter] key to exit the application
Event is System.Management.ManagementBaseObject
Event type is ProcessStoppedEvent
__GENUS:2 (SInt32)
__CLASS:ProcessStoppedEvent (String)
__SUPERCLASS:ProcessManagementEvent (String)
__DYNASTY:__SystemClass (String)
__RELPATH: (String)
__PROPERTY_COUNT:8 (SInt32)
__DERIVATION:System.String[] (String)
__SERVER: (String)
```

```
    __NAMESPACE: (String)
    __PATH: (String)
    Description:This informational event is raised to notify that a process has
been
      stopped. (String)
    EventLevelId:1 (SInt32)
    EventTypeDescription:This informational event is raised to notify that a
process
      has been stopped. (String)
    EventTypeId:1000 (SInt32)
    OccuranceTime:633612541595756077 (SInt64)
    ProcessName:Testproc (String)
    SECURITY_DESCRIPTOR: (UInt8)
    TIME_CREATED:128701597595756077 (UInt64)
```

Browsing Performance Counters

BizTalk RFID uses a variety of performance counters to track key metrics related to performance, events, processes, and devices. Tables 10-2 and 10-3 provide a breakdown of the key performance counters in the RFID:Devices and RFID:Processes groups.

Table 10-2. *Performance Counters in the RFID:Devices Group*

Counter Name	Description
# of Errors Raised	The total number of errors raised by devices. This value can be monitored to analyze error trends.
# of Errors Raised/Sec	The rate at which errors are raised by devices. This value can be monitored to flag error rate spikes as an indication of serious system issues.
Downtime	The duration for which a device has been down after a connection error. This counter value is incremented while connection attempts are active, but before the device is switched into a disabled state. This value may be monitored to flag preemptive alerts for a device that is about to be switched over to a disabled state.
Tags Read/Sec	The rate at which tags are read by the device (or an aggregate across all devices). This is useful to monitor in scenarios with an expected tag read rate (such as a conveyor belt).
Tags Written/Sec	The rate at which tags are written by the device (or an aggregate across all devices). This is useful to monitor in scenarios with an expected tag write rate (such as an applicator on a conveyor belt).
Total Tags Read	The total number of tags read by the device (or an aggregate across all devices). This can be used to analyze traffic across devices and servers.
Total Tags Written	The total number of tags written by the device (or an aggregate across all devices). This can be used to analyze traffic across devices and servers.

Table 10-3. *Performance Counters in the RFID:Processes Group*

Counter Name	Description
Process Uptime	The amount of time elapsed since a process was successfully started. This value may be monitored to analyze if any processes are unexpectedly restarting or terminating.
Tags Being Processed	The number of tags currently flowing through the pipeline for a given process. This is a crucial metric in determining if the event handlers are not processing events quickly enough (and thus causing a backlog of events).
Tags In Queue	The number of tags waiting to be fed into a given RFID process. This is the other crucial metric in determining if the event handlers are not processing events quickly enough (and thus causing a backlog of events).
Tags Processed	The total number of tags processed by an RFID process. This value may be used to track the workload for a given RFID process.
Tags Suspended	The total number of tags that have been sent to the suspended queue (i.e., the tags that have caused processing failures). This is a vital metric to recognize error trends in processing events.

Exercise 10-4 provides a walkthrough of how to view the RFID process counters using Windows Performance Monitor.

Exercise 10-4. Viewing RFID Process Counters

This exercise will demonstrate how to view RFID related process counter information using Performance Monitor (perfmon).

1. From the Vista search bar or a console window, type **perfmon**, and then press Enter.

2. From the Reliability and Performance Monitor, select Monitoring Tools, and then Performance Monitor.

3. From the Performance Monitor, click the Add button (or press Ctrl+Shift+I) to bring up the Add Counters dialog, as shown in Figure 10-1.

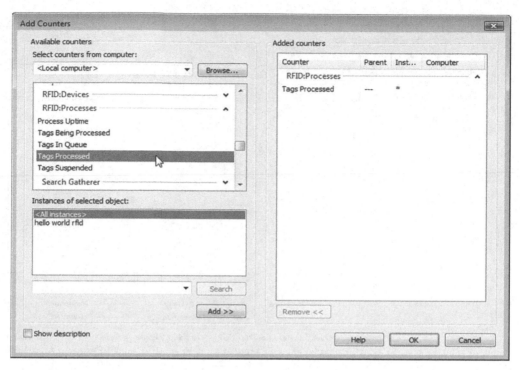

Figure 10-1. *The Add Counters dialog*

4. From the list of available counters, click the caret (^) to open the list of individual counters in the RFID:Processes group. Click the Tags Processed counter. Under the "Instances of selected object" list, click <All instances>. Click Add to add that list to the "Added counters" list.

5. After adding all of the counters you want to track, click OK.

6. Using any of the techniques you've learned throughout the course of this book, push some tags through any process (either with a real or simulated reader, or by using the View Tags ➤ Send Tags function from RFID Manager).

7. As tags are added to the process, the results should be reflected in the performance counter graph, as shown in Figure 10-2.

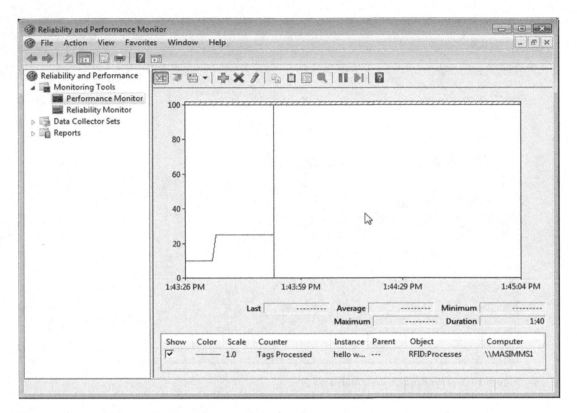

Figure 10-2. *Displaying the Tags Processed performance counter*

Tailing a Log File

Another important tool to have when developing or diagnosing issues with BizTalk RFID is one that allows you to view the contents of a log file as they appear (i.e., viewing the "tail" of the file). There are a number of utilities that provide this functionality; one that we have found to be very useful is BareTail, from Bare Metal Software (www.baremetalsoft.com/baretail/).

This utility (which comes in free and registered versions) provides several useful features, such as dynamic viewing of file contents, keyword highlighting, and the ability to view multiple files in a tabbed format. Since BizTalk RFID performs log file rotation during restart, the ability to automatically reopen a file is very useful (i.e., when the log file is rotated, open the new log file without requiring any user intervention). Figure 10-3 shows BareTail being used to trace the RfidServices log (the BizTalk RFID service log file) and a provider log, with error records highlighted in red.

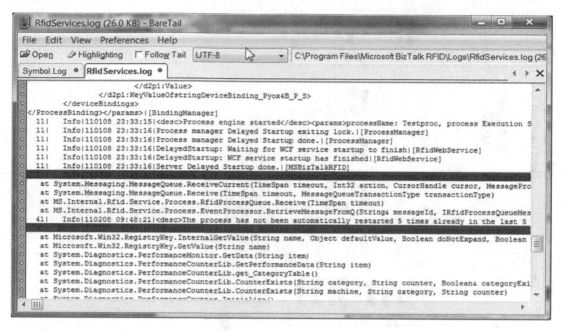

Figure 10-3. *Using BareTail to view server log files*

Peeking Inside a BizTalk RFID Application

BizTalk RFID applications have a lot of moving parts; both physical (readers, tags, assets, networking equipment, power) and virtual (providers, logical devices, processes). Trouble-shooting these systems can be challenging without knowing the available diagnostic tools and instrumentation, as well as how to approach troubleshooting in a consistent, methodical manner.

This section provides an overview of all of the available data-gathering points that allow you to get a glimpse of the inner workings of an RFID application running on top of BizTalk RFID. These information sources will be used in subsequent sections to track down and resolve issues in your applications.

As shown in Figure 10-4, there are many moving parts in a typical BizTalk RFID application, in addition to the management interfaces exposed by RFID Manager and rfidclientconsole.exe (as covered in Chapter 4), and the synchronous command API (as covered in Chapter 6).

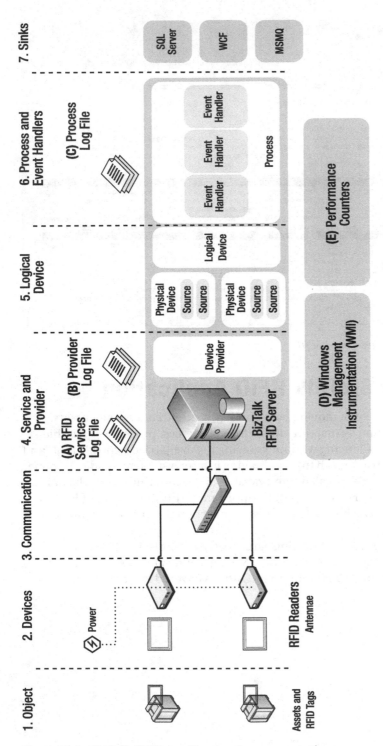

Figure 10-4. *BizTalk RFID application instrumentation*

The information available from each of these sources is described following.

BizTalk RFID Server Log Files

The BizTalk RFID Server log file (found in `BizTalk RFID Server\Logs\RfidServices.log`) is the primary source of information about the workings of the underlying RfidServices service. The logging level for the BizTalk RFID service may be adjusted between error, warning, info, and verbose, as demonstrated in Chapter 4 via RFID Manager.

For example, as shown in Figure 10-5, the services log directory contains the current `RfidServices.log` log file, as well as all of the previous provider log files. The provider log files are rotated when the service is restarted.

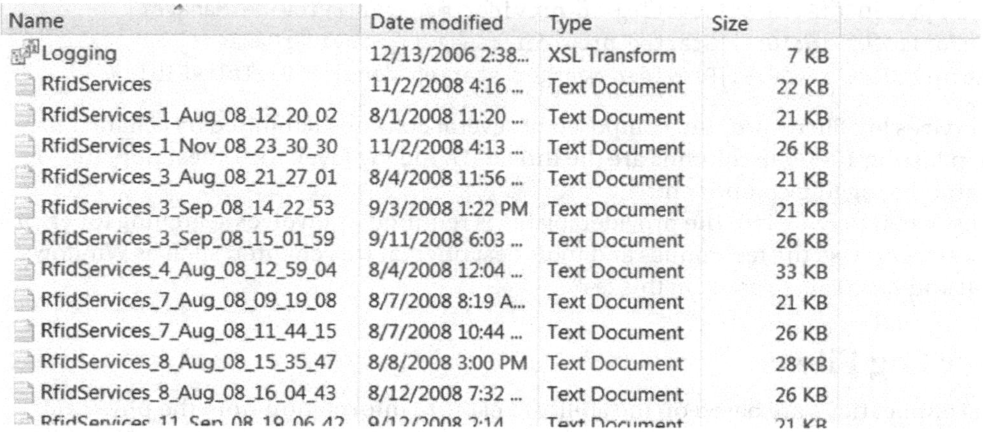

Name	Date modified	Type	Size
Logging	12/13/2006 2:38…	XSL Transform	7 KB
RfidServices	11/2/2008 4:16 …	Text Document	22 KB
RfidServices_1_Aug_08_12_20_02	8/1/2008 11:20 …	Text Document	21 KB
RfidServices_1_Nov_08_23_30_30	11/2/2008 4:13 …	Text Document	26 KB
RfidServices_3_Aug_08_21_27_01	8/4/2008 11:56 …	Text Document	21 KB
RfidServices_3_Sep_08_14_22_53	9/3/2008 1:22 PM	Text Document	21 KB
RfidServices_3_Sep_08_15_01_59	9/11/2008 6:03 …	Text Document	26 KB
RfidServices_4_Aug_08_12_59_04	8/4/2008 12:04 …	Text Document	33 KB
RfidServices_7_Aug_08_09_19_08	8/7/2008 8:19 A…	Text Document	21 KB
RfidServices_7_Aug_08_11_44_15	8/7/2008 10:44 …	Text Document	26 KB
RfidServices_8_Aug_08_15_35_47	8/8/2008 3:00 PM	Text Document	28 KB
RfidServices_8_Aug_08_16_04_43	8/12/2008 7:32 …	Text Document	26 KB
RfidServices_11_Sep_08_19_06_42	9/12/2008 2:14	Text Document	21 KB

Figure 10-5. *RFID service log files*

A snippet of the content of this sample services log is shown in Listing 10-4. Therein you can see a snippet of the standard startup sequence.

Listing 10-4. *Snippet of a Sample Services Log*

```
4|   Info|110208 16:16:44|Server Info:
BANNER
SERVER NAME: MASIMMS1
SERVER VERSION: 3.6.0.0
SERVER LOCATION: C:\Program Files\Microsoft BizTalk RFID\bin\RfidServices.exe
FILE VERSION: 3.6.5022.0
OS VERSION: Microsoft Windows NT 6.0.6001 Service Pack 1
NT PROCESS ID: 3340
SERVICE ACCOUNT: MASIMMS1\RfidSvcAcc
STORE LOCATION: MASIMMS1
STORE NAME: RFIDSTORE
|[MSBizTalkRFID]
    4|   Info|110208 16:16:45|Got store Info: RFIDSTORE status: 65536 status2:
1627389952|[MSBizTalkRFID]
```

```
   4|    Info|110208 16:16:50|SKU information: Type=Developer,
MaxDeviceCount=-1|[MSBizTalkRFID]
   4|    Info|110208 16:16:50|SKU information: IsClusteringSupported=True,
IsMachinePartOfCluster=False|[MSBizTalkRFID]
   4|    Info|110208 16:16:50|SKU: The expiry date in the registry (as a string)
is -1|[MSBizTalkRFID]
   4|    Info|110208 16:16:50|SKU: This SKU has no expiry date|[MSBizTalkRFID]
   4|    Info|110208 16:16:50|Using data dir C:\Program Files\
Microsoft BizTalk RFID\|[MSBizTalkRFID]
   4|    Info|110208 16:16:50|Resource Manager Startup done|[MSBizTalkRFID]
   4|    Info|110208 16:16:50|Component Manager Startup done|[MSBizTalkRFID]
   4|    Info|110208 16:16:50|Starting up security manager|[SecurityManager]
   4|    Info|110208 16:16:50|Starting up provider manager|[ProviderManager]
   4|    Info|110208 16:16:51|Started provider manager|[ProviderManager]
   4|    Info|110208 16:16:51|Provider manager startup done|[MSBizTalkRFID]
```

The services log file records are composed of several columns delimited by | characters. As shown in Listing 10-4, the columns are the thread ID, the log level, the timestamp, the log message, and the logging component.

Usually, when delving into the provider log file is required, it involves searching for error codes or messages. Use the techniques and tools described in this chapter, such as Windows PowerShell and BareTail, to assist in this task.

Provider Log Files

As all RFID applications are based on the ability to capture information from the physical world via RFID readers and tags, the ability to connect to these devices and receive data is critical to every RFID system. Each registered provider on a BizTalk RFID server has its own log file. (Even if two copies of the same provider are registered, each will have its own log file.) The logging level for each provider may be individually adjusted between error, warning, info, and verbose, as demonstrated in Exercise 4-3 via RFID Manager.

Each vendor has complete control over the information written in the provider log file, including how much information is written at each logging level. These files typically contain information about DSPI layer calls made into the provider for a given reader.

■Note All readers running on a specific provider will write into a single log file. The reader name will be one of the header columns for each log file entry.

These log files are found in the BizTalk RFID\Providers*Provider Name**Provider Name*.log directory. For example, as shown in Figure 10-6, the LLRP provider directory contains the current LLRP.log log file, as well as all of the previous provider log files. The provider log files are rotated when the provider (or service) is restarted.

Name	Date modified	Type	Size
bin	10/20/2008 11:5...	File Folder	
global	5/2/2007 11:09 ...	ASP.NET Serve...	3 KB
LLRP	11/2/2008 4:17 ...	Text Document	2 KB
LLRP_1_Nov_08_23_...	11/2/2008 4:13 ...	Text Document	2 KB
LLRP_20_Oct_08_12_...	10/20/2008 11:5...	Text Document	2 KB
LLRP_21_Oct_08_22_...	10/21/2008 9:01...	Text Document	2 KB
LLRP_22_Oct_08_20_...	10/26/2008 2:06...	Text Document	2 KB
LLRP_26_Oct_08_10_...	10/26/2008 9:12...	Text Document	2 KB
LLRP_26_Oct_08_19_...	10/28/2008 2:07...	Text Document	2 KB
LLRP_28_Oct_08_08_...	10/30/2008 4:32...	Text Document	2 KB
LLRP_30_Oct_08_17_...	11/1/2008 10:26...	Text Document	2 KB
web	6/11/2007 11:10...	XML Configur...	6 KB

Figure 10-6. *Provider log file list*

A snippet of the content of this sample provider log is shown in Listing 10-5. Therein you can see a sequence of commands executed against a particular reader.

Listing 10-5. *Snippet of a Sample Provider Log*

```
18|    Info|110208 16:17:24|Server Info:
BANNER
SERVER NAME: MASIMMS1
SERVER VERSION: 3.6.0.0
SERVER LOCATION: C:\Windows\assembly\GAC_MSIL\Microsoft.Rfid.Util\
3.6.0.0__31bf3856ad364e35\Microsoft.Rfid.Util.dll
NT PROCESS ID: 3340
SERVICE ACCOUNT: MASIMMS1\RfidSvcAcc|[LLRP]
   18|    Info|110208 16:17:24|LogLevel: Info|[LLRP]
   18|    Info|110208 16:17:41|About to start dedicated thread
GetProviderMetadata13|[LLRP]
   13|    Info|110208 16:17:42|DedicThr About to invoke GetProviderMetadata|[LLRP]
   13|    Info|110208 16:17:47|DedicThr Finished invoke GetProviderMetadata|[LLRP]
   18|    Info|110208 16:17:47|Successfully regained control from dedicated thread
GetProviderMetadata13|[LLRP]
    3|    Info|110208 16:17:47|LLRP being intialized|[LLRP]
    3|    Info|110208 16:17:51|Using port 5084 to listen for incoming Llrp connection
|[LLRP]
    3|    Info|110208 16:17:51|Supports IPv4 for listening connection|[LLRP]
    3|    Info|110208 16:17:51|Supports IPv6 for listening connection|[LLRP]
    3|    Info|110208 16:17:52|Found a unicast IPv4 addresses adapter name:Wireless
Network Connection. Address:192.168.1.2|[LLRP]
    3|    Info|110208 16:17:52|Found IPv4 adapter, that is up and supports multicast.
```

```
adapter name:Wireless Network Connection, index:33663168|[LLRP]
    3|    Info|110208 16:17:52|Number of relevant NICs found:1|[LLRP]
    3|    Info|110208 16:17:52|selectedAdapterId:{F1BBA902-024B-44C6-AFA2-
AACAE9B56A8A}|[LLRP]
   15|    Info|110208 16:18:02|Starting the WS-Discovery|[LLRP]
```

The provider log file records are composed of several columns delimited by | characters. As shown in Listing 10-5, the columns are thread ID, log level, timestamp, log message, and logging component (in this case, the name of the provider).

Process Log Files (Event Handlers)

The third key log file when performing diagnostics on a BizTalk RFID application is the process log file, found in BizTalk RFID\Processes*Process Name**Process Name*.log. As with the other log files, the file contents are rotated when the process (or service) is restarted. The logging level for each process may be individually adjusted between error, warning, info, and verbose via RFID Manager in a fashion similar to changing a provider's logging level.

The contents of these process files are an aggregate of the logging output from each of the event handlers registered in the process. Since multiple instances of the event handlers in a given process may be running in parallel, strictly looking at the log file in temporal order may be confusing (especially in higher-volume scenarios). In these cases, it may be useful to filter by thread ID when tracing the path of a specific event through a process.

Listing 10-6 provides a snippet of the content of a process log, showing the output from the SqlServerSink component. Of particular note are the bolded lines in the log file, showing the received tag ID and data.

Listing 10-6. *Snippet of a Sample Verbose Process Log Using the SqlServerSink Component*

```
    1|Verbose|110308 13:52:17|PostEventToSink called with
<tag>
  <rfidEventBase>
    <VendorSpecificInformation>
      <properties></properties>
    </VendorSpecificInformation>
  </rfidEventBase>
  <observation>
    <time>11/3/2008 1:52:17 PM</time>
    <sourceName></sourceName>
    <deviceName>West Door</deviceName>
  </observation>
```

```
    <tagId>g4k=</tagId>
    <tagType>EPC Class 0 tag</tagType>
    <tagData>q82DiQ==</tagData>
    <tagSource></tagSource>
    <tagTime>11/3/2008 1:52:17 PM</tagTime>
    <dataSelector>
      <tagDataSelector>
        <isId>True</isId>
        <isData>True</isData>
        <isType>True</isType>
        <isTime>True</isTime>
        <isNumberingSystemIdentifier>True
        </isNumberingSystemIdentifier>
      </tagDataSelector>
    </dataSelector>
  </tag>|[SqlServerSink]
|[SqlServerSink]
    1|Verbose|110308 13:52:17|Executing command PostTagReadEvent
Parameters
Name @tagID Value System.Byte[] Dir Input
Name @tagType Value 1 Dir Input
Name @tagTypeDescription Value EPC Class 0 tag Dir Input
Name @tagSource Value  Dir Input
Name @tagTime Value 11/3/2008 1:52:17 PM Dir Input
Name @tagData Value System.Byte[] Dir Input
Name @processName Value Test Dir Input
Name @deviceName Value West Door Dir Input
Name @logicalDeviceName Value West Door Dir Input
Name @extData Value
 <VendorSpecificInformation
     xmlns:i="http://www.w3.org/2001/XMLSchema-instance" xmlns="http://schemas.dataco
System.IO.SensorServices.Rfid.Client">
     dictionary xmlns:d2p1="http://schemas.microsoft.com/2003/10/
  Serialization/Arrays" />
</VendorSpecificInformation> Dir Input
 |[SqlServerSink]
    1|Verbose|110308 13:52:17|Removing item 7563067 from the processEventFTQ q|[Test]
```

> **■Note** One practical impact of enabling verbose logging on a process is that the volume of information logged can become very large very quickly. This can have substantial performance implications, especially in low-latency applications.

WMI for RFID

BizTalk RFID–related management events and information live in the `\root\Microsoft\Rfid` namespace within WMI. This management space contains a number of different events that are raised when the triggering BizTalk RFID event is raised, either through a provider or the server itself. Similar to how data-related events are surfaced and channeled through event handlers in processes, management events are surfaced through the WMI channel.

> **■Note** Some events are available through both channels; however, event handlers are primarily focused on data-related events in the context of a business process, as opposed to managing a server.

Troubleshooting BizTalk RFID

Since there are so many moving parts in an average RFID system, a methodical or component-centric approach is often helpful in ruling out the usual suspects. While many of the checklists in the following sections may seem terribly obvious, it has been our (sometimes painfully gained) experience that the simplest and most obvious assumptions often cause the most pain.

One other observation you might draw from these checklists is that certain symptoms may be a factor of any number of root causes. The checklists are broken down as shown in Figure 10-7.

> **■Note** If you had to pick one thing to remember from this book, remember this: always test your application with real readers, real tags, and real assets in as close to a real environment as you can. All of the bench-top testing with simulators and software can test how the logic of your application will behave. It *cannot* tell you how your readers will perform on site with noise, dust, and errant forklifts. All of the software in the world cannot help if the readers don't read in the real world.

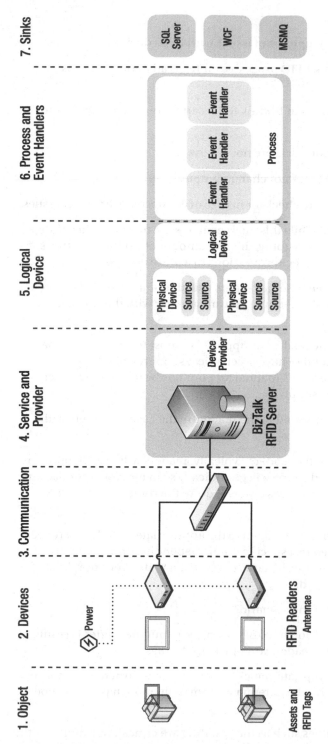

Figure 10-7. *Functional components of an RFID system*

RFID Devices

The following list details some common symptoms of issues with RFID devices:

- Tag reads are not received in BizTalk RFID processes, or tag read performance is inconsistent.

- Processes or synchronous applications in BizTalk RFID cannot open connections to registered readers.

- Input events, such as breaking a light stack, are not received.

- Output changes, such as light stacks, are not changing state.

The following list outlines some things to check for in case of connectivity or device issues:

- Is the RFID reader receiving power? While this may seem like the most obvious of steps, if the readers don't have a stable power supply, then no amount of troubleshooting software will result in a working system. Specific questions to ask are as follows:

  - Is the status LED of the reader green? Some readers use different LEDs and different light codes to indicate their state—make sure you are familiar with the specifics of your chosen readers.

  - Is the power supply secured to the reader? As opposed to most forms of consumer electronics, fixed RFID readers tend to have mechanical supports for the power supply. Be sure to review the operator's manual for your hardware for the proper method of connecting the power supply.

- Are the antenna cables properly connected to the reader (in the case of readers with external antennae)?

  - Are the antenna ports enabled on the reader? Typically, readers will disable ports to which antennae are not connected. Some will periodically scan for new antennae and reenable the ports automatically, whereas others require the ports to be manually enabled.

  - Are the correct number of antennae connected to the appropriate ports? Most readers require antennae to be connected in a specific order. Depending on whether the antennae configuration is monostatic, bistatic, or multistatic, different numbers of antennae may need to be connected.

- Is the reader properly configured for the scenario?

  - Is the correct protocol enabled? If you have EPC Gen 2 tags but the reader is configured for older UHF protocols, the reader won't pick up the tags.

  - Is the antenna gain set to an appropriate value? If the antenna is turned down too low (or the attenuation is set too high), the antenna will not emit enough power to energize tags.

  - For EPC Gen 2 scenarios, key values such as the Q setting are critical. Be familiar with how the various configuration settings for your particular reader affect read performance.

- Are the digital I/O ports properly wired, powered, and grounded?

  - Some readers require that the digital I/O ports be supplied with an independent power source. Make sure this source is properly wired and connected.

  - Use a meter (such as a multimeter or oscilloscope) to determine if the output ports are changing state (i.e., do not depend on the light stack—it may be nonfunctional).

  - If using a switch to test the input port trigger, ensure it is properly grounded to the same ground plane as the I/O ports.

Tags and Objects

After verifying that the reader is powered, the antennae are properly connected, and the reader is properly configured for your tag type and scenario, the next issue sources to investigate are the tags and tagged objects themselves.

Here are some common symptoms of issues with tags and tagged objects:

- Tag reads are not received in BizTalk RFID processes, or tag read performance is inconsistent.

- Writing to tags (commissioning) fails or is inconsistent.

And here are some things to check for:

- Can the RFID reader read the tags in "free space"?

  - When holding an RFID tag up to the antenna to check to see if it can be read, be sure not to hold onto the antenna directly. If you do, your body becomes part of the antenna (in an electromagnetic sense) and can soak up the energy that would be used to power the tag.

  - If the tag cannot be read in free space, make sure the reader is properly configured (as per the previous section) and the tag itself is valid (either by validating on another reader or using a larger set of test tags).

- Are the tags properly aligned in the read field of the antenna?

  - When working with linear antennae (either horizontal or vertically aligned), if the tags are passing through in a perpendicular manner, they won't receive enough RF to energize. If your scenario has tags passing through in an inconsistent orientation, switch to using circular antennae.

  - Is *tag shadowing* occurring? If you have multiple tags passing through the read field simultaneously but you only see some of the tags, it may be a result of shadowing. Shadowing refers to the situation wherein two adjacent tags are either touching or close enough for their antennae to "meld." If this is the case, change the orientation and application of the tags to prevent tags from butting up against each other. This issue is common in pallets with stacked boxes.

- Is the material or content of the tagged object interfering with the tag?

  - A common result of tagging objects containing metal or water, these materials can detune the tag's antenna or absorb the RF energy needed by the tag.

  - If tags can be read in free space but a drastic performance drop is observed when the tag is applied to the asset, experiment with alternate placement on the object (look for air pockets and other areas on the object that may have a lower water or metal content) or investigate the use of tags with special encapsulations designed for such applications.

Communication

Assuming that the readers are properly reading tags, the next step in the chain is to confirm that there is a valid communication path between the BizTalk RFID server and the reader. Most of this section assumes Ethernet and IP, with special notes for USB and Bluetooth connections.

The following are some common symptoms of issues with communication:

- Applications can execute synchronous commands through BizTalk RFID, but RFID processes do not receive tag read events.

- Processes or synchronous applications in BizTalk RFID cannot open connections to registered readers.

Here are some things to check for:

- For an Ethernet interface, is the link valid? Check the hub and the cable to ensure that the link is active.

- If the RFID reader is using DHCP to receive its address (*not* recommended without a static lease), does it have the expected address, net mask, and gateway? Most fixed readers support a serial connection—if you cannot get into the reader's network management console, use the serial console to double-check network settings.

- Can the RFID reader receive a ping from the BizTalk RFID server? Can a telnet connection to port 80 be established (assuming the reader supports an HTTP management interface)?

  - If a connection cannot be established, check the appropriate routing tables between the BizTalk RFID server and the RFID device.

  - If a connection cannot be established, check the firewall on the BizTalk RFID server.

  - If a connection can be established, but no events are received in an RFID process, check the firewall on the BizTalk RFID server. Most RFID readers use a separate notification channel that pushes events into the BizTalk RFID server.

Note Most fixed RFID readers support an RS232 (serial) connection. While this may seem like an old-school throwback, it is often the first and best available option for troubleshooting network connectivity issues. From the serial interface, most readers will allow configuration of the network settings (DHCP, static) as well as the ability to view low-level reader diagnostics.

Service and Providers

After having confirmed that the reader side of the system is working correctly (readers are available and tags are being read), the next step is to confirm that the BizTalk RFID service and connectivity layer are functioning correctly.

Here are some common symptoms of issues with services and providers:

- In the RFID Manager MMC snap-in, no connection can be established to the target BizTalk RFID service.

- The connection to the reader fails during initial setup in RFID Manager.

- The service is running, but providers or processes start up and immediately shut down.

Here are some common things to check for:

- If the BizTalk RFID service isn't running, start it either from Administrative Tools ➤ Services, or by right-clicking the machine name in RFID Manager.

  - Information about service failure on startup will be in the event log and the RFID Services log.

- If you have verified network connectivity with the reader but cannot connect through BizTalk RFID, then the provider/reader firmware may not be compatible.

  - Check the provider installation documents to ensure that your firmware version is compatible with the provider version.

  - Download and install new versions of the provider and/or firmware if necessary.

  - An excellent resource to inquire about hardware- and provider-related issues is the MSDN forum for BizTalk RFID (http://social.msdn.microsoft.com/forums/en-US/biztalkrfid/threads/).

- One of the specific challenges that can arise is on Windows Server 2003 installations, in which IIS acts as the isolated process host. In some situations (especially on shared boxes with other IIS-hosted applications), the application pool that supports BizTalk RFID may be corrupted or changed. One of the key symptoms of this is that the bits hosted in IIS (the processes and providers) start up, but immediately shut down again. To diagnose if IIS changes are related to weirdness in the BizTalk RFID application, look at the IIS version log to determine if any recent changes have been made. To enable configuration change versioning (formally known as metabase auditing) on IIS 6.0 or greater, please consult the IIS documentation.

■**Note** One practical result of the dependency on IIS is that backing up the IIS metadata store is an important part of backing up your BizTalk RFID configuration. Especially when working in a shared server environment with other administrators in which users have access rights to the IIS server, ensure that the IIS metabase and application pool settings are not corrupted.

Logical Devices and Process Binding

At this point, we have validated that the readers are reading and connected to BizTalk RFID. Logical readers are used to create logical groupings of information sources that are abstracted from the physical readers and antennae. Used properly, logical devices are a powerful tool for mapping event sources into processes and creating metadata based on that association (such as a location or portal).

However, if the appropriate sources or devices are not properly bound to the target RFID process, events (e.g., `TagReadEvent` and `TagListEvent`) will not show up in said process. Some common symptoms of issues with logical devices and binding are as follows:

- Tag read events are visible from the View Tags dialog, but are not processed by your event handlers.

- Given a reader with two antennae bound to an RFID process, tag read events from one antenna are received, but not the other.

Here are some things to check for:

- If using a hard link, are the sources explicitly bound to the process?

    - Open up the process definition in RFID Manager and examine each logical device.

    - Verify that the individual sources are hard-linked into at least one of the logical devices.

Event Handlers

At this point, events are flowing through into your process and being picked up by the event handler. However, the event handlers do not appear to be processing, filtering, enriching, or posting to sinks properly. At this point, be happy—it's a software problem. Here are some common symptoms of issues with logical devices and binding:

- Events are flowing into a process, but are not properly filtered (all tags are filtered, the wrong tags are filtered, etc.).

- For the stock `SqlServerSink` event handler, events are not being posted to the rfidsink database.

- The process starts up, but shuts down with an exception message in the process error log.

- For custom event handlers, the event handler code never seems to trigger.

Here are some things to check for:

- Event handlers deemed "sinks" are intended to be the end of the line for events; that is, they do not pass events on to the next handler in the chain. If you have a component that is not receiving any events, make sure that it is not chained after a sink.

- The OOB event handler `SqlServerSink` is the usual suspect of sinks in most applications. It's a very robust event handler, but there are a couple of things to watch out for:

  - The `SqlServerSink` event handler creates the rfidsink database. This means that the RfidSvcAcc account (or the hosting process account identity) needs to have sufficient privileges in the target database to create the database, establish the schema, and so on.

  - If portions of the incoming tags are invalid (such as an empty `DateTime` field or a value of `DateTime.MinValue`), the `SqlServerSink` event handler will throw an unhandled exception and kill the process.

- When developing custom sinks, there are a couple of important considerations, especially if you aren't seeing events show up:

  - The most efficient way to debug an event handler during development is to attach the Visual Studio debugger. On Windows XP/Vista machines, this is fairly simple (attach to `RfidServices.exe`); however, on Windows Server 2003 machines, the process name can be somewhat difficult to track down.

  - The best way to handle this is to embed a `Debugger.Launch()` statement within the `Init` method of your event handler (*only* during development).

  - Ensure that you have event handler methods assigned to each of the appropriate event types you want to capture (`TagListEvent`, `TagReadEvent[]`, etc.).

  - When filtering tags, remember that the event collections you receive cannot be directly edited. You need to create a new collection, add in the tags you want to keep, and pass the new collection along the pipeline.

  - Logging is the lifeblood and dynamic savior of your event handler. If the event handler takes an action that would be a valuable diagnostic tool in the field, log it.

- The only exceptions that an event handler is allowed to throw are those derived from `RfidException`. Exceptions not deriving from `RfidException` that are uncaught and bubble up to the service will cause the process to be shut down.

  - When calling into other pieces of code, ensure that all exceptions are caught and rethrown wrapped in an `RfidException`.

- The event handlers are running with the identity of the hosting account (usually RfidSvcAcc). When making calls to external services or data stores (such as SQL, MSMQ, WCF, etc.), the privileges that the event handler has while running are different from those that your development account has during testing.

  - Ensure that the RFID process account has all of the requisite permissions to access external services and data stores. This is a very common source of security and permissions issues.

- Event handlers are inherently multithreaded (i.e., multiple instances of the event handler run in parallel to improve throughput). If the event handler uses any shared resources (such as a tag table), make these resources thread safe through a `Monitor` or other synchronization object.

Sinks and External Applications

By this point, all of the RFID-specific aspects of your application should be working. However, until events can be reliably delivered to external systems, the application isn't truly complete. Most of the issues encountered when posting data to external applications are security- or connectivity-related. Here are some common symptoms of issues with logical devices and binding:

- Events are flowing into a process, but do not show up in a target MSMQ queue.

  - This is either a formatting or a permissions issue. By default, when an MSMQ queue is created, permissions need to be explicitly added. Ensure that the RfidSvcAcc account is added with write permission.

- Events are flowing into a process but do not show up in a target SQL table.

  - Ensure that either the RfidSvcAcc account has the appropriate privileges in the target table (for Windows authentication in the connection string) or the connection string contains the correct embedded user authentication.

  - Ensure that the SQL commands are valid.

Conclusion

Diagnosing issues in a BizTalk RFID application can be potentially overwhelming. However, by breaking down the system into its components and isolating issues, the complexity can be managed and overcome.

Always test in as real an environment as possible before going live—this means real hardware, real tags, real objects, and as real a physical environment as possible. RFID applications aren't just software projects—the "physics" side of RFID can sink any project if due care and attention are not given.

In any troubleshooting scenario, always remember these basic principles:

- Challenge every assumption. Continually question what you know and how you know it. Positive thinking, such as "of course that outlet has power," may help you feel better about the situation, but it won't get you any further toward resolving the problem.

- Start with the basics, work from the tags out, and independently verify each link in the chain. Validate that readers can see tags, readers can communicate with middleware, and middleware can process events.

- Use the right tool for the job. Each of the links in the RFID application chain have hooks for observing and validating their behavior. Use the hook—be it a log file, interactive RFID reader console, or network trace—that provides the highest amount of information for the least amount of noise.

The techniques and processes demonstrated in this chapter are an excellent starting point in identifying, understanding, and resolving issues with RFID applications.

Through the course of this book, you have learned how to develop, deploy, and diagnose an end-to-end RFID-enabled distributed system. Take this new knowledge and go forth into this untamed vastness, bringing the order of asset visibility where now lies only the chaos of clipboards!

All melodrama aside, you should now have a solid foundation for implementing real-world asset visibility applications using RFID on the BizTalk Server platform. Put this knowledge to work developing applications that bridge the digital and physical worlds. For more information about RFID and BizTalk Server, visit the BizTalk Server Developer Center on MSDN at `http://msdn.microsoft.com/en-us/biztalk/default.aspx`.

CASE STUDY: TRACING FISH FROM THE CRADLE TO THE OVEN

Industry: Fishing.

Overview: An Asian fish producer uses BizTalk RFID to track fish from the hatchery, through the sales channel, to the end customer. Additionally, it tracks core information pertaining to the life cycle and environment of the fish itself. An RFID tag is embedded on the fish while alive, and travels with it during its life, through the time it is caught, up until the delivery to the purchasing distributor or restaurant. Key environment variables are tracked, including water temperature, chemical content of the water, air temperatures, and feeding history. All of this information is available through a reporting dashboard that enables all parties involved to have insight into all available details about the individually purchased fish.

Results: Having detailed information about the individual fish allows for a greater price margin to be placed on it, especially for high-end lines. End customers, who value specific traits in what they are about to digest, are inclined to pay a premium for fish that are of a specific quality with a known history. Additionally, having the ability to track the fish from the hatchery to the end destination ensures improved efficiencies in handling, distribution, and delivery.

CHAPTER 11

■ ■ ■

Enterprise Planning and Deployment

Now that you have finished the process of designing, developing, and debugging your RFID application, it is time to deploy it to production. In this chapter, we cover the crucial task of moving an RFID business process from a development environment to a staging server or a production machine. The chapter will focus on enterprise deployment scenarios, including centralized provisioning, monitoring, and high availability. Many of the topics listed here are relevant only after you have reached a certain critical mass in terms of the number of instances installed in your enterprise, but it is good to know the enterprise scalability features that exist in the base product, if and when you have to deploy large numbers of servers.

From Development to Production

To move your RFID business process from development to production, you have to perform the following steps:

1. Exporting the XML definition for the RFID business process from the development machine. You can do this from RFID Manager or the command-line console.

2. Copying the assemblies from the development machine to the production machine. The assemblies need to be in the %RFIDDATADIR%"\Processes\[ProcessName]\bin directory on the target machine.

■**Note** The `rfidclientconsole.exe` tool contains a command called `CopyProcessFile` that can be used to copy files to the `bin` directory for a process. To use this command, you need to run the `rfidclientconsole.exe` program on the same machine that the BizTalk RFID server is running on.

---

3. Moving over any application-level configuration settings by copying the `Web.config` file from the RFID process runtime directory.

4. If your business process uses business rules, exporting the rules from the development machine.

5. Any additional steps that are required by your event handler, including creating database objects or installing other components that your application depends on, including business rules, if you are using the BRE.

■**Note** If you need to export BRE artifacts from the development system, use the command-line utility sample that is on the BizTalk RFID CD.

---

6. Creating the correct devices and device groups. If your production devices and device groups have different names from the development machine, you have to rebind the process on the production machine.

7. Importing the process definition into the target machine.

Exercise 11-1 illustrates how to export an RFID process definition.

Exercise 11-1. Exporting an RFID Business Process Definition

This exercise will demonstrate how to export an RFID process definition.

1. From RFID Manager, use the Export option on the Processes node to identify and export the process to an XML file. Figure 11-1 shows the Export option on the context menu.

2. Next, make sure that the Export Bindings check box is checked (see Figure 11-2). This ensures that both the process structure and the process bindings are exported. The process bindings contain the current values for all the event handler parameters, as well as the bindings from the logical devices to the physical devices. It is a good idea to always export both pieces. You can decide later whether you are going to import both processes and bindings, or just the process definition. Figure 11-3 shows an example of an exported file.

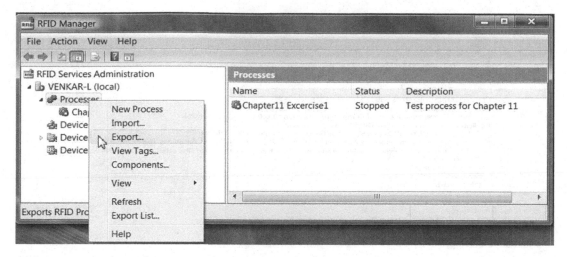

Figure 11-1. *Exporting the process definition*

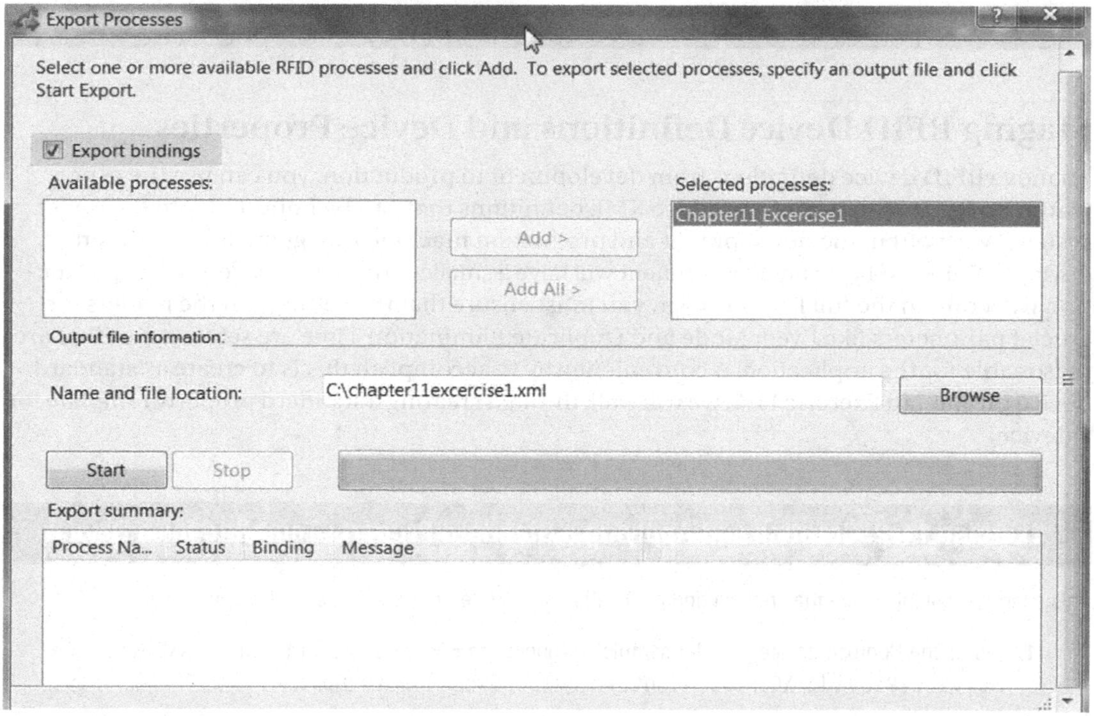

Figure 11-2. *The Export Processes dialog*

```
- <ArrayOfProcessComplete xmlns:i="http://www.w3.org/2001/XMLSchema-instance"
    xmlns="http://schemas.datacontract.org/2004/07/MS.Internal.Rfid.ClientUtilities">
  - <ProcessComplete>
    + <m_processBinding xmlns:d3p1="http://schemas.datacontract.org/2004/07/Microsoft.SensorServices.Rfid.Design">
    - <m_rfidProcess xmlns:d3p1="http://schemas.datacontract.org/2004/07/Microsoft.SensorServices.Rfid.Design">
        <d3p1:description>Test process for Chapter 11</d3p1:description>
      - <d3p1:logicalSource>
        - <d3p1:componentList>
          - <d3p1:EventHandlerDefinition>
              <d3p1:componentName>store in db</d3p1:componentName>
            - <d3p1:eventHandlerInfo>
                <d3p1:assembly>Microsoft.Rfid.OobComponents, Version=3.6.0.0, Culture=neutral,
                    PublicKeyToken=31bf3856ad364e35</d3p1:assembly>
                <d3p1:className>Microsoft.SensorServices.Rfid.ProcessComponents.SqlServerSink</d3p1:className>
                <d3p1:description>This component writes event data to a Microsoft SQL Server database. The location of the database
                    is specified by using the event handler parameters. For information about the sink schema, see the Microsoft BizTalk
                    RFID documentation.</d3p1:description>
              </d3p1:eventHandlerInfo>
            </d3p1:EventHandlerDefinition>
          </d3p1:componentList>
        + <d3p1:logicalDeviceList>
          <d3p1:logicalSourceList />
        </d3p1:logicalSource>
        <d3p1:messageHandlingReliability>Transactional</d3p1:messageHandlingReliability>
        <d3p1:name>Chapter11 Exercise1</d3p1:name>
      </m_rfidProcess>
    </ProcessComplete>
  </ArrayOfProcessComplete>
```

Figure 11-3. *Fragment of an XML file created by the process export operation*

Staging RFID Device Definitions and Device Properties

To move RFID device definitions from development to production, you can use the export feature in RFID Manager and produce XML definitions that can be imported into the target system. Most often, the development and production machines are going to have different device definitions. Typically, development will have a smaller number of readers, while production will contain the full list. However, you must ensure that the settings on the readers for crucial parameters like Event Mode and Duplicate Elimination Time are set to values that are reasonable for the application. A convenient way to accomplish this is to create a "standard device profile." In Exercise 11-2, we will walk through creating a standard property template for a device.

Exercise 11-2. Creating and Applying a Standard Property Template for a Device

This exercise will introduce the creation and application of a property template using the Contoso provider.

1. Install the Contoso device provider sample by running `%rfidinstalldir%\Samples\Device Service Provider\Contoso\ContosoEndToEnd\contososetup.cmd`.

2. Run the Contoso device simulator from `ContosoDeviceSimulator\runContososimulator.cmd`. Now you should have a running process and a device that shows up as open.

3. Using the export option on the Devices node of RFID Manager, export the properties for the ContosoTestDevice to a location on the file system (see Figure 11-4).

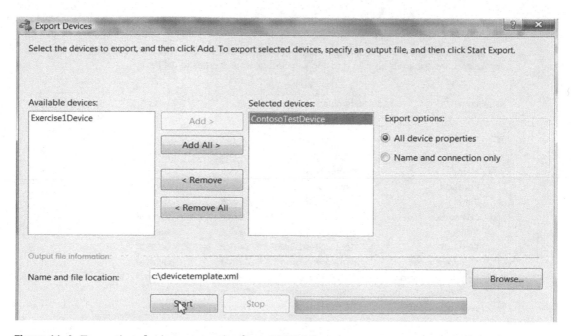

Figure 11-4. *Exporting device properties from RFID Manager*

4. Now that you have successfully created a template file, you can use it to reset the properties for a device to a known configuration from any point in time. As an example, right-click the ContosoTest-Device and choose Apply Template, as shown in Figure 11-5.

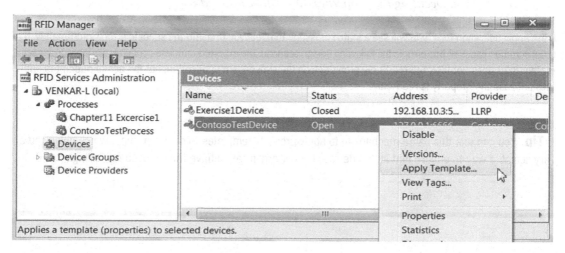

Figure 11-5. *Applying templates on a device*

5. You will be presented with a dialog that lets you see the properties that are going to be applied. Apply them, as shown in Figure 11-6.

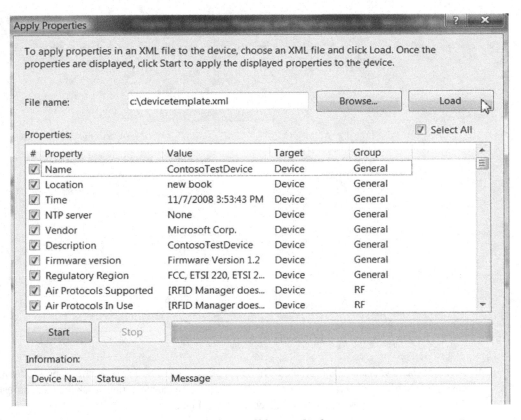

Figure 11-6. *Deciding the properties that will be applied*

If the apply operation fails, you will see a status message that lets you drill into the specific error. Unfortunately, the most common cause of this error is the following benign scenario: the exported template contains read-only properties; BizTalk RFID does not filter out read-only properties on the subsequent application, but the actual attempt to apply fails because the property is read-only!

■**Tip** You can use this same mechanism to apply property templates to device groups, which gives you a very scalable way to ensure that all the devices in your organization have the exact same settings.

Planning for Disaster Recovery

If you ever plan on restoring the state of a BizTalk RFID instance after a hardware failure or you need to switch production machines because of some other disaster, you need to know about the places BizTalk RFID stores configuration and runtime information. Each such place represents an item that must be backed up by you and restored to the second machine. Here are some best practices that will help you with this process:

- Use a domain account with "roaming profile" enabled when you install BizTalk RFID on your production machine. This will let you restore settings and state that were encrypted with the credentials of the RFID service account.

- Periodically export all the process definitions and device definitions to the file system.

- Periodically export the server-level configuration settings by using the GetServerConfiguration command on the rfidclientconsole.exe tool.

- Under the hood, most of the configuration information used by BizTalk RFID is stored in the RFIDSTORE SQL Server database. Make sure that you are backing up this database on a regular maintenance schedule (using a SQL Server Agent job if required).

- It is also a good idea to back up the %RFIDDATADIR% directory on the machine. This directory contains the executables for the providers and processes, along with the file system configuration files and the recent log files, which are handy if you need to report a problem to your development team.

- Notice that there are no MSMQ queues or IIS artifacts on this list. Both of these are automatically recreated by BizTalk RFID when the new instance starts up, so you don't have to plan for them during disaster recovery.

BizTalk RFID Footprint

We will now dive deeper into the various artifacts that are created under the hood when processes and providers are deployed. You should treat all the information in this section as subject to change in the next version of BizTalk RFID. This information largely amounts to implementation details, but knowledge of their existence and relationships should help you troubleshoot and understand the inner workings of the system.

File System Artifacts

If you are deploying a process called MyProcess, BizTalk RFID will create a directory called %RFIDDATADIR%\Processes\MyProcess. On my default installation, this translates to C:\Program Files\Microsoft BizTalk RFID\Processes\MyProcess. Think of this directory as the top-level directory that holds all the file system artifacts for your process. It is also the base directory of the application domain that is used to execute your process.

Tip At runtime, if you need to access this directory location from within your event handler code, use AppDomain.CurrentDomain.BaseDirectory.

Under this directory, you will find the files global.asax and Web.config, along with a bin directory. If you have done any ASP.NET programming, you will realize that these are the same artifacts created in an ASP.NET application. So, what is the connection between BizTalk RFID and ASP.NET? BizTalk RFID uses ASP.NET as its "application host" when running on Windows Server. When it is running in Windows XP or Windows Vista, the process is hosted in an application domain that is running inside the BizTalk RFID NT service. However, to keep the differences between the hosting environments to a minimum, the artifacts and configuration files are the same on both platforms.

■**Tip** The `global.asax` file contains code that is run whenever the application is launched inside IIS. If you add your own application code to it, your code will execute when running only on Windows Server, not on Windows XP or Vista, where IIS is not used by BizTalk RFID. If you want your application code to run on all platforms, you are better off using the event handler initialization, which will always happen, regardless of the host.

■**Tip** If you are using a component that must be configured using a .NET configuration file setting (such as enabling network tracing or using WCF in your application), you can use the `Web.config` file for this purpose. The `Web.config` file is created by BizTalk RFID as part of process creation if the file does not already exist in the application folder for the process. If you plan to use this mechanism, you should start from the file that BizTalk RFID creates and incorporate your changes into it. We recommend that you use event handler properties wherever possible to configure event handlers—they represent the path of least complexity for you and your administrator.

Event Handler Assembly Location

Once you implement your event handler, you need to decide how you are going to distribute the component. The main consideration for you is whether multiple processes are going to use your event handler, or if a single process is going to use it. If multiple processes are going to use your event handler, you should consider adding the event handler to the global assembly cache (GAC), since it simplifies the servicing and upgrading of your component, where you have to upgrade a single copy of the DLL on the machine. If you are going to add the assembly to the GAC, you have to meet the requirements for the same, including signing your assembly with a strongly named signature and requiring administrative privileges for the user who will be installing your assemblies in the GAC. BizTalk RFID uses the term "shared components" to refer to components that are loaded from the GAC.

■**Tip** If you are going to be using your objects from within the Business Rule Composer (e.g., if you have a new event type and you intend to support users creating rules and policies that refer to the event type), you must add your component to the GAC for the composer to find it.

If you are not going to be creating a shared component, you can just copy your DLLs to the bin directory of the process, and BizTalk RFID will automatically find them at runtime. Such components are called *private components*.

■Tip BizTalk RFID includes an entity called ComponentManager that provides design-time support for browsing private event handlers available to a process. This manager is just a design-time service; at runtime there are no requirements that an assembly must be registered with the ComponentManager to be available. RFID Manager has a cool feature for browsing shared components by enumerating the GAC and displaying the assemblies to you. However, this feature is limited to the local machine on which the tool is running.

RFID Store Artifacts

The actual process definition, process bindings, and error information for each process are saved in the SQL Server database that is being used for the RFID store. This guarantees consistency of the process and its subcomponents when it is modified or retrieved from BizTalk RFID. The contents of the XML in the tables are not intended for end users to manipulate directly, but the knowledge that BizTalk RFID stores configuration information in a SQL Server database is useful, especially for creating a maintenance plan or troubleshooting failures.

IIS Artifacts

The artifacts created in IIS include the virtual directory and the application pool. Since the application is running within IIS and uses WCF to communicate with the BizTalk RFID server, there are a number of things that you need to be aware of as they relate to IIS. For instance, ASP.NET 2.0 must be registered correctly, WCF must be correctly configured on the machine, the default web site must have anonymous authentication set up correctly, and so on. There is an excellent section on IIS troubleshooting in the product documentation that you should start with if you are seeing random WCF failures in your application.

■Tip IIS automatically monitors the bin directory of an application for changes. If it detects changes, it will restart the application. This could cause event processing to be restarted at unexpected times for your application. Make sure you don't have any writable files in the bin directory of your application. Also, make sure that if you have antivirus software running, you exclude this bin directory from the antivirus scan. To troubleshoot this issue, look at a log file called shutdowns.log in the application directory. That should contain the reason for the shutdown, and is very useful for troubleshooting will-o'-the-wisp IIS application pool restart issues.

MSMQ Artifacts

BizTalk RFID makes heavy use of MSMQ as an internal store-and-forward mechanism. The usage of MSMQ is not directly exposed to the application, and you should not make any assumptions regarding the internal implementation: if Microsoft chooses to change the queuing mechanism in a subsequent release, you should not be affected as long as you are using the public APIs to access the event stream.

Enabling Cold Standby

If you have a good strategy for moving artifacts from development to production and a sound plan for disaster recovery where you understand all the moving parts that need to be backed up, you are well on the path to enabling a cold standby configuration with minimal additional effort. *Cold standby* configurations are usually simpler and more economical solutions for enabling high availability in a number of real-world deployments. The level of availability, of course, will not be as automatic or flexible as what you would get with a premium high-availability option such as what is enabled by Microsoft Cluster Service, but you have to make the trade-off between the degree of high availability required and the cost in accomplishing the same.

To enable a cold standby configuration of BizTalk RFID, you need to ensure that your secondary server is up to date, with all the required RFID business process definitions, device definitions, and device properties. One of the unique aspects of an RFID deployment is that you need to pay close attention to the connections to devices.

When the secondary machine is on standby, it must not attempt to connect to devices that the live machine is connected to. Depending on the specific provider and the device that is being used, simultaneous connections can lead to very complicated troubleshooting scenarios. They could end up causing the device to get into an error state or the RFID process to lose events, since the events will get delivered to the wrong server.

Conversely, when the machine comes out of standby mode, you need to ensure that the primary machine is really shut down, so that its device connections are closed. An easy way to accomplish both objectives is to have the RFID processes on the secondary machine in a stopped state, and start up the processes as part of the cutover process.

■**Caution** Whenever you move the state of BizTalk RFID from one machine to another in this manner, all the "in-flight" events that are still in the local MSMQ queues (i.e., events reported by devices but not yet delivered to the RFID processes) will be lost. Since the event processing pipeline assumes near-real-time processing, this should not be of concern in most scenarios.

Running BizTalk RFID Under Microsoft Cluster Service

The enterprise edition of BizTalk RFID supports high availability while running under Microsoft Cluster Service. Following is a brief description of the logical way in which BizTalk RFID supports clustering. However, please note that detailing all the steps to actually enable a clustered instance is outside the scope of this chapter. We recommend that you start with the product whitepaper if you are going to do this.

At a high level, BizTalk RFID supports clustering in an *active-passive* configuration (i.e., only one of the nodes in the cluster is active, or online, and the other nodes in the cluster are passive, or offline, and waiting to take over when the active node fails and cluster node failover happens). The actual failover is managed by the administrator, or automatically by Microsoft Cluster Service, when a fatal condition is detected. This implies that you have to install BizTalk

RFID on all the nodes of the cluster individually. Also, from an installation perspective, you must install and configure the Microsoft Distributed Transaction Coordinator (MSDTC) and the MSMQ components to be in the clustered configuration. There are excellent whitepapers on MSDN for both topics, but they are fairly detailed and not for the faint of heart.

You have the option of using either a clustered or a remote instance of SQL Server for the RFID configuration database. In either case, you have to make sure that all the instances are configured to point to the same RFID store. Similarly, you must ensure that a domain account with an enabled roaming profile is used for the RFID service account and the RFID process account. Additionally, the data directory must be set up to be on a shared disk that is accessible to the new active node on failover.

■Note There are two primary advantages to using clustering for high availability instead of cold standby: the failover is automatic and in-flight events are not lost. The trade-off is increased cost in hardware, software, and complexity of installation, configuration, and ongoing management. Typically, we recommend cold standby for spoke installations of BizTalk RFID in branch locations such as manufacturing shop floors or retail outlets, and clustering-based failover for hub installations of BizTalk RFID that can be brought under more traditional IT management processes.

Enterprise Deployment

Most enterprise deployments of RFID have a hub-and-spoke deployment architecture. The spokes are the physical extremities of the business—typically warehouses, manufacturing plant floors, or retail outlets. The tags and readers (and hence BizTalk RFID) are deployed at the spokes. Typically, the role of BizTalk RFID is as follows in such architecture:

- It enables real-time decision-making. The real-time decisions are made at the spoke, without direct intervention or calls to the hub. Examples include sending commands to GPO devices such as stack lights, boom barriers, buzzers, and alarms; and local verify/ accept/reject human workflows in response to a physical event read such as a tag read or GPI event detect. The decisions are made by components that are typically custom event handlers or BRE policies. Both kinds of components need to be managed centrally and distributed to the spoke whenever changes happen.

- It collects information and automatically forwards it to the central hub to enable cross-spoke visibility and detailed business analytics, and to update back-end line-of-business (LOB) applications. In this scenario, the right integration and store-and-forward technologies have to be used to transfer the information from the spoke to the hub. Choices include SQL Server Integration Services, BizTalk Server, MSMQ, and WCF-based services.

- In certain deployments, the spokes themselves directly update the LOB system, but this is unusual and is limited to scenarios where the LOB is the warehouse or inventory management system, and the LOB is already coordinating or participating in the business process that is happening on the spoke.

Servicing RFID Device Providers

If you need to update an existing device provider with a new version, you can use the following steps: stop the provider, update the DLLs, and restart the provider. Under the hood, the device connections will be stopped and started automatically by BizTalk RFID. There is no need to drop device definitions and recreate them, unless your hardware manufacturer explicitly asks you to do so; which could be required if they have made any breaking changes to existing properties or property metadata.

Servicing RFID Processes

If you need to service an event handler implementation DLL, you can do so in an online fashion. Since there is an internal event queue between the RFID device and the RFID process definition, events can continue to be queued for the process, even when the code for the process is not running. When the process starts up again, all such pending events are delivered to the process. To put the process in this event collection mode, you need to pause the process from within RFID Manager. When the process is paused, the event handler DLLs can be updated, after which the process can be started normally. Using this sequence lets you service the process without losing events.

■**Caution** Event collection mode turns out to have one interesting side effect: most of the time, event handlers can be expected to process near-real-time events only. However, because of event collection mode, an event handler may occasionally have to deal with processing events from the past. If your event handler is responsible for taking some physical action, like opening a gate, you need to ensure that it ignores events from the past correctly.

Changing Device Bindings for a Process

There is another kind of change that you may need to make to a process: you may need to change the process properties or the set of devices that a process is currently bound to. Both of these come under the category of changing the bindings for a process, and can be done in an online fashion, without dropping events. Under the covers, when event handler parameters are changed, BizTalk RFID will put the process in event collection mode, change the parameters, and restart.

Distributing and Upgrading Business Rules

One of the key benefits of using the BRE integration is the built-in support for *dynamic policy morphing*—or, simply put, the support for the automatic update of business rules that is baked into the BRE. The BRE uses its own versioning scheme, and its own publishing and caching mechanism to make sure that the correct version of a particular policy is being used by an instance of the rule engine. When you create an event handler that will execute a business rule using a policy, you should usually check the policy flag that tells the engine to use the newest available version of a policy.

Figure 11-7 shows the BRE event handler configuration dialog. Once the "Use latest version" flag has been set, the Rule Engine Update service automatically checks for new policy versions, and informs all existing rule engine instances when it finds a new version of a policy. All this is transparent to the administrator and the end user.

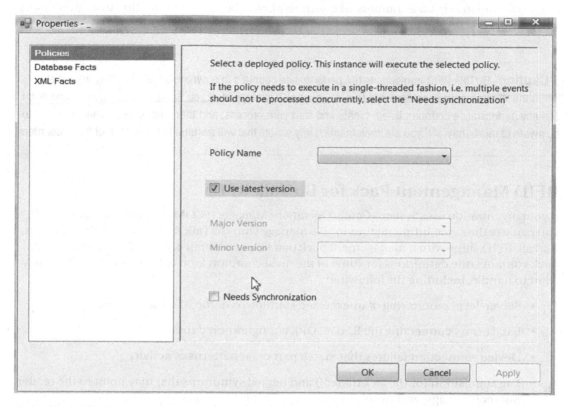

Figure 11-7. *The BRE event handler configuration dialog*

Enterprise Monitoring

BizTalk RFID provides the following ways to monitor its own health and potential problems on each installation (multiinstance monitoring is covered in the "RFID Management Pack for BizTalk RFID," section, which follows):

Windows event log messages: BizTalk RFID logs messages in the event log under the application directory. Nearly every administration operation results in a Windows event log message, so that is the first place that you should go to look for additional information on an error.

Log files: The BizTalk RFID Windows Service logs all of its operations to a file located at `%rfiddatadir%\logs\rfidservices.log`. The individual process and provider log files can be found in the respective provider and process directories.

Windows Management Instrumentation (WMI) events: BizTalk RFID raises WMI messages under the root/microsoft/rfid namespace. You can also receive the same events in your RFID business process.

Performance counters: Device- and process-level performance counters can be used to track statistics such as number of events read, number of events waiting to be processed, and uptime for the process.

■**Caution** BizTalk RFID implements the performance counters in a dynamic fashion. They are created when the RFID process is created and torn down when it is stopped. If you fire up perfmon.exe and don't see any performance counters listed, create and start your process, and then check back. You also need to be aware of this behavior if you are implementing any scripts that will assume the presence of these counters.

RFID Management Pack for BizTalk RFID

If your organization uses Systems Center Operations Manager (SCOM) for centralized monitoring, you can use the same infrastructure to also manage your BizTalk RFID server. Out of the box, BizTalk RFID ships with a management pack that you can install on your SCOM server. This pack contains rule definitions for some of the most common kinds of scenarios that you may want to handle, including the following:

- Server-level monitoring of unexpected shutdowns of the RFID service itself

- Fatal errors connecting the RFIDSTORE configuration database

- Device connection failures that match particular patterns of activity

- Tag acquisition (or the lack thereof) and related symptoms that may point to the reader not reading tags, and so on

- Custom monitoring rules—you can customize the management pack to detect conditions that are particular to your deployment and have them alert an administrator

If you browse the contents of the RFID management pack (RMP), you will see that it supports certain very specific errors, but is also intended to be customizable to take into account various criteria that are deployment-specific. This customization is done using the SCOM extensibility hooks that can operate off the lower-level health-monitoring queries over the event logs, WMI events, and performance counters mentioned in the previous section.

From an action perspective, you can use the SCOM scripting extensibility to launch RFID Manager directly from within the context of an alert from a specific server, or run one of the canned tasks that are part of the RMP. The tasks in the RMP are scripts that wrap the rfidclientconsole.exe tool to perform common tasks such as importing/exporting devices and processes, and querying for the current status of the devices and processes in the system.

Device Versioning

With the device versioning feature, as a system administrator, you can keep track of all the changes made to devices, find out exactly what property was changed, and quickly revert a change that had an adverse behavior. Exercise 11-3 looks at the device versioning management feature.

Exercise 11-3. Device Versioning Walkthrough

In this exercise, you will use the Contoso device to modify a device property and browse the version history for the device using RFID Manager.

1. Install the Contoso device provider sample by running `%rfidinstalldir%\Samples\Device Service Provider\Contoso\ContosoEndToEnd\contososetup.cmd`.

2. Run the Contoso device simulator from `ContosoDeviceSimulator\runContososimulator.cmd`. Now you should have a running process and a device that shows up as open (see Figure 11-8).

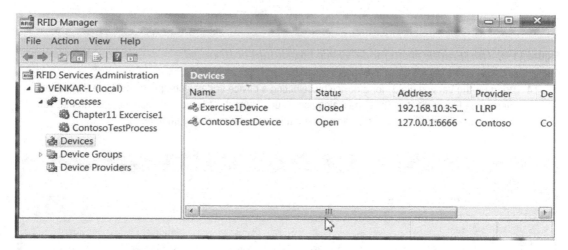

Figure 11-8. *The running device*

3. Bring up the device properties, click the Notification tab, and turn off the event mode property by unchecking the "Enable event mode" check box (see Figure 11-9). The event mode controls whether the device will deliver events autonomously to processes, and its being off is the number one reason that processes fail to receive events.

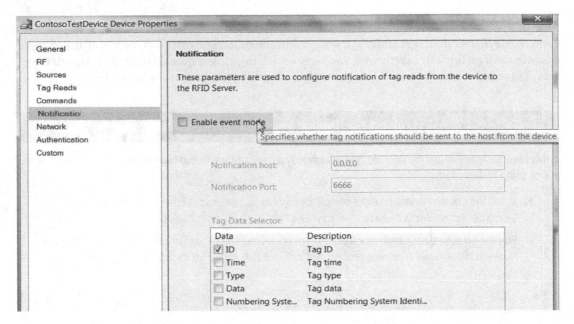

Figure 11-9. *The "Enable event mode" check box should be disabled.*

4. Bring up the Version dialog for a device by selecting a device and selecting Versions from the context menu (see Figure 11-10). Once the dialog comes up (Figure 11-11), you can see the change that you made in the topmost version. You can also see the user who made the change.

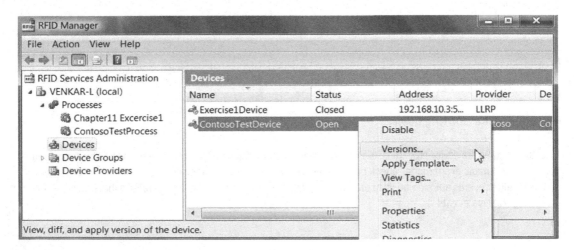

Figure 11-10. *Launching the device version browser*

5. Next, pick the latest version and diff it against the previous version, as shown in Figure 11-11.

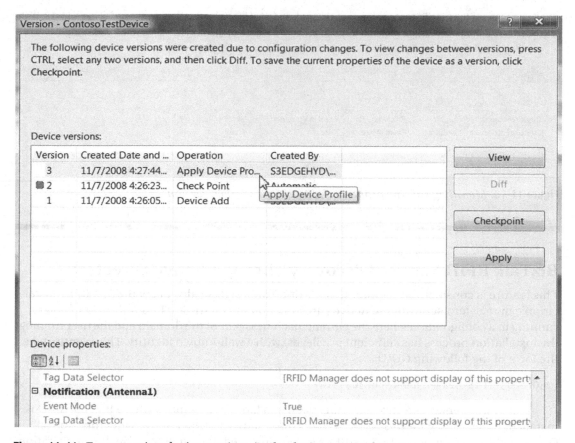

Figure 11-11. *Enumerating device versions in the device version browser*

6. Select any two versions, and then click the Diff button, as shown in Figure 11-12.

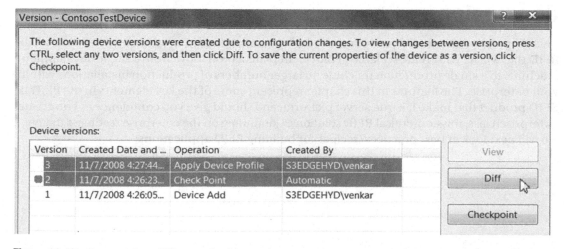

Figure 11-12. *Comparing different device versions*

Finally, you can see the specific property that was changed, and what the new value was, as shown in Figure 11-13. With this, you have all the information required to troubleshoot "the case of the device that worked yesterday."

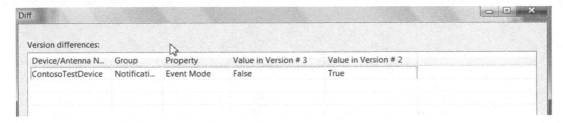

Figure 11-13. *Identifyig specific property changes across device versions*

BizTalk RFID Service Discovery Through Active Directory

This feature is considerably simpler than its title implies. Basically, every BizTalk RFID installation can register itself with the Active Directory domain controller (assuming that you are running in a configuration where the current machine is part of the domain and the user running the installation process has sufficient privileges) with a well-known identity. This identity takes the form of the following GUID:

{230F80B3-7F28-4219-89D0-6966F3C4931C}

This feature enables Active Directory clients to look for machines where BizTalk RFID is installed, by searching for this service connection point (or SCP in Active Directory–speak). Once you have a number of BizTalk RFID servers installed in your enterprise, this registration mechanism will let you find servers that match a bunch of interesting criteria, including service name and service version.

Conclusion

This chapter has introduced you to some of the high-end enterprise readiness features in BizTalk RFID that will let you create scalable deployment plans as you move from a single development machine, to a single production machine, to larger numbers of production installations within your enterprise. The features in this chapter represent some of the key elements in the BizTalk RFID product that make it a true server platform, and should give you confidence as you create enterprise-class, mission-critical RFID solutions. Continuing on the enterprise readiness theme, we will next look at best practices/recipes for building RFID applications.

CASE STUDY: EXPLOSIVE EXCEPTION HANDLING

Industry: Mining.

Overview: In South Africa, a mining company has been investigating the use of RFID to increase safety in relation to explosives and detonations. Miners and explosives are equipped with RFID tags, while RFID readers are placed every 100 feet within the mine shaft. As miners and explosives pass through the underground shafts, the readers record their movements, and the data is passed back to a server where the movement can be monitored.

Results: Since all of the explosives and miners can be tracked, operators know when all personnel are cleared from an area and the detonation of an explosive is safe to proceed with.

CHAPTER 12

■ ■ ■

BizTalk RFID Recipes

The purpose of this chapter is to expand on a number of concepts that have been introduced throughout the course of this book. Due to the prevalence and importance of these topics, it will be valuable to see more details about each so you can better understand how to incorporate them into your own architectures. These concepts will be written in a "problem-solution" format: the problem will be presented and a solution will follow. The solution will be a discussion that will go into varying degrees of detail aimed at allowing you to properly approach such challenges on your own.

The recipes that are included in this chapter are as follows:

Transport Protocols Within Event Handlers: This recipe looks at additional techniques for the communication of information from RFID event handlers to external components and services.

RFID Data, XML, and SQL Server: This recipe will help you discover approaches to dealing with data in XML to simplify the integration of different applications and platforms with BizTalk RFID.

Debugging Tips: There are a variety of components in a typical BizTalk RFID implementation, and it is valuable to understand how some of the most common can be tracked and debugged.

Integration with BizTalk EDI Functionality: It is fairly common to need to initiate the creation and delivery of EDI documents from an RFID read. This section will give an overview of how to deliver an EDI document in response to an RFID tag event.

Creating an XSD Based on RFID XML: Automating schema generation is an important skill when working with any type of XML.

12.1. Transport Protocols Within Event Handlers

Problem

There are a variety of protocols (HTTP, MSMQ, SOAP, FTP) that can be used within event handlers to post RFID information to external targets. How can I determine the appropriate protocol to use when architecting my solution?

Solution

Chapter 5 went into detail on how to work with event handlers, and Chapter 8 presented the steps needed for publishing information to an MSMQ from an event handler. The problem at hand is not how to build a custom event handler, but rather how to interact with external components, applications, and platforms using different transport protocols. The key to working with data publication within event handlers is understanding that the handoff portion of the code is easy to modify—an event handler can be swapped from posting to an MSMQ to posting to a web service with relative ease.

Before working through the different protocols, it is important to note that it is best practice not to put business rules and complex logic into an event handler. A simple handoff to a web service can be greatly complicated when taking into account things like exception handling, retries, transaction support, messaging patterns, and backup transport logic. When BizTalk Server is available, it is most appropriate to push the event publication to this platform using a transport protocol that is unlikely to present errors—for example, the path of the MSMQ (if the queue is on the local machine, it is highly unlikely that exceptions will occur). Letting BizTalk Server take on the workflow logic and the exception handling—for example, sorting and de-duplicating events— is an excellent way to keep BizTalk RFID event handlers simple and performant.

Architectural discussions aside, there are times when event handlers need to communicate directly using services (both web and WCF), file transports, HTTP, TCP/IP, and other protocols. Given what has already been illustrated around the MSMQ event handler (see Exercise 8-1), our solution will start with referring to this code base, and from there reach out to other protocols and handoff methods. The code of interest in the event handler is really contained in a single method, PostEvent. There is some code in the Init method that initializes the queue, and this should certainly be taken into account for other transport protocols; but the PostEvent method, with the single line of code that pushes a serialized version of the RfidEventBase object to the queue, is the primary point of interest (see Listing 12-1). With a reference to where the handoff is occurring for an MSMQ base event handler, you can now look at other protocols and substitute the MSMQ handoff with the new transfer protocol code.

Listing 12-1. *The Original Post to an MSMQ in the PostEvent Method*

```
private void PostEvent(RfidEventBase evt)
{
  ...
  try
  {
   destinationQueue.Send(SerializeEvent(evt)
    ,MessageQueueTransactionType.Single);
  }
  ...
}
```

WCF Services Transport

Consuming WCF services is quite easy, since the bulk of the work is done by a Visual Studio wizard. The first step to consuming WCF is to add a reference to the service in the event handler project. This can be done by right-clicking the project, selecting Add Service Reference (see

Figure 12-1), and locating the WCF service to consume. This process will add a generated file to the project, with class definitions that can be instantiated from the event handler code.

Note The .NET 3.5 Framework or later must be installed. Visual Studio 2005 can reference WCF services with the proper extensions deployed, but additional steps must be taken to add a service reference (i.e., this option is not available in the project context menu).

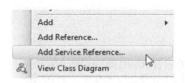

Figure 12-1. *The Add Service Reference option in Visual Studio*

Once the WCF service has been referenced, it can be called easily from the event handler. Assuming that the name of the client class is WCFClient, the code shown in Listing 12-1, which is the MSMQ post, could be replaced with the WCF code in Listing 12-2.

Listing 12-2. *Updated PostEvent Using WCF*

```
private void PostEvent(RfidEventBase evt)
{
 ...
 try
 {
  WCFClient client = new WCFClient();

  // the SerializeEvent will need to be based on what is
  // expected in the ProcessRfidMessage method.  In this
  // case, if the SerializeEvent remains the same as it was
  // for the MSMQ post, it will pass an XML document version
  // of the event to the method.
  client.ProcessRfidMessage(SerializeEvent(evt));
  client.Close();
 }
 ...
}
```

Web Services Transport

Consuming web services is similar in nature to consuming WCF services. The difference is simply to select Add Web Reference from the project context menu instead of Add Service Reference (see Figure 12-2). In the dialog box, point to the web service to consume—and Visual Studio will take care of the rest. It will create all of the class reference information needed to call the web service. If you're calling a web method with the same definition as ProcessRfidMessage in the previously described WCF service, the code update to the event handler will look identical to that shown in Listing 12-2.

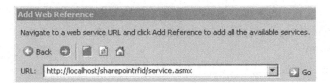

Figure 12-2. *Adding a web service reference in Visual Studio*

File Transport

In the MSMQ event handler, log information is written directly to a file. It could easily be extended beyond the methods available in ILogger to those in System.IO. The method of delivering information by file could be valuable in several scenarios, but is generally relegated to logging information to a text file.

In truth, it would make sense to remove this logging from the event viewer and push it into a commonly referenced assembly or a BizTalk orchestration, so that all event handlers and other components can use the same approach to logging. Logging to a file today may need to be extended to include a database table tomorrow. Rather than having to update all of the event handlers separately, the single point of common logging (the assembly or the orchestration) could be updated.

Discussion

It should be quite clear from the protocols outlined in the discussion that swapping from one transport protocol to another in an event handler should be extremely easy. There are no technical limitations to how information is pushed from an event handler to an external application or client. The art is in determining the appropriate architecture—whether an event handler should call directly to a web service or not depends on the amount of workflow and exception handling that may need to be performed.

12.2. RFID Data, XML, and SQL Server

Problem

There is a lot of information I would like to store in a database related to BizTalk RFID information, but I am not sure of the most appropriate way to do this. Additionally, I am trying to determine how best to query the data to return it to external systems. Some of the information is stored in XML and some in traditional table format.

Solution

Chapter 9 briefly outlined how to interact with BizTalk RFID's databases using XML and XQuery. There is much to be learned from this outline, and it should be stressed that the more done to structure data correctly on the database side, the easier data transformation and routing will be outside of the database. This means that for the majority of communications with enterprise applications, formatting information as XML at the database level will greatly improve the overall development and maintenance experience on external components and applications.

There are varying arguments about how to incorporate XML into databases and data structures. Some say that databases should never be involved in data transformations. One way to look at it is to say that the structure of data should reside solely in the database, whether that structure represents how the data is stored (e.g., in traditional tables) or how the data is presented to external clients (such as through stored procedures). For purposes of this solution, relying on XML as the chief way of presenting data to the external world is the ideal enterprise integration architecture.

Storing and retrieving data as XML is easy to accomplish in SQL Server 2005 and later editions. There is an `XML` data type available, and this type allows for full XML structures to be stored in a single column. This means that the data structure of an object can remain flexible and change without impacting the structure of the underlying table. To illustrate this, turn to the RFIDSTORE database and look at the `tagevents` table. Most of the columns are typical types of `nvarchar` and `int`. Executing a standard `select *` against this table shows results similar to those in Figure 12-3.

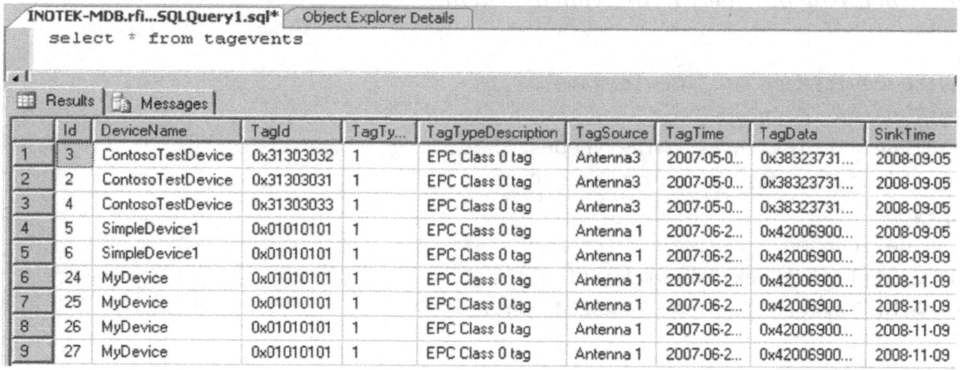

	Id	DeviceName	TagId	TagTy...	TagTypeDescription	TagSource	TagTime	TagData	SinkTime
1	3	ContosoTestDevice	0x31303032	1	EPC Class 0 tag	Antenna3	2007-05-0...	0x38323731...	2008-09-05
2	2	ContosoTestDevice	0x31303031	1	EPC Class 0 tag	Antenna3	2007-05-0...	0x38323731...	2008-09-05
3	4	ContosoTestDevice	0x31303033	1	EPC Class 0 tag	Antenna3	2007-05-0...	0x38323731...	2008-09-05
4	5	SimpleDevice1	0x01010101	1	EPC Class 0 tag	Antenna 1	2007-06-2...	0x42006900...	2008-09-05
5	6	SimpleDevice1	0x01010101	1	EPC Class 0 tag	Antenna 1	2007-06-2...	0x42006900...	2008-09-09
6	24	MyDevice	0x01010101	1	EPC Class 0 tag	Antenna 1	2007-06-2...	0x42006900...	2008-11-09
7	25	MyDevice	0x01010101	1	EPC Class 0 tag	Antenna 1	2007-06-2...	0x42006900...	2008-11-09
8	26	MyDevice	0x01010101	1	EPC Class 0 tag	Antenna 1	2007-06-2...	0x42006900...	2008-11-09
9	27	MyDevice	0x01010101	1	EPC Class 0 tag	Antenna 1	2007-06-2...	0x42006900...	2008-11-09

Figure 12-3. *Selecting the results in standard format*

If you add a `FOR XML AUTO` directive to the `select * from tagevents` query, the results will be formatted in XML. With a little more effort, not only can the results be formatted, but the overall structure of the data can be improved. This can be shown by first selecting the results using the following statement, which results in the XML shown in Listing 12-3:

```
select top 1 (*) from tagevents FOR XML AUTO
```

Listing 12-3. *Simple Single Result Formatted Using FOR XML AUTO*

```
<tagevents
 Id="3"
 DeviceName="ContosoTestDevice"
 TagId="dbobject/tagevents[@Id='3']/@TagId"
 TagType="1"
```

```
TagTypeDescription="EPC Class 0 tag"
TagSource="Antenna3"
TagTime="2007-05-04T04:48:54.433"
TagData="dbobject/tagevents[@Id='3']/@TagData"
SinkTime="2008-09-05T11:14:44.373"
ProcessName="ContosoTestProcess"
ExtData="[EDITED FOR CLARITY]"
LogicalDeviceName="mylogicaldevice"
TagIdAsHex="0x31303032"
TagDataAsHex="0x383237313838303231303239"
/>
```

Using this approach forces each row in the table to be produced as an individual XML document. But what if all of the results should be treated as a single XML document? What if the structure of the document needs to be modified such that each of the devices has its information rolled up—for example, all of the ContosoTestDevice events are rolled up under a single ContosoTestDevice node? In this case, the structure of the XML can be explicitly defined, with the result matching that shown in Listing 12-4.

Listing 12-4. *Restructuring the Query with Explicit Structure*

```
select NULL
,(SELECT device.DeviceName As "@DeviceName"
  ,device.TagType As "@TagType"
  ,device.TagTypeDescription As "@TagTypeDesc"
  ,(SELECT Cast(tag.TagIdAsHex as varchar(100))
    FROM tagevents tag
    WHERE tag.devicename = device.devicename
    GROUP BY Cast(TagIdAsHex As varchar(100))
    FOR XML PATH('TagRead'), BINARY BASE64, TYPE
  )
  FROM tagevents device
  GROUP BY DeviceName
          ,TagType
          ,TagTypeDescription
  FOR XML PATH('Device'), BINARY BASE64, TYPE)
FOR XML PATH('ResultSet'), BINARY BASE64
```

The results of this query are shown in Listing 12-5.

Listing 12-5. *Structured Result Formatted Using FOR XML PATH*

```
<ResultSet>
 <Device DeviceName="ContosoTestDevice"
        TagType="1"
        TagTypeDesc="EPC Class 0 tag">
```

```
  <TagRead>0x31303031</TagRead>
  <TagRead>0x31303032</TagRead>
  <TagRead>0x31303033</TagRead>
</Device>
<Device DeviceName="MyDevice"
        TagType="1"
        TagTypeDesc="EPC Class 0 tag">
  <TagRead>0x01010101</TagRead>
</Device>
<Device DeviceName="SimpleDevice1"
        TagType="1"
        TagTypeDesc="EPC Class 0 tag">
  <TagRead>0x01010101</TagRead>
</Device>
</ResultSet>
```

Discussion

Learning to incorporate XML into your BizTalk RFID solutions will greatly improve the overall design and ease of development. Become familiar with the syntax of XQuery and FOR XML directives so that data can be structured in the way it is most appropriately presented to the external world.

12.3. Debugging Tips

Problem

I have a number of different components in my BizTalk RFID infrastructure, including .NET assemblies, web services, enterprise applications, database calls, and log files. I am at the development stage, and am struggling with a cohesive way in which to debug and track what is occurring as different components execute.

Solution

Debugging different components in an integrated environment requires varying approaches. To demonstrate a process of debugging across such an environment, this discussion will look at several components that make up a typical "integrated solution."

Debugging Event Handlers

The process of debugging an event handler is quite simple; it requires attaching to the RFID service using Visual Studio. Once an event handler has been successfully built in Visual Studio, open the Debug menu and select Attach to Process. Select the RfidServices.exe process and click OK (as shown in Figure 12-4). Set appropriate breakpoints in the event handler code. When a BizTalk RFID process executes and initiates the event handler, this code will run and the breakpoints will enable the developer to step through the code.

■**Note** Make sure that the event handler assembly has been deployed to the proper location prior to attaching to the process. If the assembly has not been deployed and is not referenced in a BizTalk RFID process, the event handler code in Visual Studio will never execute.

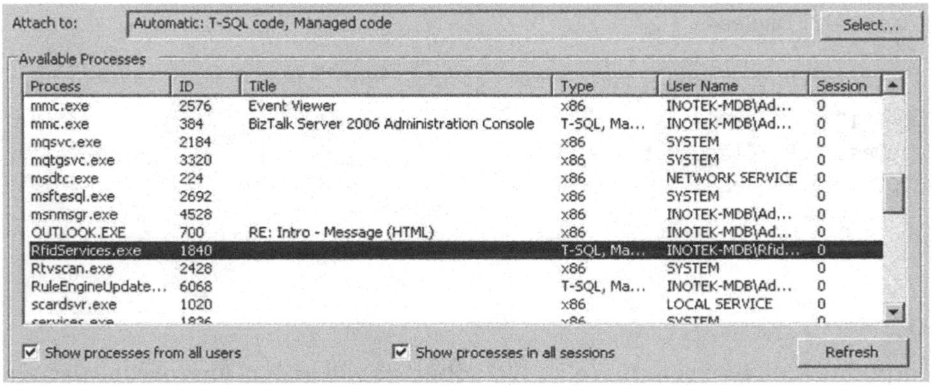

Figure 12-4. *Attaching to the RfidServices process*

Debugging Orchestrations

There are two options to debugging orchestrations. Unfortunately, there is nothing as simple as attaching to a process. Instead, a developer can either add "logging" shapes to an orchestration or use the Orchestration Debugger. The first option is as simple as placing an expression shape in an orchestration and adding logic to write to the Windows Event Viewer (or alternative logging options). The second option requires that the orchestration be fully deployed and that the Orchestration Debugger be accessed using Health and Activity Tracking (HAT).

To add simple logging using expression shapes in the orchestration, take these steps:

1. Add an expression shape to the orchestration wherever logging should take place. As shown in Figure 12-5, a number of expression shapes have been added simply to log information as steps in the orchestration are performed.

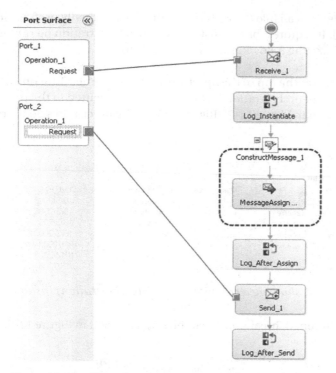

Figure 12-5. *Adding logging to an orchestration*

2. Add code to each expression shape to log to the event viewer, such as that shown in Figure 12-6.

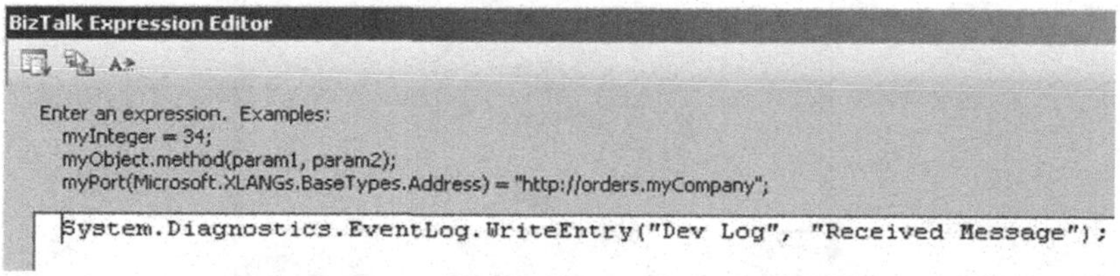

Figure 12-6. *Logging to the Windows Event Viewer from an expression shape*

The Orchestration Debugger is available through HAT, and is occasionally useful (though somewhat cumbersome to use). It requires that an instance of the orchestration be run before configuring a breakpoint in it. Take the following steps to use this tool:

1. Open HAT. From the menu at the top of the application, click Queries. Run one of the queries, which will return an orchestration instance that has executed in the past (an example of a result is shown in Figure 12-7). Right-click the instance and select Orchestration Debugger.

100 item(s) displayed. To view more details on an entry, right-click the cell and select **Orchestration Debugger** or **Message Flow** (requires Service Instance ID column).

Service/Name	▼	Service/Type ▼	ServiceInstance/State ▼	StartTime
Microsoft.BizTalk.DefaultPipelines.XMLReceive		Pipeline	Terminated	10/3/2008 8:26:
Microsoft.BizTalk.DefaultPipelines.XMLReceive		Pipeline	Terminated	10/3/2008 8:24:
Microsoft.BizTalk.DefaultPipelines.XMLReceive		Pipeline	Terminated	10/3/2008 8:21:
Microsoft.BizTalk.DefaultPipelines.XMLReceive		Pipeline	Terminated	10/3/2008 8:11:
Microsoft.BizTalk.DefaultPipelines.XMLReceive		Pipeline	Terminated	10/1/2008 11:23:
▶MSMQTesting.BizTalk_Orchestration1		Orchestration	Terminated	8/14/2008 1:49:
MSMQTesting.BizTalk_Orchestration1		Orchestration	Terminated	8/13/2008 12:22:

Figure 12-7. *HAT query results showing terminated service (orchestration) instances*

2. When the debugger has opened, breakpoints can be set, as shown in Figure 12-8.

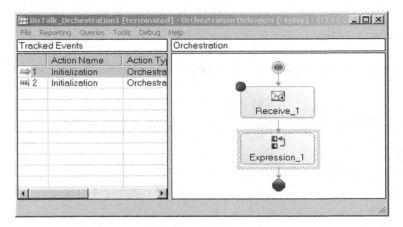

Figure 12-8. *Setting breakpoints in the debugger*

The next time that an orchestration instance runs, the breakpoints will be encountered. The instance can be accessed through HAT (the state of the instance will show In Breakpoint). Values associated with different parameters and messages within the orchestration will be accessible through the debugger.

Debugging Web Services and Web Parts

Debugging web services, SharePoint web parts, and anything else that executes under the ASP.NET service account is as simple as attaching to the appropriate service in Visual Studio. To do this, open the web service project in Visual Studio and click the Debug menu. Select Attach to Process, and click the appropriate process (generally w3wp.exe for SharePoint and aspnet_wp.exe for web services, though these may change depending on environments). Set breakpoints within the Visual Studio project and force the code to execute (either by running SharePoint from Internet Explorer or consuming the web service from a .NET application or other source). An example of attaching to the w3wp.exe process is shown in Figure 12-9.

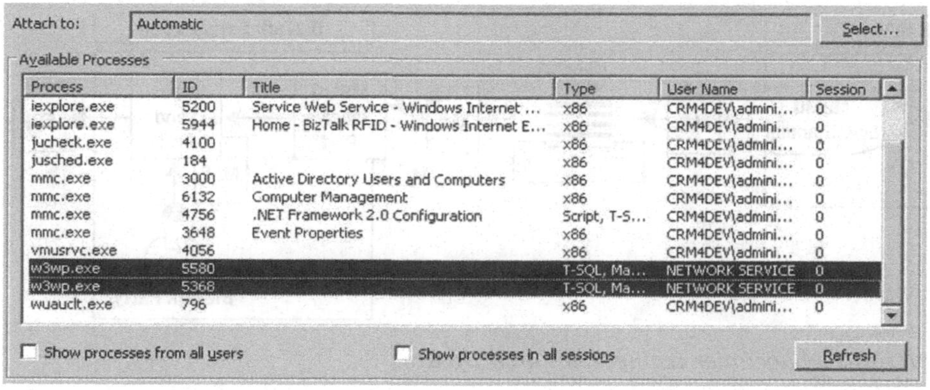

Figure 12-9. *Attaching to the w3wp process to debug a SharePoint web part*

Discussion

Debugging in an integrated environment can be somewhat overwhelming when first initiated— but breaking down the integrated components into the constituent parts leads to a much more focused and simplified experience. There is no single, universal way to debug components, but there is a similarity in the way most .NET applications function.

12.4. Integration with BizTalk EDI Functionality

Problem

I want to trigger the creation of an EDI document from BizTalk Server when certain RFID events are fired. I understand the basic interaction between BizTalk RFID and BizTalk Server, but I don't understand how to integrate the BizTalk Server EDI components.

Solution

A common scenario for triggering EDI documents from RFID readings is to send advance shipping notifications (EDI document type 856). For example, when a case of products is scanned by an RFID reader as it is loaded onto a truck for shipment, you may want to immediately send an 856 to the appropriate trading partner. The process for sending an EDI document starts with publishing the appropriate information in BizTalk RFID to BizTalk Server. Once the data is in BizTalk Server, the EDI components are used to format and route the document to the appropriate destination. To demonstrate how to configure each of the components, we'll discuss the architecture outlined in Figure 12-10.

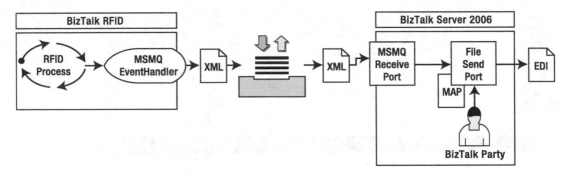

Figure 12-10. *RFID-to-EDI document component architecture*

Preparing the Foundation

Chapter 8 presented an extensive outline of how BizTalk RFID and BizTalk Server can communicate with one another. Rather than rehash this discussion, we will start from the point of handoff to an MSMQ—where a BizTalk RFID event handler places an XML document on the MSMQ and BizTalk Server receives the data using an MSMQ receive port. The following components need to be in place for the flow of information from BizTalk RFID to BizTalk Server to take place:

- The BizTalk RFID event handler that pushes information to the MSMQ. See Exercise 8-1 for details on publishing to an MSMQ.

- BizTalk Server, set up to receive data from the MSMQ using a receive port. See Exercise 8-2 for details on subscribing to an MSMQ.

Assuming these steps have been taken based on the exercises from Chapter 8, the information that will be posted to BizTalk Server will look similar to Figure 12-11.

```xml
<?xml version="1.0" ?>
- <tag>
- <rfidEventBase>
  - <VendorSpecificInformation>
    - <properties>
      - <property>
          <vendorKey>ItemID</vendorKey>
          <value>1234</value>
        </property>
      - <property>
          <vendorKey>PONumber</vendorKey>
          <value>PO123456</value>
        </property>
      </properties>
    </VendorSpecificInformation>
  </rfidEventBase>
- <observation>
    <time>6/22/2007 12:07:10 AM</time>
    <sourceName>Antenna 1</sourceName>
    <deviceName>MyDevice</deviceName>
  </observation>
  <tagId>AQEBAQ==</tagId>
  <tagType>EPC Class 0 tag</tagType>
  <tagData>QgBpAHoAVABhAGwAawAgAFIARgBJAEQA</tagData>
  <tagSource>Antenna 1</tagSource>
  <tagTime>6/22/2007 12:07:10 AM</tagTime>
- <dataSelector>
  - <tagDataSelector>
      <isId>True</isId>
      <isData>True</isData>
      <isType>True</isType>
      <isTime>True</isTime>
      <isNumberingSystemIdentifier>True</isNumberingSystemIdentifier>
    </tagDataSelector>
  </dataSelector>
  </tag>
```

Figure 12-11. *Sample output XML*

With the send port successfully writing out the XML that was posted to the MSMQ, the solution is now ready to be built upon to include the EDI components. This will require taking the following steps:

1. Add an XSD schema that represents the incoming RFID XML and modify the XML receive pipeline.

2. Create the map that transforms the data from the RFID XML to the EDI representation of an 856 document.

3. Configure a BizTalk party to represent the target trading partner.

4. Prepare the send port to use the EDISend pipeline, the newly created map, and the configured trading partner properties.

Preparing the Receive Port

The first step is to create a schema that matches the RFID XML on the MSMQ—currently the data is simply passing through the receive and send ports, since both are using the default PassThru pipelines. A schema can be created by using the XML that is output by the send port (shown in Figure 12-11) using the Add Generated Items wizard (see Recipe 12.5 for more details). A schema that represents this data is shown in Figure 12-12. Once the schema has been created and deployed, the receive port must have its PassThruReceive pipeline changed to XMLReceive.

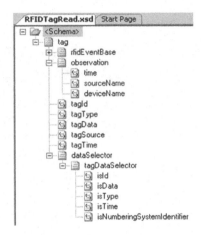

Figure 12-12. *XSD generated from the RFID XML*

Creating the Map

The second step is to perform the transformation of the source RFID XML into the target EDI 856. This will require three BizTalk artifacts:

The source schema: This was created in the previous section—it is the RFIDTagRead.xsd schema.

The target schema: This is the EDI 856 schema. When the BizTalk EDI components are installed, a directory is created that contains thousands of EDI-related schemas. In the case of the 856, it is included in the X12 folder.

▪Note For purposes of this discussion, the 862 document that will be used will be the 4010 version, which is located in $:\Program Files\Microsoft BizTalk Server\XSD_Schema\EDI\X12\00401.

The map: This is the actual map the defines the rules of data transformation between the source and target schemas.

Using Visual Studio, create a project with both the source and target schemas, and a new custom map. The mapping rules should be based on the EDI implementation guide provided by the trading partner. This discussion won't go into detail about how to perform the mapping, aside from showing the key elements in the source schema mapped to the target. Information that is not available in the source schema will need to be gathered through database lookups, .NET assembly callouts, functoid configurations, or other means available through the BizTalk mapper.

An example of mapping the purchase order number to the target 856 is shown in Figure 12-13. The functoid combination states that if the vendorKey element in the source document is equal to PONumber, then map the value element to the PRF01 node. Since there are multiple property nodes on the source document, a loop functoid is added to ensure all of the source values are worked through.

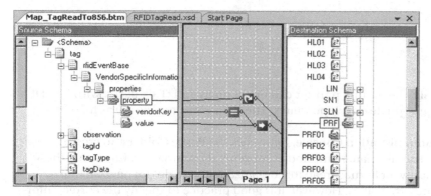

Figure 12-13. *Create the map to create the 856.*

Once the full mapping has been completed, deploy the source, target, and map so that they are accessible in the BizTalk Administration Console. The map will eventually be added to the send port that is associated with the target trading party.

Configuring a BizTalk Party

The next step is to configure a BizTalk party with the information needed to correctly create the envelope of the EDI document. The mapping of the 856 leads to the body of the document being created—but no envelope information is added until the information is sent through the EDISend pipeline. In the case of the 856, the envelope consists of the ISA, GS, and ST blocks at the start of the document, and the SE, GE, and IEA segments at the end. For purposes of argument, assume that the document shown in Listing 12-6 is a valid instance of what is to be delivered to a trading partner. This figure shows the envelope information that will be configured in the BizTalk party.

Listing 12-6. *A Valid 856 Envelope*

```
ISA*00*          *00*            *01*001234567        *01*098765432
*081028*0603*U*00301*000007911*0*T*>~

GS*PD*001234567*098765432*20081028*0603*1390*T*004010~

ST*856*000001390~

...

...

SE*60*000001390~

GE*1*1390~

IEA*1*000007911~
```

Using this as a basis, the trading partner can be set up as a BizTalk party, with its EDI properties set to the appropriate envelope values. The basic steps to take are as follows:

1. In the BizTalk Administration Console, right-click the Parties folder and create a new party. Give it the appropriate name and other general information. Know that these values are primarily for human-readable organization, and do not have an impact on how envelopes are routed. However, it is good practice to specify the correct information. An example of a party's general information, based on the envelope's ISA06 element (the target trading partner), is shown in Figure 12-14.

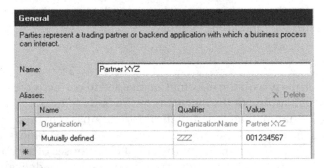

Figure 12-14. *Sample of the party's general information*

2. Once the party has been created, right-click it and select "EDI properties." A window will open where all EDI envelope information is entered. Since the direction of information is flowing from BizTalk RFID through BizTalk Server to the trading partner, the values that will need to be configured are those related to Party as Interchange Receiver. The important values, shown in the ISA, GS, and ST segments in Listing 12-6, can be input directly into the property sheets. An example of this is shown in Figure 12-15.

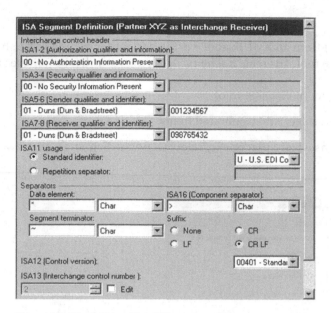

Figure 12-15. *Setting the ISA properties*

Setting Up the Send Port

With the party configured and the map and schemas deployed, the final step is to configure the send port. Begin by adding the new 856 map (created earlier in this discussion) to the send port. Next, change the send port's pipeline to EDISend. After this, set the filter on the send port to subscribe to the receive port (BTS.ReceivePortName). Finally, tie the party to this send port by double-clicking the party and setting it on the Send Ports tab.

■**Note** There are a large number of options for configuring the send port's filter. Using the BTS. ReceivePortName is just one easy-to-implement option.

Discussion

This solution laid out the specific steps to setting up the EDI components of BizTalk Server to deliver an EDI document. It was intended to give an overview of the components, not to give an exhaustive look into BizTalk EDI. Some important topics to look further into are configuring acknowledgments (997s indicating that the 856 was received), EDI reporting (through the Group Hub page in the BizTalk Administration Console), and document tracking.

12.5. Creating an XSD Based on BizTalk RFID XML

Problem

I have an XML representation of RFID data that is ready to be posted to BizTalk Server. To successfully process this, I need to create an XSD. What is the simplest way to create this?

Solution

You can generate an XSD schema from an XML instance using a wizard available through Visual Studio, or using the XSD.exe tool. To create a schema using the wizard, follow these steps:

1. Create a new BizTalk project in Visual Studio.

2. Right-click the project and select Add Generated Items.

3. In the Add Generated Items wizard that opens, select Generate Schemas, as shown in Figure 12-16.

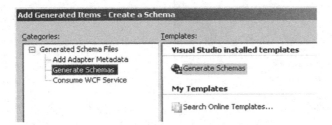

Figure 12-16. *The Add Generated Items wizard*

4. On the next screen, select Well-Formed XML from the first drop-down, and select a valid instance of the XML to base the XML on in the second field (see Figure 12-17).

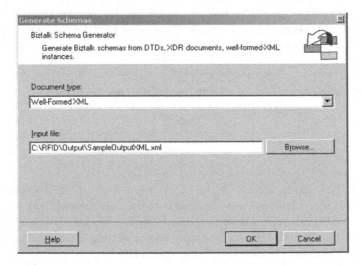

Figure 12-17. *Selecting a well-formed XML document as the input*

■**Note** The first time this is performed, an error may pop up indicating that a script must be run before a schema based on a well-formed XML instance can be generated. Pay attention to this warning, as it states the exact location of the script that needs to be run (it is included in the installation of BizTalk Server).

---

5. Click OK on the final screen, and a schema will be generated.

Discussion

The ability to create a schema from a well-formed instance is essential in facilitating communication between BizTalk RFID and BizTalk Server. There are two things you should note in the generation of a schema:

- The schema generation wizard will try to determine field types based on the input instance of the XML. Often, these are incorrect types, and need to be manually converted. For example, the item ID of an RFID read may be an integer value of 1234 in one XML instance, and ABCD in another. Both are valid, but since the schema was generated from the instance with 1234 in the node, the schema forces a field type of xsd:integer—which is incorrect. The appropriate value should be xsd:string. Because of this, you must validate several instances against the schema that was generated prior to moving forward with using it.

- The schema will be created with a name based on the input instance's file name. Make sure to change this name to an appropriate value.

Conclusion

The goal of this chapter was to present a number of problems that are common when building out BizTalk RFID solutions. The recipes in this chapter introduced additional functionality across BizTalk Server, including handling different transport protocols, extending the communication with the underlying SQL database, and implementing EDI-based solutions. As you begin to work on your own implementations, the ability to architect a solid infrastructure that will meet the long-term needs of an organization is of critical importance. There are numerous ways to architect and implement a solution, but only experience and exposure to a variety of problems will ensure that the chosen architecture is the correct one. The key phases of a successful implementation always include the following:

Technical design and architecture: Integration projects always require extensive technical architecture. BizTalk Server implementations are generally 80 percent architecture and design, and 20 percent development and build.

Development: There are a large number of components and concepts to understand with BizTalk Server, but once these are fully realized, actual development time is generally very short in duration. There is a fairly substantial learning curve at first.

Testing and quality assurance: Test phases are always important, but when integrating enterprise systems and data, they are of even higher priority. The test phase must include business analysts and data owners, and should not be left solely to a developer.

Deployment: BizTalk deployments are generally quite easy, and include the ability to import and export MSI files and binding files. Building a staging environment that mimics production will facilitate a much easier transition to a live environment.

CASE STUDY: COUNTERING TERRORISM

Industry: State security.

Overview: A trial system was put into place in Germany to track and scan facial features using RFID technologies. Volunteers were asked to carry RFID tags with them as they commuted to work, where they passed by several camera systems. These camera systems would record the faces of the individuals carrying the RFID tags, and upload the data to a centralized server where analysis could be performed. The system would measure features—such as the jawbone—and compare them with photographs already on file. Metrics were created to prove the validity of the comparisons.

Results: The test results were deemed promising, but wide-scale deployment has not yet occurred. In a real-world deployment, RFID would likely not be part of the system. Its primary purpose in this test system was to ensure that only those individuals carrying the RFID tag would be recorded, allowing the public at large to pass by the camera systems without being recorded. In an actual implementation, all individuals passing by the camera systems would be recorded.

Index

You Need the Companion eBook

Your purchase of this book entitles you to buy the companion PDF-version eBook for only $10. Take the weightless companion with you anywhere.

We believe this Apress title will prove so indispensable that you'll want to carry it with you everywhere, which is why we are offering the companion eBook (in PDF format) for $10 to customers who purchase this book now. Convenient and fully searchable, the PDF version of any content-rich, page-heavy Apress book makes a valuable addition to your programming library. You can easily find and copy code—or perform examples by quickly toggling between instructions and the application. Even simultaneously tackling a donut, diet soda, and complex code becomes simplified with hands-free eBooks!

Once you purchase your book, getting the $10 companion eBook is simple:

❶ Visit **www.apress.com/promo/tendollars/**.

❷ Complete a basic registration form to receive a randomly generated question about this title.

❸ Answer the question correctly in 60 seconds, and you will receive a promotional code to redeem for the $10.00 eBook.

2855 TELEGRAPH AVENUE | SUITE 600 | BERKELEY, CA 94705

Offer valid through 9/09.